SHALL WE KNOW ONE ANOTHER IN HEAVEN?

GUY N. WOODS

GOSPEL ADVOCATE
A TRUSTED NAME SINCE 1855

Gospel Advocate Company
P.O. Box 150
Nashville, Tennessee 37202

Books in Print by

GUY N. WOODS

The Second Coming and Other Sermons

How to Read the Greek New Testament

Questions and Answers, Vol. 1

Questions and Answers, Vol. 2

Commentary on the Gospel of John

Commentary on the Epistles of Peter, John and Jude

Commentary on James

Woods–Cogdill Debate

Woods–Britnell Debate

Shall We Know One Another in Heaven?
Gospel Advocate Reprint Library Edition, 2001

Published by Gospel Advocate Co.
P.O. Box 150, Nashville, TN 37202
www.gospeladvocate.com

ISBN: 0-89225-473-4

DEDICATION

To
The memory of my dear father and mother, whom I
confidently believe to be with the Saviour
they so long and so faithfully served,
George Emmet Woods
and
Eula Estelle Woods
Who kept ever before me from childhood's earliest
memory the high honor and blessed privilege
of being a faithful and active gospel
preacher; whose faith in me that
this goal would be attained
never faltered; whose
sacrifices made
it possible,
is this
book

LOVINGLY DEDICATED

FOREWORD

Paul the greatest, by far, of all the apostles of the Lord, in his marvelous epistle to the saints in Rome, described his sense of duty and obligation that constrained him to preach the gospel to all whom he could reach in this moving and impressive fashion: "I am debtor both to the Greeks, and to the barbarians; both to the wise and the unwise. So much as in me is, I am ready to preach the gospel to you that are at Rome also. For I am not ashamed of the gospel of Christ: for it is the power of God unto salvation to every one that believeth; to the Jew first, and also to the Greek. For therein is the righteousness of God revealed from faith unto faith: as it is written, The just shall live by faith" (Romans 1:14-17).

The readiness of that incomparable servant of the Cross to proclaim the unsearchable riches of divine grace, and the conditions on which these blessings are secured and appropriated, to a world lost in sin, under certain condemnation and destined to eternal destruction, should be, must be, and is, the aim and intent of every faithful and earnest preacher of the Word; and, to this end I have gladly, happily and fully devoted my chief efforts, feebly and imperfectly though they have always been, for more than a half century.

These sermons are typical of the approach I have ever striven to follow in my work as an evangelist, and they therefore reflect those areas of biblical teaching as well as where I think emphasis should be placed, if the church is to maintain and preserve a true faith and faultless practice, and please him whose we are and whom we serve.

Some sermons included I have preached in meetings throughout the land, and many who read this collection will perhaps recall having heard me discuss some of the themes now included here in somewhat more exhaustive form than when orally delivered. Occasionally, brethren record my sermons; some of these have been transcribed, purely personal and local allusions excised, most introductions and conclusions eliminated because of limitations of space, then typed by me into a computer, and representing the best effort of which I am capable in the presentation of principles and precepts so sorely needed in our day.

It would please me greatly, and fully justify all the work involved in this production, if one lost soul is influenced by it to flee the wrath to come, or one member of the church is drawn back from the abyss of compromise, liberalism and unbelief toward which I sadly believe many are drifting.

No words of mine can possibly express the gratitude I feel to the hundreds of churches and elderships which have invited me for meetings—many of them regularly over a period of thirty years or more—and to that great multitude of sincere saints who have listened patiently and encouragingly to my presentation of the great truths of the gospel. My hearty thanks to sister Virginia Phillips, secretary at the Gospel Advocate, for her usual efficient help in proofreading, and all the other arduous tasks incident to a publication of this kind.

Scripture quotations are from the King James Translation, except in a few instances where reference is made to the American Standard Version of 1901.

Guy N. Woods
P.O. Box 150
Nashville, TN 37202

CONTENTS

SHALL WE KNOW ONE ANOTHER IN HEAVEN?

The mystery of life and the ever-present problem of death have alike occasioned the wonder and the constant concern of the wisest from the early morning of the race. Despite man's constant probing into the phenomena which obtain, many questions clamor for solution, and each generation carries on the constant quest.

The means by which to make the search have become more numerous with the passing of the years, and each has been utilized to the fullest in an effort to push back the barriers of the unknown and to read the riddle of the universe. Biology has sought to offer a scientific explanation; philosophy a rational view. History testifies to its universality, and poetry attempts to soften its effects. Despite these aids, there hovers over death an impenetrable shroud to all who seek to solve the problems of life and death without revelation.

The eloquent Ingersoll gave expression to the despair which must characterize all who ignore or disregard inspiration when, at the tomb of his brother, he uttered these cheerless words: "My friends: I am going to do that which the dead often promised he would do for me. The loved and loving brother, husband, father, friend, died where manhood's morning almost touches noon, and while the shadows still were falling toward the West. He had not passed on life's highway the stone that marks the highest point, but being weary for a moment he laid down by the wayside and, using his burden for a pillow, fell into the dreamless sleep that kisses down his eyelids still. While yet in love with life and raptured with the world, he passed to silence and pathetic dust. Yet, after all, it

1

may be best, just in the happiest, sunniest hour of the
voyage, while eager winds are kissing every sail, to
dash against the unseen rock, and in an instant hear
the billows roar over a sunken ship. For whether in
mid-sea or among the breakers of the farther shore, a
wreck must mark at last the end of each and all. And
every life, no matter if its every hour is rich with love
and every moment jeweled with a joy, will, at its close,
become a tragedy, as sad, and deep, and dark as can
be woven of the warp and woof of mystery and death
. . . Life is a narrow vale between the cold and barren
peaks of two eternities. We strive in vain to look
beyond the heights. We cry aloud, and the only answer
is the echo of our wailing cry. From the voiceless lips
of the unreplying dead there comes no word."

Such is the helplessness of unbelief, the despair of
those who deliberately draw the curtain of inspiration
and refuse to regard the lessons which it alone can
teach.

But little better is the philosophy of those who, while
confessing to the belief of life after death, yet deny the
plain lessons of truth regarding its nature. Some
indeed seek to question the fact of death itself, in
disregard of the universal observation of all men, and
the eventual experience of all the race. Such are the
so-called Christian Scientists. Others, in the realm of
materialism, declare that all there is of man dies, and
that in death complete, utter dissolution occurs. The
truth is with neither. Granting that in death the body
returns to the dust out of which it is constructed,

"This is not the whole sad story of creation
Told by toiling millions o'er and o'er'
One day, then black annihilation,
A sunlit passage to a sunless shore,"
                                    —Emerson.

Still others err in assigning a wrong cause to the occasion for suffering and death in this dispensation. True it is that death and all its associated sorrows entered into the world through the door of sin; it is not true—and it is a serious sin to so affirm—that all affliction and death are the result of some particular sin or sins. In his effort to find a cause for every effort he observes, man has been very prone to see in the trials of humanity tokens of punishment. The so-called friends of Job were sure that his sufferings were the result of sins of which they were ignorant. The Jews were particularly obsessed with the idea, and the disciples of Christ exhibited traces of it. "Now there were some present at that very season who told him of the Galilaeans, whose blood Pilate had mingled with their sacrifices. And he answered and said unto them, Think ye that these Galilaeans were sinners above all the Galilaeans, *because they have* suffered these things? I tell you, Nay: but, except ye repent, ye shall all in like manner perish" (Luke 13:1-3).

With reference to the blind man whose eyes the Lord opened, the disciples inquired: "Master, who did sin, this man, or his parents, that he was born blind? Jesus answered, Neither hath this man sinned nor his parents: but that the works of God should be made manifest in him" (John 9:2,3). In these two instances, Jesus settles once and for all the question of personal guilt as a necessary consequence of infirmity or death. That suffering and death may result as an immediate consequence of sin is admitted; a man, for example, through intoxication, may suffer an automobile accident and die; but the mere fact of suffering and death does not entail, as a necessary consequence, the commission of sin. Infants, the purest and best of earth, are incapable of sin, yet they die. Some of the most godly, consecrated souls in life have as their inescapable lot the problem of pain; and release from pain-ridden bodies comes only by death. We must learn to distinguish between the *guilt* of sin and the consequences which attend it. Adam's sin brought death upon the race; we suffer its consequence, though not guilt of the actual transgression. "Therefore, as through one man sin entered into the world, and death through sin; and so death passed unto all men, for that all sinned:—for until the law sin was in the world; but sin is not imputed when there is no law. Nevertheless death reigned from Adam until Moses, even over them that had not sinned after the likeness of Adam's transgression who is a figure of him that was to come" (Romans 5:12-14).

Often, well-meaning but misguided individuals add to the burdens of the faithful by attributing their infirmities to personal transgression; and the sufferers themselves, in seeking for some explanation thereof, often ask, "What is it that I have done that the Lord afflicts me in such fashion?" It is appointed unto men "once to die," and this results from the fact that death has been passed upon all the race of which we are a part. We should be careful lest we imbibe the unbelief which characterized the superstitious who continually pore over the events of life to see in them tokens of their superstitious awe. John Greenleaf Whittier, in his lovely poem, The Eternal Goodness, reveals the faith that should characterize us all:

"Within the maddening maze of things
And tossed by storm and flood,
To one fixed trust my spirit clings,
I know that God is good."

"I know not what the future hath
Of marvel or surprise;
Assured alone that life and death
His mercy underlies."

"And so beside the silent sea
I wait the muffled oar;
No harm from him can come to me
On ocean or on shore."

"I know not where his islands lift
Their fronded palms in air,
I only know I cannot drift
Beyond his love and care."

"And thou, O Lord, by whom are seen
Thy creatures as they be,
Forgive me if too close I lean
My human heart on thee."

What Is Death?

Some terms, notwithstanding the fact that they are often on our lips and frequently recur in our phraseology, are not easy of definition. Such are the words, *life* and *death*. Though we are in possession of the one and shall eventually experience the other, and despite the fact that their manifestations are ever about us, it is not easy to define them. True it is that our dictionaries say that life is "a vital force"; "existence"; "way or manner of living"; and death is "loss of life"; "state of being dead"; "cessation of existence"; etc.; but notwithstanding this, we instinctively feel that all such attempts at definition are inadequate and defective— far short of the demands of the case. In contemplation of these efforts to clarify the life and death, and conscious of their inadequacy, we are made to inquire, What is a vital force, what is existence, what is a way or manner of life; and what occurs in the loss of life, what is the state of being dead, and what is cessation of existence? Clearly, the definitions of the dictionaries do not satisfy.

On this, as on all matters relevant to man's origin and destiny, man must turn to the only source of information thereon: the Bible. From its pages the most humble and obscure person may learn more regarding his earthly life and its termination than the wisest philosophers have been able to discover in centuries outside its pages.

In a simple, but wonderfully comprehensive statement, James said, "*The body apart from the spirit is dead*" (James 2:26). By deduction we discover from this that *life* is that state or condition which exists while the body and the spirit are united; *death* is that state or condition resulting when the spirit is no longer in the body. Life, then, is the union of the body and spirit; death, their separation. Death *is not* non-existence, it *is not* cessation of life or of existence, it *is not* extinction. It is simply and solely separation—separation of body (the flesh) and the spirit (the immortal entity). James declares that, under the condition which he contemplates, "the body . . . is dead." The qualifying phrase is "apart from the spirit." Thus, death is the condition obtaining when the body is apart from the spirit. But when the body is apart from the spirit, the body and the spirit are separated. Death, then, is the separation of the body and spirit. This conclusion seems certain.

The penalty of Adam's sin was death—first, spiritual death, consisting in the separation from God which he suffered as the result of his transgression in Eden, and occurring the moment he partook of the forbidden fruit; and second, physical death in consequence of having been separated from the "tree of life" by which alone it was possible for him to perpetuate his physical existence. In view of the fact that the essential characteristic of death is separation, it follows that one may die in just as many senses as he can be joined to that which, as a result of such connection, produces life. These facts have long been recognized, and have often been demonstrated in our debates with materialists.

Death is not cessation of existence, it is not dissolution of the body, it is not annihilation. *It is the separation of the body and the spirit.* The body, when separated from the spirit, is said to be dead, not because it is inactive, cold, or even returning to the dust—these are the effects which attend death. The *cause* is that the spirit which animated it and gave it life is no longer there. Throughout the sacred writings the departure of the spirit (or soul, when regarded as synonymous with the spirit) is regarded as the occasion of death. The following instances will illustrate this fact:

1. Genesis 25:8: "And Abraham *gave up the ghost,* and died in a good old age, an old man, and full of years, and was gathered to his people."

2. Genesis 35:18: "And it came to pass, as her soul *was departing* (for she died)."

3. 1 Kings 17:22: "And the Lord heard the voice of Elijah; and the soul of the child came into him again, and he revived."

4. Psalm 90:10: "The days of our years are threescore years and ten; and if by reason of strength they be fourscore years, yet is their strength labour and sorrow; for it is soon cut off, *and we fly away.*"

5. Acts 7:59: "And they stoned Stephen, calling upon God, and saying, Lord Jesus, *receive my spirit.*"

In giving up the ghost, Abraham died; the departing of Rachel's soul from her body resulted in her death; the child for whom the prophet prayed was dead and revived only when the soul returned to its body; the days of our years are terminated when that which is immortal flies away, and the martyr Stephen expired when his spirit left his bruised and broken body. The conclusion from this collation of scripture (which might be greatly extended) is irresistible, and establishes beyond reasonable doubt that death is simply the condition subsisting when the spirit is no longer in the body.

Does the spirit survive apart from the body as a conscious entity? In a remarkable testimony to this fact, Paul wrote: "Being therefore always of good courage, and knowing that, whilst we are at home in the body, we are absent from the Lord . . . and are willing rather to be absent from the body, and to be at home with the Lord" (2 Corinthians 5:6-8). The original is even more striking: *Those who dwell in the body are at a distance from the Lord: those who have traveled out of the body reside with the Lord.*

Whether we shall know each other in heaven is truly a question of more than merely curious interest. Every thoughtful person who has suffered the poignant pain of parting from those near and dear and has tenderly laid their physical forms to rest in the tomb is vitally and absorbingly interested in the implications which this question raises. He knows that he shall see them no more in this land of the living; that they have passed beyond the door of death to return to this world no more. If there is no future recognition, the moment of parting at the grave, however forbidding the thought may be, becomes the hour of final separation. Soon we, too, shall divest ourselves of the mortal robe with which we are clothed here, and go to join the teeming millions of our race who have lived and loved and at last gone to take their places in the silent halls of death. On the morning of the resurrection day we shall rise to stand in judgment and to hear the pronouncement of our eternal destiny. If there is to be no recognition, we shall there be among total strangers; every memory we now possess will have been obliterated and every bond here severed, and as strangers we shall enter heaven and so live there forever and ever.

If a careful study of the sacred writings should lead us to such a conclusion, it will, it must be acknowledged, greatly alter our conceptions of heaven and the abode of the sainted dead. Whether fully aware of all the implications which attach to the matter or not, our hope of heaven and our expectation of future bliss have been conditioned on the understanding that some wondrous day we shall be privileged to gather up the sundered threads of this existence so rudely severed in death, and in the company of dear loved ones and valued friends gone on before enjoy the ineffable bliss of paradise forever and ever and ever.

Are we prepared for such a conclusion?

Our whole being instinctively and unhesitatingly shrinks from such a supposition. We are, in the first place, *unwilling* to accept the conclusion that heaven will be peopled with those who are utter strangers to them here, that every vestige of memory will have been obliterated there, and that we shall never again be privileged to see and know those we have loved a while and lost here. And, secondly, we find ourselves *unable* to visualize a place of perfect happiness as heaven is alleged to be thus stripped of what is surely one of its sweetest joys and most fondly anticipated delights.

The view is opposed to reason, (a) because it ignores one of the most deep-seated and well-recognized desires of the heart: a glad reunion with the precious loved ones on the golden shores of the heavenly city. The separation which death inevitably brings is physical and outward and visible only; the ties of affection, regard, and memory are as tangible and definite and real as any which subsist in life. Our loved ones are gone from us in bodily presence only; they live on in our hearts with immortal and imperishable vigor. The granite stones which we erect to their precious memory, the tears which fall from our eyes on their graves, and the flowers which we place on their sacred mounds bear unmistakable testimony to the love and affection we feel for them, and the memory which is enshrined in our hearts. "She was going unto the tomb to weep there," is the record of not only Mary, but of millions of others in every age and country and clime. The soul longs for assurance of a happy reunion beyond the door of death, and diligently searches (and not in vain, we shall later see) for evidence in the scriptures that such a longing is not a delusion and fantasy.

(b) The wisest and greatest and best of all ages have confidently looked beyond the sombre curtains of death and thought that there is such a place as the scriptures reveal heaven to be. Among the heathens the most enlightened and elevated minds, though without the full light of truth, while groping in the feeble glimmer of reason and grasping for whatever truth they might thus imperfectly see, were able to visualize a place of pleasure where a communion with the departed dead would be possible. Socrates, one of the wisest and best of the Grecian philosophers, condemned to death by unjust judges, calmly submitted to his fate, and talked with his friends almost to the moment when he took the fatal hemlock cup. In his speech to his judges following his sentence of death, he said: "If death is a removal to another place, and what is said to be true—that all the dead are there—what greater blessing can there be than this, my judges? Or if, on arriving at Hades, released from those who pretend to be judges, one shall find those that are true judges, and who are said to be there—Minos and Radamanthus, Aeacus, and Tripotolemus? . . . Would this be a sad removal? . . . At what price my judges, would not any one estimate the opportunity of questioning him who lead that mighty army against Troy, or Ulysses, or Sisyphus, or ten thousand others whom one might mention, both men and women? with whom to converse and associate, and to question them, would be an inconceivable happiness."

Such would indeed be "an inconceivable happiness," and when to the opportunity afforded of interviewing the great and illustrious characters of all ages, we add the unspeakable privilege of talking with and seeing those nearest and dearest to our hearts, our innermost being thrills with joy at the anticipation of such, and heaven glows with undying lustre as we long for its joys and rich delights. Whose soul is it which does not go wild at the prospect of *seeing* and *knowing* illustrious prophets, priests, and kings; of being associated with the great and wise and good of all ages: of sitting at the feet of Peter and Paul and the Lord? And when to this we add the wondrous prospect of seeing our dear loved ones in their immortal state, no longer weary and sad and worn and sick, no longer clothed in bodies weak with pain and ravaged by disease, but arrayed in the imperishable splendor which shall ever characterize the good, the pure, and the blest, who can avoid the conclusion of the peerless apostle that it is "very far better" there?

No. The hope of a glad and happy reunion "just over there" is not a cruel delusion, a vain and empty fantasy. Those who silently weep in loneliness may take comfort in the fact that they sorrow not in vain, or as others who have no hope. Inspiration has not left us comfortless in this matter; on the contrary, the warmest assurances of the reality of such a hope abound on the sacred page; and that we may confidently expect to mingle with, converse, and walk again with those we have loved and lost in a land where songs will be infinitely sweeter than any we have rendered here, where handclasps will be warmer than any we have ever experienced in this life, and where tears, heartaches, and sorrows are unknown.

Scriptural Evidence of Future Recognition

Thus far attention has been directed to the philosophical and reasonable basis of the doctrine of future
recognition in the heavenly sphere. While neither
philosophy nor reason constitutes the *final*, or, for that
matter, even an *authoritative*, word on any matter of
divine providence, it will be admitted by thoughtful
persons that when each approves and endorses the
idea, such amounts to corroborative and presumptive
evidence of the matter under consideration; and when
to such presumptive proof is added the infallible
testimony of sacred writers, faith and reason combine
to establish the truth beyond reasonable question.
Having, in this inquiry, listened to reason, we are now
to hear revelation on the subject of future recognition.

In this field, the evidence is so abundant, the proof
so varied, and the references so numerous one
wonders where to begin. By this it is not meant that
the doctrine is taught in formal propositions or
announced in direct statements. One will search in
vain for any positive affirmation thereon by any Biblical
writer. On this subject, as on a great many matters of
equal importance, we are dependent on incidental
allusion, logical deduction, and necessary inference for
the proof with which we hope to sustain our
proposition. Such evidence, as every one skilled in
evaluating it knows, is no less credible or relevant
because undesigned. And, it is, in the nature of the
case, all the more abundant, for this reason.

1. There is, for example, the incidental allusions to
impending joy which Paul expected to experience in
the life to come because of the faithfulness and
devotion of those to whom he had preached and
among whom he had labored. They were his "joy and
crown" (Philippians 4:1), those whom he fondly and
confidently expected to afford him with the occasion
for "rejoicing . . . in the day of the Lord Jesus" (2

Corinthians 1:14). "For what is our hope, or joy, or crown of rejoicing?" he asked, and then answered his question thus: "Are not even ye in the presence of our Lord Jesus Christ at his coming?" (1 Thessalonians 2:19). But what would be the manner of his realization of such rejoicing? Again he answers: "He which raised up the Lord Jesus shall raise up us also by Jesus, and shall present us with you" (2 Corinthians 4:14). Who among us can believe that these who were to be raised would be total and utter strangers to Paul, and he to them, with no memory of any former association, with the recollection of their great obligation to him completely blotted out, not even knowing that it was he who led them out of darkness into light and from the power of Satan unto God? Truly, the words, "shall present us with you," must signify more than the mere gathering of unfamiliar personalities, the assembly of strangers!

2. The comforting assurances of holy writ, penned by inspired men for the purpose of soothing sorrowful hearts and comforting the sad and grief-stricken, imply a reunion and consequent resumption of association in a better land: "But we would not have you ignorant, brethren, concerning them that fall asleep; that ye sorrow not, even as the rest, who have no hope. For if we believe that Jesus died and rose again, even so them also that are fallen asleep in Jesus will God bring with him. . . . Wherefore comfort one another with these words" (1 Thessalonians 4:13,14,18). Two classes of the dead are here contemplated: (1) Those who died in Christ; (2) those who died out of Christ. Loved ones of the former class are not, as those of the latter, without hope; on the contrary, their loved ones will reappear with the Lord when the sign of the Son of man is seen in the clouds, and be privileged again to be associated with those whom, in death, they left behind. In consequence, we are admonished and

encouraged to (a) entertain hope and (b) to find
comfort in this fact. But, on the assumption that the
personality of those we have loved and lost is
obliterated, their memories of us, and ours of them
forevermore gone and with no tangible marks of
identity remaining, how is *hope* possible and where is
there occasion for comfort in such a circumstance?
Before such a prospect, the mind quails, hope fades
into despair, words calculated to comfort become
empty mockery, and the passage is without significance.

3. The doctrine of rewards and punishments, taught
so clearly and at such great length in the scriptures,
implies and necessitates the conclusion that future
recognition is an assured fact. In the field of criminal
jurisprudence, for example, a man is regarded as
worthy of punishment for unsocial acts committed,
only when it appears that he is mentally capable of
recognizing the nature of his deed. However violent
the act and vicious the deed, when it is shown that the
one having committed it is mentally incompetent,
penal processes are immediately suspended, and the
man is committed to an institution for the insane. Are
we, in the light of this humane and reasonable
consideration of law—a law which affects itself to be
founded on the law of God—to assume that a benign
Father will, nevertheless, disregard the competency
of the culprit, and administer punishment *for acts of
which the person being punished has no recollection
whatsoever?* We shrink from the very suggestion of
such an imputation.

Moreover, the scriptures clearly establish the fact
that in judgment men will be possessed of the memory
of deeds done here, and will allege such in extenuation
of, and in protest to, the decision there to be handed
down: "Many will say to me in that day, Lord, Lord,
did we not prophesy by thy name, and by thy name

cast out demons, and by thy name do many mighty works?" (Matthew 7:22). Further, in numerous instances individuals, now in the disembodied state, are declared to be possessed of a distinct and vivid recollection of events occurring on earth prior to their passing: "I saw under the altar the souls of them that were slain for the word of God, and for the testimony which they held: and they cried with a loud voice, saying, How long, O Lord, holy and true, dost thou not judge and avenge our blood on them that dwell on the earth?" (Revelation 6:9,10). These were (a) personalities in the spirit realm; (b) they had an awareness of their surroundings; (c) they knew why they were there: they had been murdered; (d) they inquired when judgment would be exercised on those guilty of their murder. If there is not here a clear and convincing demonstration of consciousness following death; if this passage does not establish a definite and mental connection between this life and the next; if it is not shown that there is a positive and certain retention of memory with reference to events occurring here, then there is an end to all reasonable exegesis, and we may as well be done with any effort to ascertain the meaning and significance of any passage in the scriptures by the usual and ordinary rules of interpretation.

4. The case of the rich man and Lazarus (Luke 16:19-31), whether a parable or not, supplies us with a glimpse of the state of the dead, lifts the curtain of the future, and enables us to look for a moment on the scenes of the yet-to-be. The consciousness which each of the characters possessed, their awareness of their surroundings, and the memory which they retained of the world from which they had but lately left all point irresistibly to the conclusion which we have reached. And, couched in the two words, *"Son,*

remember," is a necessary inference for all for which we contend.

5. Paul, in a chapter designed to deal at length with the resurrection state, represents the risen saint as standing on the verge of his empty grave and shouting the song of triumph: "O death, where is thy victory? O death, where is thy sting?" (1 Corinthians 15:55). This consciousness of triumph is possible only on the supposition that memory is able to carry across the chasm of death the recollection of the destiny with which all men, until the Lord comes, are faced.

6. A phrase of peculiar significance, and especially relevant to our present study, occurs in connection with the record of Abraham's death. In a passage poignantly pathetic, one which simply touches the heart with its simplicity and pathos, and picturing the passing of the venerable patriarch, his demise is recorded thus: "And Abraham gave up the ghost, and died in a good old age, an old man, and full of years; and was gathered to his people" (Genesis 25:8). The phrase, *"And was gathered to his people,"* occurs with slight variation in the chronicle of Ishmael's death (Genesis 25:17), the death of Isaac (Genesis 35:29), Jacob (Genesis 49:29,33), Moses and Aaron (Deuteronomy 32:50). This phase cannot properly be understood as referring to the burial of their bodies, for Moses, as an example, was buried in a secret place "in the valley in the land of Moab," far from the sepulchres of his fathers. The reference must, therefore, be to his spirit, and to its reunion with the spirits of his ancestors gone on before. Jacob was "gathered unto his people," while in the land of Egypt, and thus long before he was borne to Canaan and entombed in the soil of his homeland (Genesis 49:33-50:1-3). It seems certain, in the light of these facts, that the phrase, "gathered unto his people," refers, not to the fact of death, nor to the place

thereof, but to the journey of the spirit to the unseen world.

The grief-stricken David, with the body of his dead child yet unburied, said, "Can I bring him back again? *I shall go to him, but he shall not return to me"* (2 Samuel 12:23). The question which the humbled king raised in rhetorical, the answer obvious. He could not bring the child back. He was aware that the spirit of the child was not there, though the body yet remained. The comfort which he derived was conditioned on journeying to the place where the child was. Are we to conclude that the monarch believed that, on the occasion of such a reunion, this child would be to him no more than any other child, that he would, indeed, be unable to know whether it was his own child or not? We cannot believe it.

Jesus, in a discourse dealing with the wickedness of his contemporaries, affirmed that the men of Nineveh, who repented at the preaching of the fiery prophet Jonah, would rise up in judgment and condemn those of his generation. In order to do what is affirmed of them, it will be necessary for the men of Nineveh to be in judgment; to be in judgment in their own characters and clothed with the personalities which they possessed here: to retain the detailed and minute memory of events then occurring, and particularly, of the waywardness, rebellion, and perverseness characteristic of those about whom the Savior spoke (Matthew 12:38-41). Only on the supposition that the memory of men in the next world extends to this is such a circumstance as these verses relate possible.

Objections to the Doctrine of Future Recognition Answered

Despite the abundance of evidence which obtains and the consolation which the doctrine of future recognition brings, objections have been raised and arguments against it offered. That such arguments are offered and objections raised does not establish a presumption that the doctrine is false, or that the evidence by which it is sustained is insufficient or weak. Objections have been, and are being, offered against every cardinal doctrine of the Christian religion. When the mind is disposed to cavil, human perverseness is such that it finds at hand unbelief on which to feed and grounds which to itself is sufficient to oppose that against which it arrays itself.

The objections which are filed against the doctrine of future recognition have their origin in a defective concept of the nature of the next life or in projecting the limitations of this life into the next, or both.

1. It is, for example, alleged that we will have lost, in the next world, the physical characteristics and recognizable distinctions which we possess in this; and that with these gone and with ourselves nothing but "spirit beings" there will be nothing with which to identify us with this existence. By "spirit beings" is usually meant ghost-like wraiths of the same nature as a child imagines fairies to possess. How may such intangible and immaterial beings be recognized, it is asked.

In reply it should be said that such concepts as the foregoing grow out of a gross misapprehension of the teaching of the scriptures with reference to the nature and characteristics of the resurrected saint. The resurrection of the body—this body changed from a mortal to an immortal one—is taught in the fullest, most explicit, and satisfactory manner. "It is sown in corruption, it is raised in incorruption" (1 Corinthians 15:42). What is the antecedent of the "its" of this entire passage? "For this corruptible must put on incorruption, and this mortal must put on immortality" (1 Corinthians 15:53). What corruptible, what mortal?

Corruptibility and mortality are affirmed of some part of us. Of what part? Not the spirit, certainly; for it is neither mortal nor corruptible. Reference is, therefore, to the body. But the affirmation of the text is that "this" mortal shall put on immortality. What mortal? The one we now possess. What is it about us that we now possess that is mortal? *This* body. The "manner of body" which it pleases God to give us is that which undergoes the change thus indicated (1 Corinthians 15:35-38).

Job said, "For I know that my Redeemer liveth, and that he shall stand at the latter day upon the earth: and though after my skin worms destroy this body, yet in my flesh shall I see God: whom I shall see for myself, and mine eyes shall behold, and not another" (Job 19:25-27). Here, in the most positive fashion, the resurrection of the body, the preservation of the personality, and the identity of the individual are taught, Job believed that *he* (as Job) would see God; that he would see God in the flesh (with the change implied through which bodies must pass in the resurrection), and that it would be Job who experienced this with his own eye, and not another.

But to set the matter at rest once and for all we have only to examine the references respecting the resurrection of the Lord's body. He was "the firstfruits of them that are asleep," the pledge and token of the resurrection of all the rest. (1 Corinthians 15:20). When he shall appear, "we shall be like him" (1 John 3:2). But the body in which Jesus came forth possessed the same distinctive features as that which was buried. The disciples looked with transfigured gaze upon his lovely form; they thrilled with rapture to his familiar voice; with wonder and reverent joy they touched him with their hands and examined the cruel spear thrust in his side. So full and satisfactory was the evidence thus afforded them that ever thereafter they had the fullest assurance of his identity, and from this conviction they never wavered. If then his resurrection is indeed a demonstration of the certainty of ours; if we are truly to be as he was; does it not follow that those who know us as well as the disciples were acquainted with him before his death will see in us the same recognizable characteristics?

2. Others based an objection to the doctrine of future recognition on the Lord's reply to the Sadducean cavil that "in the resurrection they neither marry, nor are given in marriage, but are as angels in heaven" (Matthew 22:30). But this, far from sustaining the objection, establishes its opposite; for it asserts that the risen saints will be as "angels in heaven," who surely must possess the faculty of memory and who are undoubtedly acquainted with each other. This statement of our Lord was a reply to the Sadducees who, in objecting to the doctrine of the resurrection, presented a hypothetical case which was designed, if not to make the doctrine of the resurrection impossible, to make it look at least ridiculous. The statement was made to show that the marriage relation will not be maintained in the next life. It should be noted that this passage teaches that the relation of marriage is to be terminated; not that the recollection will be blotted out.

3. Some affect great difficulty in accepting future recognition on that ground that should we know each other there, and some of our loved ones are not there, the consciousness of this fact would mar the bliss of heaven. But this supposition, instead of solving the difficulty, increases it; for, if we are unable to recognize *any* of our loved ones there, we must then be uncertain whether any of them are there, even if they are, in which case we should worry about *all* of them, though there! Much better, on this hypothesis, for some of them to be there, and know them, than for all of them to be there and not know any of them. The conclusion

which those who offer this objection reach is grounded in an erroneous concept with references to the attitude which shall characterize us in the next world. It assumes that we shall ignore the manner of life characteristic of those who have failed to reach heaven and desire their presence in spite of the way in which they have lived. When the mists have cleared, and all imperfect conceptions are gone, we shall be able fully to acquiesce in the righteous judgments of God. We shall then be able to see clearly that those who are not in heaven do not deserve to be there; that they made no effort to reach that place; that, on the contrary, they resisted every effort to lead them there. Knowing this, we shall then be able to accept without question the wise decisions of the Judge of all the universe and recognize fully that he doeth all things well.

We have earlier seen that death is the separation of the body from all that involves life. This would include the mind and all of its operations, as well as the soul or spirit—the immortal nature. This being true, and thoughtful people will not question it, it must follow that a disembodied spirit is without any relationship of time and space, along with all material matters. It seems quite clear that if the physical organs are absent—and they are in death—the senses are no longer operative, and all functions necessarily have terminated. This is not to say that there is no communication between spirits in the spiritual world; it is to say that there is not, because there cannot be such communication between those of that world and this, the means of and avenues through which such communication would be achieved are no longer present.

This consideration, were there no others—and there are numerous ones to be drawn from the scriptures, clearly and irrevocably establishes the falsity of claims increasingly being made of communication with the dead by those yet living. Any hope thereto is destined to certain failure, and any offer by spiritualistic mediums to establish such contact is a cruel hoax engineered by those who would prey on the sorrowful and the sad, those who still long for "the touch of a vanished hand, and the sound of a voice that is still." Alleged accounts of such intercommunication bear on their face their fictitious character, purportedly claiming sensations through senses no longer present in death. The claims are thus not only opposed to the scriptures, but to common sense, and are simply figments of imagination, the result of which is to deceive and delude.

Spirits, out of their tabernacles of flesh (2 Corinthians 5:1), are, therefore without the faculties of sensing the materialistic effects always alleged to be characteristic of these seances, and any impression, dependent on physical powers must, in the absence of such powers, be regarded as impossible, and the effort to achieve it resulting from superstitious imagination.

It is at this point that another matter of absorbing interest arises, and the satisfactory solution of another problem appears. It must follow that the spirit—the immortal nature which is not subject to death, and which survives it—is, in its disembodied state, without awareness of the passing of time. The thoughtful person must have pondered, with no little concern, the question of the alleged lapse of time, if such there be, and its effects on the spirit, from the moment of death until the resurrection, between which millenniums of years, as time is reckoned on earth, may intervene. It has been thousands of years, for example, since the death of the illustrious patriarch Abraham, the consummation of all matters is not yet, and could possibly not be for untold centuries; for multitudes, time as measured in centuries on earth, moves slowly by; are those now in the spirit world, and all of us who are to follow, destined to wait out the passing of the ages, through seemingly endless periods, before receiving the reward of a life of service here?

It should be kept in mind that time cannot be contemplated, indeed, does not exist apart from the events by which it is determined and measured. A day, for example, is calculated by the rotation of the earth; the hours are arbitrary divisions of the day, as minutes are of the hour and seconds are of the minute. The spirit, at death, wings its way into the Hadean world to wait for the resurrection of the body, the final judgment and the end of the world. For it time no longer exists, since neither the means by which it is determined, nor the conceptions by which it is recognized are present. How, for example may a spirit, released from its body, and gone from the earth, be aware of the seasons, of hot and cold, of night and day, or other impressions possible only to those yet on earth?

I must say to you, in the light of these facts, that I incline strongly to the view that the spirit, free of its body and all fleshly limitations, is wholly unaware of the passing of the years, the centuries or the millenniums men use to mark off time here! It is not out of order to draw a parallel from our own experiences in dreams that accompany sleep (our Lord and the apostles did in comparing death to sleep), by noting that utter unawareness of the passing of time in dreams—surely the nearest we can come to apprehending being apart from time. In such experiences there is complete absence of any consciousness of the passing of time—dreams may, and often do, bridge great chasms of time, and involve vivid experiences and impressions of the long ago which nonetheless seem but yesterday. These, and other considerations into which time does not now allow, lead me, at least, to conclude that those in the spirit world are not bound

by the restrictions of time, and that the "period" of
their sojourn in Hades will pass for them in what to
us on earth is but a moment.

I rejoice to believe that loved ones, now awaiting
our coming, will not languish through long periods for
the happy moment of glad reunion on golden shores,
neither shall we be required to wait through endless
ages in Hades for the blissful joys of the heavenly city;
stripped of the limitations of time and space, we'll live
in eternity when the "past" the "present" and the
"future," are all before us in one grand and wonderful
view! This seems clearly deducible from that comforting and consoling statement of Paul to the Thessalonians: "But I would not have you to be ignorant,
brethren, concerning them which are asleep, that ye
sorrow not, even as others which have no hope. For if
we believe that Jesus died and rose again, even so them
also which sleep in Jesus will God bring with him. For
this we say unto you that we which are alive and
remain unto the coming of the Lord shall not prevent
(literally, 'go before') them that are asleep. For the Lord
himself shall descend from heaven with a shout, with
the voice of the archangel, and with the trump of God:
and the dead in Christ shall rise first: then we which
are alive and remain shall be caught up in the clouds,
to meet the Lord in the air: and so shall we ever be
with the Lord. Wherefore comfort one another with
these words" (1 Thessalonians 4:13-18). Though penned
primarily to assure sorrowing saints in the Thessalonian church that their loved ones who died before the
return of the Lord would not be left behind in the
catching up of the saints to heaven at the last day, it
nonetheless clearly implies that none will exceed
others in the joys and blessings of salvation which
would hardly be the case if there are indeed long
periods of waiting for some saints before the realization
of all their hopes and longings, as would characterize

Abraham and all the ancient saints, in that event. I rejoice to believe that all of the blessed dead, though they died centuries ago, will not be any more disadvantaged than the last faithful disciple who shuffles off his mortal coil of flesh moments before the trumpet sounds, heralding the end of the world and the consummation of all things.

Objections raised to the doctrine of future recognition are not valid. It is grounded in hope, it is sustained by faith, and love longs for its realization. *It is the truth.* Let us derive great comfort and consolation in it.

DEGREES OF REWARD
AND PUNISHMENT

There are many incentives in the sacred writings prompting us to greater devotion and to increased activity in the service of the Saviour. Love for the Lord, a longing for salvation, the desire for a heavenly home, and the fear of punishment and the eternal fires of hell, are among the many inducements in the Bible to influence us to strive earnestly for a higher and more noble life.

Strong though these promptings are, it seems to me that there is another that exceeds all others in its appeal to the human mind, since it speaks directly to our sense of personal values, and involves self interest in the most positive and direct fashion. This motivation, of matters directly related to our own well being, happiness, and status in the world to come, about which I wish to speak to you in some detail this evening, is so powerful, so persuasive, and so potent in its effects, that were it possible to induce our people throughout the brotherhood to believe it and to recognize its implications, there would be an immediate end to most problems besetting us; and a measure of faithfulness, dedication and zeal not before known among us would at once appear. Thoughtful and intelligent people, mindful that the choice is theirs whether they shall enjoy heaven and to what degree, or suffer the torments of the damned and to an extent aggravated by their actions here, will not be indifferent to these sobering matters. I hope therefore that you will consider these themes carefully and come to share with me the profound feeling of importance to us all I fervently believe they deserve.

26

Judgment awaits us all. The Bible abounds with affirmations to this end, some of which are these: "And many of them that sleep in the dust of the earth shall awake, some to everlasting life, and some to shame and everlasting contempt" (Daniel 12:2). "Marvel not at this: for the hour cometh, in which all that are in the tombs shall hear his voice, and shall come forth; they that have done good, unto the resurrection of life; and they that have done evil, unto the resurrection of judgment" (John 5:28, 29). "So then every one of us shall give an account of himself to God" (Romans 14:12). For we must all be made manifest before the judgment seat of Christ; that each one may receive the things done in the body, according to what he hath done, whether it be good or bad" (2 Corinthians 5:10).

"And I saw a great white throne, and him that sat upon it, from whose face the earth and the heaven fled away; and no place was found for them. And I saw the dead, the great and the small, standing before the throne; and books were opened; and another book was opened, which is the book of life: and the dead were judged out of the things written in the books, according to their works. And the sea gave up the dead that were in it; and death and Hades gave up the dead that were in them: and they were judged every man according to their works. And death and Hades were cast into the lake of fire. This is the second death, even the lake of fire. And if any was not found written in the book of life, he was cast into the lake of fire" (Revelation 20:11-15).

These passages—and the list might be greatly lengthened, since the scriptures often warn of these awesome events—clearly evidence an eventual and inevitable day of judgment for all accountable beings, in which number we certainly are. From this representative induction of the scriptures we may properly deduce the following irresistible conclusions:

(1) A judgment day, for us all, is certainly coming.
(2) There all of us must appear, and in our own persons, and not by proxy.
(3) The record of our lives will be unfolded and examined.
(4) From that record, now being entered, our eternal destiny will be determined.
(5) Those who have faithfully served the Lord here will be bidden to enter heaven's happy home.
(6) Those who have not will be thrust into hell, there to remain through endless ages.

We have seen, from passages already presented, that a judgment day inevitably awaits us. If it can be shown that in that solemn hour, the people who appear in that tribunal will be required to answer for their actions in proportion to the guilt they sustain, and if it can be further shown that this guilt will be proportionate to the privileges and opportunities they enjoyed here, I will have shown you that this, the United States, and this the "Bible Belt" of this great land will be, beyond doubt, the *worst possible place* from which to go the judgment *unprepared*, since the opportunities we enjoy here are surely equal to the best in the world and certainly superior to most.

Is this conclusion a proper one, and does it follow from the premises advanced? More importantly, for us, do the scriptures teach it? I am unable to see how it could be otherwise. Before offering for your consideration scriptures leading, in my opinion, irresistibly to this conclusion, let us, for the moment, examine the reasonableness of it. Do not men generally recognize this principle as a valid one, and accept it as an accurate method of determining the degree of guilt to be assigned to wrong doers?

It is recognized that some crimes and offenses against mankind result from greater depravity than others, and consequently deserve more severe punishment. This may be clearly seen in the wrongful taking of human life, ranging all the way from involuntary manslaughter, where someone dies through the carelessness of another, but not through intent; voluntary manslaughter, where the law considers that there are extenuating circumstances; murder in the third degree; murder in the second degree; murder in the first degree—each degree representing a greater amount of intent and premeditation, and therefore indicating greater guilt. Our legislative bodies, in recognition of this, have accordingly adapted the punishment to the crime, in harmony with the concept that the more advanced one's guilt is, the more severe the punishment attending it should be. This appears to be a reasonable and proper approach, and has been exercised judicially by human tribunals from the dawn of the race. Will this principle be applicable in the Court of the Last Great Day, and before the Judge of the quick and the dead? What do the scriptures teach regarding this momentous matter?

I can give but a tithe of the evidence therein found regarding this vital matter, but more—much more—than enough, I think, to establish, for all reasonable and thoughtful persons, the only proper conclusion which may be drawn from the Holy Spirit's simple and unmistakable statements touching the subject. In a sharp rebuke to certain Palestinian cities, Jesus said, "Woe unto thee, Chorazin! woe unto thee, Bethsaida! for if the mighty works had been done in Tyre and Sidon which were done in you, they would have repented long ago in sackcloth and ashes. But I say unto you, it shall be more tolerable for Tyre and Sidon in the day of judgment, than for you" (Matthew 11:21,22).

Chorazin and Bethsaida were *Jewish cities* located on, or near the Sea of Galilee, not far from Capernaum where the Lord, during the period of his public

ministry, lived. But little, indeed, is said regarding
them in the gospel narratives, evidencing again what
we often have occasion to note in our study of the New
Testament, how much of our Lord's activities during
his busy career on earth were not recorded. John, by
hyperbole, wrote: "And there are also many other
things which Jesus did, the which if they should be
written every one, I suppose that even the world itself
would not contain the books that should be written"
(John 21:25). Chorazin and Bethsaida had been blessed,
not only by the Lord's visits into their midst, but also
with the privilege of witnessing "mighty works" he did
while there, and they were "upbraided" for not having
repented, as would have Tyre and Sidon—*Gentile cities*
located in Western Palestine on the Mediterranean
Sea—had they enjoyed equal opportunities. Jesus lived
for approximately thirty years in Nazareth, only a few
miles north of Tyre and Sidon, but no mention is made
of his having visited in these cities, since their people
were Gentiles and his ministry was to the Jews
(Matthew 15:24).

"Then began he to upbraid the cities wherein most
of his mighty works were done, because they repented
not." To "upbraid" is to reproach, and the verb
appearing here is so translated in Luke 6:22, Romans
15:3 and 1 Peter 4:14. It does not involve bitter or
vengeful speech; on the contrary, there is discernible
great regret and sorrow and tears in the wail of woes
pronounced. Had Tyre and Sidon enjoyed equal
privileges, notwithstanding their admittedly corrupt
condition, they would have "repented long ago in
sackcloth and ashes," as in the case of Ninevah in the
long ago.

It should be observed that the superiority ascribed
to Tyre and Sidon did not result from any inherent
merit on their part, because they were corrupt peoples,
and are often denounced as such in the Bible (Jeremiah

25:22; Ezekiel 26:3-14). However, the disposition they possessed would have prompted them to claim for themselves the blessings ignored by Chorazin and Bethsaida, had they enjoyed the same opportunities. Jesus once said of their counterparts, "But woe unto you, scribes and Pharisees, hypocrites! because ye shut the kingdom of heaven against men: for ye enter not in yourselves, neither suffer ye them that are entering to enter" (Matthew 23:13). The kingdom of heaven came near to these men, but they distanced themselves from it! We must not overlook the fact that these people were condemned by our Saviour, not because of persistence in sin—he offered them a way out of their corruption and ungodliness—but because of their apathy, indifference, and unconcern. They did not persecute, ridicule and otherwise evilly treat him, they simply ignored him! A complacency which simply disregards responsibility is more fatal than a corrupt life. The latter is easily recognized, and by all admitted to be wrong; but, a self-satisfied life, whether resulting from self righteousness or simply from indifference and neglect, often lulls one into complacency, yet this disposition was condemned by the Lord more severely, and for these reasons, than overt sins (John 8:1ff).

People in Palestine often wore sackcloth—a coarse and crude garment out of cloth made from goat's hair—in times of mourning, and to evidence the total absence of happiness and contentment. Job's experiences will immediately come to mind in demonstration of the practice. Ashes were sprinkled on the head in order to symbolize further the miserable and wretched state it was designed to reflect.

The Saviour's application of the principle involved is clear and unmistakable: "But I say unto you, it shall be more tolerable for Tyre and Sidon in the day of judgment, than for you." It will be more tolerable, that is, *it will fare better* with Tyre and Sidon *in the day of judgment* than it will with Chorazin and Bethsaida, since Tyre and Sidon's opportunities were fewer and their guilt correspondingly less. When will the measure of guilt be determined? *In the day of judgment.* The answer admits of no doubt, and demonstrates fully the principle I have earlier set out: *The greater the opportunity, the greater the guilt; the greater the guilt, the greater the punishment, in the day of final accounting.*

In further illustration of this principle, Jesus turned to his own city, Capernaum, in which he lived for approximately three and a half years, where he often taught in her streets and performed mighty works in the presence of her peoples, and said to her, "And thou, Capernaum, shalt thou be exalted unto heaven? Thou shalt go down unto Hades: for if the mighty works had been done in Sodom which were done in thee, it would have remained unto this day" (Matthew 11:23). They were not to suppose that the privileges that were theirs—and these blessings exceeded that of all others in that period during which he sojourned there—would enable them to enjoy heaven; on the contrary, they were to be brought down to Hades (and into that part of the unseen world of the dead into which wicked spirits go) because they treated with indifference, disinterest and apathy the immeasurable blessings of the Lord's personal presence and work among them. Sodom, an Old Testament city so corrupt that Abraham was unable to find ten righteous people among its entire populace, will fare better in judgment, because she would have seized the opportunities and profited by them which Capernaum indifferently passed by.

Does not this historic incident demonstrate beyond reasonable doubt the absolute truth of the principle we are considering? There is more, a great deal more, evidence to this end in the sacred writings, some of which we now examine: "And let us consider one another to provoke unto love and to good works: not forsaking the assembling of ourselves together, as the manner of some is; but exhorting one another: and so much the more, as ye see the day approaching. For if we sin willfully after that we have received the knowledge of the truth, there remaineth no more sacrifice for sins, but a certain fearful looking for of judgment and fiery indignation, which shall devour the adversaries. He that despised Moses' law died without mercy under two or three witnesses: of how much *sorer* punishment, suppose ye, shall he be thought worthy, who hath trodden under foot the Son of God, and hath counted the blood of the covenant, wherewith he was sanctified, an unholy thing, and hath done despite unto the Spirit of grace?" (Hebrews 10:24-29). Let the word "sorer," a comparative adjective, be carefully noted. If there is a "sorer" punishment, there must be one of lesser intensity, properly described as a "sore" punishment; others, more guilty, will be punished in a "sorer" fashion. Here, again, as so often elsewhere in the scriptures, we clearly see the divine intent to punish sin proportionately to the guilt of those involved—guilt determined by opportunities available to them in this life.

The book of Hebrews appears to have been written to stem an impending apostasy, on the part of some Jewish disciples, to Judaism. Among them false teachers had appeared, teaching that Jesus was not the true Messiah—that the Messiah was yet to come and by this alleged coming Messiah—and not Jesus— salvation would be attainable. Throughout the book of Hebrews, the author shows the fallacy and falsity of this contention by emphasizing the deity of Jesus and the superiority of the law of Christ to the law of Moses, and anything that preceded it. Among these arguments is that presented here: If those who disobeyed God under former dispensations and fell out of his favor, were the objects of severe punishment, (and the Old Testament abounds with them), how much greater will the punishment be—and ought to be—of those under an admittedly superior system who have trodden under foot the Son of God, counted the blood of the covenant an unholy thing and done despite (treated with contempt) the Spirit of grace?

We have certainly not been left without warnings to this end: "Therefore we ought to give the more earnest heed to the things that were heard, lest haply we drift away from them. For if the word spoken through angels proved steadfast, and every transgression and disobedience received a just recompense of reward; how shall we escape, if we neglect so great a salvation? which having at the first been spoken through the Lord, was confirmed unto us by them that heard; God also bearing witness with them, both by signs and wonders, and by manifold powers, and by gifts of the Holy Spirit, according to his own will" (Hebrews 2:1-4).

Impressive as are these affirmations and the conclusions to be drawn from them, our Lord's parable of the Wicked Servant, and his own comments thereon, absolutely lift the matter, for thoughtful and sincere students, above the level of doubt, and establish, beyond all reasonable question, the truth of the proposition that the greater the opportunity, the greater the guilt; the greater the guilt, the greater the punishment awaiting the finally disobedient.

"Then Peter said unto him, Lord, speakest thou this parable unto us, or even to all? And the Lord said, Who then is that faithful and wise steward, whom his lord shall make ruler over his household, to give them their portion of meat in due season? Blessed is that servant, whom his lord when he cometh shall find so doing. Of a truth I say unto you, that he will make him ruler over all that he hath. But and if that servant say in his heart, My lord delayeth his coming; and shall begin to beat the menservants and maidens, and to eat and drink, and to be drunken; then the lord of that servant will come in a day when he looketh not for him, and at an hour when he is not aware, and will cut him asunder, and will appoint him his portion with the unbelievers. And that servant, which knew his lord's will, and prepared not himself, neither did according to his will, shall be beaten with many stripes. But he that knew not, and did commit things worthy of stripes, shall be beaten with few stripes. For unto whomsoever much is given, of him shall be much required: and to whom men have committed much, of him they will ask the more" (Luke 12:41-48).

An argument more forceful, and a conclusion more obvious, could not be advanced. The servant who *knows* his master's will, yet *does it not*, shall be beaten with *many stripes;* the servant who *knows not* the master's will, yet *does things worthy of stripes* shall be beaten with *few stripes*. The "stripes" represent punishment; the number, the degree of severity involved in the punishment to be administered. *Many* stripes to those who "know" and do not; *fewer* "stripes" to those who "know not" and "do not." It must not be overlooked that the application of the passage is to the lost, and those of this category only. The righteous will receive no stripes at all—neither many nor few. It must then follow, as clearly as night the day, that our Lord here intended to indicate that the gravity of the sin, the guilt that attends it, and the punishment that follows are all directly related to the knowledge and opportunity of those involved.

Caution is required in not extending the application of this portion of scripture beyond that intended by the Lord. Some have assumed, based on a gross misapprehension of these verses, that ignorance of wrongdoing will excuse one and that if one avoids increasing one's knowledge, one's stripes, if any, will be few. The conclusion is an exceedingly dangerous one; God will require of all who appear before him to answer, not only for the knowledge they possessed, but *what they might properly have acquired, and did not!* It is not a sufficient answer to the charge of law violation in the courts of the land today that the accused was not aware of the law he is charged with violating; public knowledge of matters applicable to all may be presumed to be known by all, and all responsible people are, therefore, accountable thereto. A plea of ignorance, or an answer based on a refusal to acquire knowledge, merely adds to the guilt of one who so does, and for which an accounting must be made before the bar of divine justice. For the time, at least, religious freedom prevails; the Bible is available and within the reach of all; and most areas have had the gospel offered to the people thereof repeatedly. It's a grievous and an inexcusable sin to be uninformed in God's word. An awareness of this fact ought to have a sobering effect upon us, and to prompt us all to greater and more earnest study of it.

Awesome also, in the light of these facts, is the responsibility resting on those who presume to preach and to teach the Word. God, through the prophet Ezekiel, said: "Son of man, I have made thee a watchman unto the house of Israel: therefore hear the word of my mouth, and give them warning from me. When I say unto the wicked, Thou shalt surely die; and thou givest him not warning, nor speakest to warn the wicked from his wicked way, to save his life; the same wicked man shall die in his iniquity; but his blood will I require at thine hand. Yet if thou warn the wicked, and he turn not from his wickedness, nor from his wicked way, he shall die in his iniquity; but thou has delivered thy soul" (Ezekiel 3:17-19).

How great must God regard the guilt of those
professing to be preachers of the word who have
substituted gimmicks for the gospel, and whose
preaching consists of pious platitudes and witty words
for the message of life and salvation through which—
and by no other means—may sinful man be redeemed.
How great also is the contrast between these time
servers, and faithful proclaimers of the word, whose
only aim is that expressed so beautifully by Paul when
he wrote, ". . . Christ in you, the hope of glory, whom
we preach, warning every man, and teaching every
man in all wisdom; that we may present every man
perfect in Christ Jesus; whereunto I also labor . . ."
(Colossians 1:27,28). This should be our sole aim, as it
was that of the great apostle, to *preach*, to *warn*, to *teach*
every man in all wisdom, and *to present every man perfect*
in Christ Jesus!

How does this relate to the righteous in heaven in
the age to come?

Does the principle I am discussing in this sermon,
that the greater the opportunity, the greater the guilt,
and the greater the guilt, the greater the punishment,
have opposite application, and may it therefore be
affirmed, for the righteous, that the scriptures teach
that the greater the use we make of the opportunities
afforded us in this life as children of God, the greater
our spiritual attainments and the greater our spiritual
attainments on earth and in the church, the greater
our enjoyment of heaven and eternal life will be? This,
I believe with all of my heart; I am not aware of any
matter I believe to be more clearly and certainly taught
in the sacred writings. From a philosophical viewpoint
I do not see how it could be otherwise. As a matter of
fact, such is so, *in this life; indeed, in this service this*
evening! Assuming that there are five hundred people
present in this meeting tonight, would not justify the
assumption that there are five hundred levels of

enjoyment; but, of this we may be sure, there is
certainly more than one level, ranging from boredom,
on the part of a very few (I hope!), through polite
interest on the part of others, and with many others, I
am persuaded, complete absorption and enjoyment of
all the activities of this service. But, are not all of us
participating in the same service? Is not the same
spiritual atmosphere around us all? Wherein is the
difference? Does it not consist in variations of *capacity
for enjoyment*, a capacity acquired through enhance-
ment of spiritual levels through Bible study, prayer,
and persistence in all the things pertaining to the
church of our Lord? The conclusion simply cannot be
successfully controverted.

Two people listen to a musical rendition. One of
these is trained in musical matters and finds the music
delightful; the other, not thus trained, finds it
boresome. But are not both hearing the same presentation? Are not the same sounds impinging on their ears?
Wherein, then, is the difference? May any thoughtful
person seriously doubt that it consists solely in a sharp
difference in capacity for such enjoyment—a capacity
acquired through training? Do the scriptures teach that
children of God are provided with a probationary
period here on earth and in the church for the purpose
of *acquiring this capacity which will enable them to enjoy
heaven hereafter*? The evidence abounds, our time again
permitting only a tithe of that available.

Daniel wrote, "And many of them that sleep in the
dust of the earth shall awake, some to everlasting life,
and some to shame and everlasting contempt. And
they that be wise shall shine as the brightness of the
firmament; and they that turn many to righteousness
as the stars for ever and ever" (Daniel 12:2,3). To turn
people to righteousness (right doing, the keeping of
God's commandments, Psalm 119:172), is to teach
them the truth and prompt them to obey the gospel.

Those who thus do—and are successful in the effort—shall shine as the stars "for ever and ever." This is, quite obviously, a figurative statement designed to indicate the reward awaiting those who "turn many to righteousness." Will those who turn only a few to righteousness, or none at all, shine just as brilliantly? If so, why was the statement penned, since in this event it is meaningless and without significance?

Paul, to his beloved Thessalonian brethren, said: "For what is our hope, or joy, or crown of rejoicing? Are not even ye in the presence of our Lord Jesus Christ at his coming? For ye are our glory and joy" (1 Thessalonians 2:19,20). Their conversion to Christ, and their godliness, in the face of trial and suffering, greatly endeared them to the apostle; they were his "hope," his "joy," and his "crown of rejoicing." When will he derive these pleasures from their faithfulness? I have no doubt that he did so from the moment he brought to them the gospel; however, he designates specifically when he would experience these emotions: *at the coming of Christ.* Suppose at his coming it should develop that they had forsaken the faith—as did some of his converts—and were not among the redeemed? The "glory," the "joy," and the "crown of rejoicing" vested in them would no longer exist. No longer would they be an occasion of joy, in them he would find no glory, and they would have ceased to serve as a crown of rejoicing. Is it possible that any thoughtful person could conclude that should such happen it would not affect Paul's level of happiness in the hereafter? To conclude otherwise is to assume that the presence in heaven of their converts will add to the joys of those who won them to Christ, but their absence will pass unnoticed! Surely, the conclusion to thoughtful people is unacceptable.

With great tenderness and obvious affection Paul wrote to the Philippians: "Therefore, my brethren dearly beloved and longed for, my joy and crown, so stand fast in the Lord, my dearly beloved" (Philippians 4:1). Had they wavered into unbelief and eventual apostasy, would this awareness, in heaven, have influenced him in his thinking, and in the "joy" he would otherwise have experienced?

The Hebrew Christians were told to "obey them that have the rule over you, and submit yourselves: for they watch for your souls, as they that must give an account, that they may do it with joy, and not with grief: for that is unprofitable for you" (Hebrews 13:17). Contrary to concepts increasingly prevailing—which I regard as further evidence of a general trend away from positions formerly characterizing us all—it is my conviction that those who "have the rule" over us are faithful elders, that we are to "submit" ourselves to their "rule" in the congregation, and that it is their responsibility to "watch" for our souls.

I shall not pause at this juncture to contend with those among us in various places who do not believe that the words "rule," "over you," and "submit," have their usual and ordinary import and that one may, with impunity, disregard these injunctions. The Bible is not an esoteric volume, yielding its meaning only to those in cloistered halls who labor to uncover meanings not apparent to ordinary readers. The Bible was written for the unlearned and unscholarly, by worldly standards, and it yields its significance readily when allowed to do so. Usually, honest and sincere people, earnestly seeking to know the Lord's will, find their way by recognizing that the obvious import of a passage—as in the instance before us—is the correct one, and so be fully content with it. Jesus said, "If any man will do his (God's) will, he shall know of the doctrine, whether it be of God, or whether I speak of myself" (John 7:17). He has not offered us a road map designed to show us the way to heaven, yet made it so obscure and ambiguous that only the wisest and most learned of earth's creatures can correctly follow it. Isaiah, describing the characteristics of the kingdom of Christ he envisioned, wrote: "And a highway shall be there, and a way, and it shall be called The way of holiness; the unclean shall pass over it; but it shall be for those: the wayfaring men, though fools, shall not err therein" (Isaiah 35:8).

Elders are to "watch" for our souls, and they will be required to "give account" at the last day for their faithfulness and stewardship in these areas. Will the salvation, on the one hand, or the damnation of those for whom they are to watch, on the other hand, have no effect on their own happiness in heaven? To conclude that such is so is to say, in effect, that those divinely designated as watchmen for our souls here on earth, will be indifferent to the presence or absence in heaven of those from whom they were responsible on earth. I reject, without hesitation, this obviously false and objectionable hypothesis. It ought to be said, in this connection, that elders will indeed, understand why the unfaithful are excluded and fully acquiesce in the wisdom and justice of the Judge who excluded them, but this is far from saying that the elders will have no awareness of the absence of these people from heaven and no reaction, one way or other, to it.

"Then said Jesus unto his disciples, If any man will come after me, let him deny himself, and take up his cross, and follow me. For whosoever will save his life shall lose it: and whosoever shall lose his life for my sake shall find it. For what is a man profited, if he shall gain the whole world, and lose his own soul? For the Son of man shall come in the glory of his Father with his angels; and then shall he reward every man according to his works" (Matthew 16:24-27). In this precious, if paradoxical, statement, our Saviour urged his disciples to move forward in thought into the age to come and to consider whether the "gain" or the "loss" to their souls has been properly evaluated. "What shall a man give in exchange for his soul?" Money? Material things? Houses and lands? None of these one any longer has when this earth is left behind. Made crystal clear here is that in vain will one sell his soul to Satan with the expectation that he can redeem it when no longer on earth to "enjoy" its ephemeral affairs. A judgment day approaches when Jesus will "reward every man according to his works." "*According to his works*" can only mean proportionate to his works. If you have a dozen people working for you, and you pay them "according to their work," it is most unlikely that a check in precisely the same amount will be issued, by you, to each of them!

Here, again, as often elsewhere, in the Bible, is taught that each one will be required to account for one's stewardship in direct ratio to one's devotion to duty and faithfulness in discharging the responsibility assigned. Opportunity to serve, and the capacity to do so, establishes accountability. The "reward" awaiting will be determined on these grounds. This *reward* is not synonymous with *salvation*. All who enter heaven are saved; not all who go there, however, will carry with them the same "reward," since the extent of their "works," on the basis of which they are to be rewarded differs.

Some, indeed, will be in heaven who have done no work at all. Infants, idiots, insane persons will surely reach the heavenly shores, though no "works" of faith and service will accompany them. An aged man, for example, living in a distant mission field, and never having heard the gospel, attends a mission meeting, learns the truth and obeys it, but dies shortly after coming forth from the baptismal waters. Will he eventually enter the eternal city? Of this I have no doubt whatsoever. Of course he will. But this is far, very far, from saying that he will carry there the same capacity for enjoyment as will Paul, Stephen, James and countless other martyrs who suffered so long and so sacrificially for their Saviour. If so, the argument that a long life of faithfulness, sacrifice and self-denial for the Saviour will result in great blessing and warm approval by the Lord, and be richly rewarded by him in the world to come, is a fantasy and vain delusion, and all of us may as well serve Satan all of our days, and then at the end of a useless, worthless and misspent life, turn our worn-out carcasses over to the Lord by "obeying the gospel" near the end of our earthly existence, and still receive as many blessings as any saint who ever lived! Surely we all reject, without hesitation, such a conclusion, which nonetheless follows if the premises I have advanced throughout this lesson are not sound and true.

Finally, in what I regard as incontrovertible evidence leading to an irresistible conclusion of the truth of the premise I have advanced, Paul wrote, "I have planted, Apollos watered, but God gave the increase. So then neither is he that planteth any thing, neither he that watereth; but God that giveth the increase. Now he that planteth and he that watereth are one and every man shall receive his own reward according to his own labor. For we are labourers together with God: ye are God's husbandry, ye are God's building. According to the grace of God which is given unto me, as a wise masterbuilder, I have laid the foundation, and another buildeth thereon. But let every man take heed how he buildeth thereupon. For other foundation can no man lay than that is laid, which is Jesus Christ. Now if any man build upon this foundation gold, silver, precious stones, wood, hay, stubble; every man's work shall be manifest: for the day shall declare it, because it shall

be revealed by fire; and the fire shall try every man's
work of what sort it is. If any man's work abide which
he hath built thereupon, he shall receive a reward. If
any man's work shall be burned, he shall suffer loss:
but he himself shall be saved; yet so as by fire" (1
Corinthians 3:6-15).

The theme, in this remarkable passage from the
apostle, is the work of gospel preachers and the reward
attending such effort. He begins by comparing the
work of the preacher with that of a "planter," saying,
"I have planted, Apollos watered; but God gave the
increase." He then changed the figure from that of a
planter to that of a "builder," identifying himself as a
"masterbuilder," who laid the foundation, and to
which others add to the structure, and warned, "let
every man take heed how he buildeth thereon." The
building blocks are the preacher's converts; and the
degree of faithfulness and their ability to resist the
temptations of earth are represented by "gold,"
"silver," "precious stones," "wood," "hay," and
"stubble." It will be seen that this list, from the last to
the first, reflects an increasing imperviousness to fire.
Each is to be "tried" by fire, that is, tested by it, so
that its true character will be revealed. The "fire" of
this passage is not that of punishment awaiting the
finally disobedient (Matthew 25:41), since this is
designed simply to reveal the degree of faithfulness—
or lack of it—characteristic of the preacher's converts,
and not retribution for a sinful life. That retribution
will come is a settled fact (Matthew 25:46); here, the
apostle does not deal with that aspect of it. Let it be
remembered that the builder is the preacher; his
converts, the blocks of the building the preacher is
erecting; and the various materials mentioned representatives of the character of the converts.

Some converts are like stubble; so soon as fire strikes,
stubble burns and is destroyed. Converts of this

character apostatize at the first temptation. Others are like hay; hay does not burn quite as quickly as stubble—nonetheless, has little ability to resist fire and is soon consumed; some converts are like wood—wood does not burn as quickly as hay. Still others are like precious stones—which endure heat better than wood. Some are like silver which endures heat better than precious stones. And (thank God for them!), many converts are like gold—completely and totally impervious to fire!

"If a man's (the preacher's) work (his converts) abide (remain faithful), he (the preacher) shall receive "a reward." He will not only be saved he will be rewarded for the permanence and enduring quality of the work he has done. The "reward" mentioned is not to be confused with salvation—it is in addition to it. The faithfulness of my converts is not the condition of my salvation. Indeed, it is conceivable that every person I have been instrumental in leading to the knowledge of the truth and have prompted to obey the gospel, could be saved in heaven, and I could, through apostasy, be lost. The salvation of my converts will not, of itself, ensure my salvation!

"If a man's (the preacher's) work (his converts) be burned (are proved by fire to be unfaithful), he (the preacher) shall suffer "loss." Loss of what? Not his soul. As the faithfulness of my converts throughout life is not the determining factor of my own salvation, neither will their having proved to be unworthy and unfaithful at the last day result in my condemnation, unless, indeed, I am responsible for their apostasy! What then is the "loss?" Not loss of salvation for the reason just stated, and the following irresistible one, that stated in the text: "If any man's work shall be burned, he shall suffer loss; but *he himself shall be SAVED . . .*" *He shall suffer loss, yet, he shall be saved.* He shall suffer loss! Loss of what? Not his salvation, since it is said that, though suffering loss, he shall be saved. Loss of what then? Loss of *reward*. The argument, to reasonable people, must be conclusive; it is shown to be true, not only from the text, but also grammatically from the fact that the verb of the passage is used in the New Testament in a transitive sense, and thus with an object in numerous cases, rather than intransitively. See, for example, Matthew 16:26; Mark 8:36; and Philippians 3:8. Quite clearly, the object of the verb is the "reward" of the verse preceding.

Salvation from sin is the gift of God's immeasurable grace, and appropriated (not earned) through obedience to the Lord's commands—not a reward for works of merit, and achievements through human effort. We are stewards with a commitment from our Master; and, our "reward" will be conditioned on the way in which we have handled this trust. As stewards, though having lost some of the fruits of our labors, we shall still be saved, but the joy of association in heaven with those converts who, through apostasy, will not be there is, to this extent, diminished (1 Thessalonians 2:19,20).

There are those who, in an attempt to visualize heaven, unfortunately assume a simplistic concept of what it will be like on golden shores. Their assumption is that heaven is a happy place; if, therefore, they can but get there, they will be happy, too! This is an oversimplification of the matter; a more realistic view is this: Heaven will be a happy place for those who have learned how to be happy in what heaven offers! I illustrate it in this fashion: in this auditorium, it is warm, comfortable and cheery. Outside, chill is in the air, cold winds blow, and it is decidedly uncomfortable. You are outside. All that is necessary for you to be happy, therefore, is simply to move from the outside to the inside! It is not quite so simple. A better illustration is that while it is indeed a frigid evening and cold winds blow, and you are out there in the icy air, *you have acquired, or are acquiring, the characteristics*

*outside that will enable you, once you get into the building,
to be comfortable and happy.* An Eskimo, not accustomed
to the heated buildings of our culture, would not be
as comfortable inside as are we; a grizzly bear would
much prefer the cold winds to the heat from the
registers we find delightful.

Let it be impressed upon us and never forgotten:
HEAVEN WILL BE A PREPARED PLACE FOR A
PREPARED PEOPLE. A prepared people! People, who
through preparation here are adapted to the heavenly
climes. This is why the Lord has provided us with a
period of probation in order that we may be able to
enjoy heaven when we get there. In most cities of size
there are areas sometimes referred to as "skid row,"
where characters of the most corrupt and depraved
type congregate, and who find pleasure only in the
company of others of the same or similar character.
Do we suppose that if we brought one of this type into
this service and required him to sit on one of these
pews through the whole of one of our meetings, it
would be a delightful and happy hour for him, and
he would be glad he came to the services? On the
contrary, he would find it to be a miserable experience;
he would long for the moment when it was over, and
he would resist any effort to require him to repeat it.

But, let it also be asked: How can *we* expect to enjoy
heaven if we find sixty minutes of religious activity
boring and uninteresting, and we are glad when the
service is over so that we may resume our earthly and
secular pursuits? *The Lord will not force heaven on people
who are not prepared for it.* It is, therefore, an act of
self-deprivation when we turn aside from religious
activity to worldly affairs, and though we are able to
gain heaven, we have to this extent deprived ourselves
of the soul-cultivation the activity would have afforded.

The question may be raised, "Are you suggesting
some sort of caste system in heaven in which some

will occupy a higher rank and be accorded greater
blessings than others?" Of course not. All who go to
heaven will enjoy it to the fullest extent of which they
are capable; but that capability will have been determined by the amount of preparation made while on
earth. All who reach heaven will carry a full basket.
But, the size of the basket we take with us will depend
on the amount of preparation we take to heaven in it.
An elephant and a rabbit go down to a creek to get a
drink. Each fills his stomach with water. Both now
have full stomachs. But, there is considerable difference in the amount of water each has in his stomach!

It seems, in the light of the foregoing facts, not
possible to advance more compelling reasons why we
should give top priority to our duties, obligations and
responsibilities to God. "Behold, now is the accepted
time: behold, now is the day of salvation," wrote Paul
(2 Corinthians 6:2); death awaits, the grave beckons,
and the judgment day approaches. Need we be
reminded that the devil, not God, substitutes *tomorrow*
for *today!*

" 'Tomorrow,' he promised his conscience
   'Tomorrow I mean to believe;
'Tomorrow I'll think as I ought to,
   Tomorrow my Saviour receive;
'Tomorrow I'll conquer the habits
   That hold me from heaven away.'
"But ever his conscience repeated one word,
   And one only: 'Today.'
"Tomorrow, tomorrow, tomorrow—
   Thus day after day it went on;
"Tomorrow, tomorrow, tomorrow
   Till youth like a vision was gone;
"Till age and its passions had written
   The message of fate on his brow
"And forth from the shadows came Death
   With the pitiless syllable 'Now!' "

PAUL'S PRIORITY

No words of mine could possibly express to you the joy I feel in being here today. My uninterrupted and continuous association with you on the last Lord's day of the year now embraces a period of at least a quarter century. I would like for you to know that it truly warms my heart that you continue to invite me to be with you on these year-end occasions, and I look forward to each. I am not acquainted with a finer congregation than the Getwell church; I do not know of a more dedicated and capable eldership than yours; and I am sure there is not a sounder and more faithful gospel preacher living today than brother Garland Elkins.

How quickly have the days, the weeks and the months of the year now ending passed! Soon it will be gone, gone forevermore, and with it all the opportunities it afforded, whether utilized or not. Wasted hours, unused moments, a kind word unspoken, a good deed not done, are matters now beyond our power either to recall, or redeem. The painful awareness of blessings ignored, of duties disregarded, and of responsibilities shirked, are common to mankind, and are echoed in the plaintive cry of the aged Jacob: "Few and evil have been the days of the years of my life and they have not attained unto the days of my father in the days of their pilgrimage" (Genesis 47:9). It is unwise to grieve about matters over which we have no control; we ought, however, to learn from them, and to profit by them.

I am saddened by the realization that there are many who were here in earlier years but are no longer with us, and I—as do you—miss them greatly, but I confidently believe that they are now with the Lord whom they so long and faithfully served. Those of us who remain ought to be impressed with the fact that one day—very soon for some—and not long for any, we, too, must leave these realms forever and journey, as they have already done, through the gathering shadows to the place where all roads meet, and from which none may ever turn back.

How much of life remains for any of us we have no means of knowing; the span of human existence on this planet is, at best, brief; the Pale Horse and his Rider inevitably comes for all. These facts biblical writers keep ever before us. Life, they tell us, is like water poured out on the ground; a flying shadow which moves across the sky, in whose shade a weary traveler seeks rest, and looks up only to find that it has flown away; a frail and fragile flower; a dream; a handbreadth; a shepherd's tent; a tale that is told and soon over. In this way did the inspired writers deal with the ever flying years and the certainty of death as life's last event for us all.

"Gather the rosebuds while ye may,
Old time is still a-flying;
And this same flower that smiles today,
Tomorrow will be dying."

It is customary, at this season, to speak of the Old Year, soon to end, and of the New Year, as about to begin. These are really invalid descriptions—vain and meaningless efforts on our part to break time into segments, as if one portion of it can be made to stop, at a previously designated point, and another to start. Time moves inexorably on. It pauses for no one. This is God's unvarying, and unchangeable order. The swelling bud of spring becomes the full-grown leaf of summer and when the cold rains of November come, to wither, to die, and to fall into the embrace of the earth, its loveliness gone, as the season ends. And so it is with life on all levels; the babe of early morning becomes the mature man of high noon only to become the old and the stooped and the infirm, in the sunset's final glow. This is the law of nature; the history of mankind; the destiny of us all. May we never forget it. If there is any supreme folly; if there is any course in life utterly senseless, it is for a person possessed of an immortal soul to be indifferent to these facts and to make no provision for the day we must all "shuffle off this mortal coil," and face the judgment inevitably following.

"O the yesterday's moments for pleasure or woe,
Have been stealthily carried away;
I am nearer the valley of shadows, I know—
Am I nearer to heaven today?
Am I nearer? Am I nearer?
Am I nearer to heaven today?
Am I nearer the gate where the blessed ones wait?
Am I nearer to heaven today?"

Paul, (Philippians 3:13,14), having said that he had not yet reached the goal in life toward which he was journeying, wrote, "Brethren, I count not myself yet to have laid hold: but one thing I do, forgetting the things that are behind, and stretching forward to the things which are before, I press on toward the goal unto the prize of the high calling of God in Christ Jesus." I cannot imagine a finer, nobler motto. I commend to you the philosophy, as thus expressed by the great apostle, as being that which should always and in every place characterize us all.

Let us, at this point, carefully look at the apostle's words and note especially this: "I count not myself to have laid hold . . ." Remarkable, indeed, for the apostle so to affirm. It evidences, quite clearly and emphatically, that he had not attained to a status in life from which he could not fall, nor to an acceptance with God he could not lose. His words constitute a powerful

and unanswerable protest of that form of antinomian-
ism that alleges that he who has once "believed in
Christ," cannot ever sin as finally to be lost in hell.
This is the doctrine of the impossibility of apostasy. I
have engaged in many debates on this theme with
those who heartily subscribe to this, to me, distasteful
doctrine. I have in my possession a tract, the title of
which is, "Do a Christian's Sins Damn His Soul?" It
reads, in part:

> "We take the position that a Christian's sins do not
> damn his soul. The way a Christian lives, what he says,
> his character, his conduct, or his attitude toward other
> people have nothing to do with the salvation of his
> soul . . . All the prayers a man may pray, all the Bibles
> he may read, all the churches he may belong to, all the
> services he may attend, all the sermons he may
> practice, all the ordinances he may observe, all the
> laws he may keep, all the benevolent acts he may
> perform will not make his soul one whit safer; and all
> the sins he may commit from idolatry to murder will
> not make his soul in any more danger. The justification
> of the human soul is through the atonement of Christ
> and not through the efforts of men. The way a man
> lives has nothing whatever to do with the salvation of
> his soul."

The author of this incredible tract is wrong, wholly
wrong, fatally wrong, because the way one lives *does*
have something to do with the salvation of one's soul;
known sins, deliberately and willfully engaged in and
unrepented of, *will* surely and certainly damn one's
soul. This doctrine, subscribed to by all Calvinists
theologically, and by multitudes of people in practice,
rests on the false assumption that "once saved" is
"always saved," and cannot, therefore, fall from grace,
whatever one's conduct may thereafter be. It would
not be possible to image a more false, hurtful and
pernicious doctrine. There are at least twenty-five

hundred warnings of the possibility of apostasy in the
Bible; one can scarcely open its pages from beginning
to end without seeing some statement evidencing the
necessity of watchfulness and care in order to ultimate
deliverance and a home in heaven. Paul warned, "Let
him that thinketh he standeth take heed lest he fall"
(1 Corinthians 10:12), surely useless and meaningless
advice if one cannot fall, and he wrote to the Galatians,
"Ye are severed from Christ, ye who would be justified
by the law; *ye are fallen away from grace!*" (Galatians 5:4).

Only by the exercise of ceaseless and unwavering
attention to duty may one avoid the seductions of
Satan of whom Peter so pointedly warned, "Be sober,
be vigilant; because your adversary the devil, as a
roaring lion, walketh about, seeking whom he may
devour: whom resist steadfast in the faith" (1 Peter
5:8,9). Satan is called "a roaring lion," because of the
fierceness with which he stalks, and the readiness with
which he attacks. The word "roar" describes the howl
of the lion when hungry, the verb "walketh about,"
indicates his restless energy; and the word "seeking,"
denotes the persistence with which he searches out
and destroys his victims. The most favored of Jehovah
have never been immune to the allurements of the evil
one; and the great and good of the apostolic age were
ever mindful of the need for watchfulness every
moment of their lives. Paul, surely the greatest of the
apostles and, of all the others, the one most likely to
feel complete inner sufficiency, nonetheless was
fearful that he might stumble, and fall. Said he, "I keep
under my body and bring it into subjection: lest by any
means, when I have preached to others, I myself
should be a castaway" (1 Corinthians 9:27).

History, both sacred and secular, is replete with
melancholy examples of those who climbed the
dizzying heights of earthly fame and enjoyed, in full
measure, the world's acclaim, only in unguarded

moments to fall from places of eminence and often into disgrace and ruin. Moses, the great lawgiver, of whom God said, "And there arose not a prophet since in Israel like unto Moses, whom the Lord knew face to face" (Deuteronomy 34:10), and whose fame was so great his people were not privileged to have his body in death for burial, lest it become an object of worship, was refused entrance into the Land of Promise, though this was the embodiment and realization of his fondest hopes and dreams, *because of unwise words at the waters of Meribah*

David, Israel's sweetest singer, and most beloved of all the Kings of Israel, in an hour of temptation and weakness, suffered irretrievable loss of that which later he was to regard as most dear. Solomon, monarch of all of God's realms, possessed of more wisdom than any other on earth, and King of Israel in her most prosperous and glorious years, committed grievous sin in the last years of his life, and he lives in history as a sad and shocking example of how far great and once good men may fall.

Human nature is little different from what it was in those days of the long ago, and history has repeated itself again and again in the years following. The lessons of life should keep us ever mindful of the fact that he who stands may easily fall, and that unceasing watchfulness against deception through the wiles of the devil is the only certain guarantee that we shall be able to achieve successfully our goal of ultimate deliverance from sin and Satan, both here and in the world to come.

Napoleon, whose armies brought terror to all of Europe and convulsed France, was within sight of his dreams of empire only to fail at last, and to spend his last days amid the lonely scenes of St. Helena. Alexander the Great, more brilliant than the greatest of his generals, conquered the world before his 33rd birthday, wept because there were no more worlds to conquer, and died in ignominy soon thereafter. Cyrus, Caesar, Hannibal, Charlemagne, Hitler, all attained to great worldly prominence only to see their plans for global dominion fail and themselves repudiated. We must never forget that he who does not learn from history is destined to repeat it!

Paul concentrated his efforts. "This one thing I do," he said; not, "these forty things I dabble at," we may add. In order to succeed in any endeavor there must be concentration of effort. How long would it take, and how successful would the effort be, to acquire skilled training, if a student doctor, lawyer, or other professional person, regularly allowed his attention to wander from his studies, and to be largely concerned with a multitude of matters not related to that which should be his chief interest? An old Scotch cobbler, repairer of shoes, was asked what his business was. He answered, "My business in life is to go to heaven; I repair shoes only to be able to live while going there!"

This is not to say that Christianity consists only in religious activity, in the ordinary acceptation of the term. There is a philosophy in the brotherhood today that alleges that one is *serving* God only when thus engaged. It is also urged by those who so teach that we bear fruit only by converting others. I do not accept either of these conclusions. It is my conviction that he, or she, who worthily and properly carries on life's responsibilities as a mother, a wife, a husband, a school teacher, a worker in a factory, a farmer, or whatever one's calling in life may be, serves God as surely, as certainly and as acceptably as I do while standing in this pulpit and preaching!

The Saviour, in his explanation of the ground in the parable of the Sower which produced thorns ultimately choking out the wheat, said that the thorns represent, among other things, "the care of the world' (Matthew

13:22). The "care of the world" includes the multitudinous duties, the daily tasks, the manifold obligations
that claim attention and, at times, dissipate the
energies of us all. It is a part of God's plan for the world
that worldly tasks, essential to the ongoing of the race,
be performed; and in engaging therein we simply serve
his purpose in this respect. Up to, but not beyond, a
certain point. Beyond this, they become thorns which
choke the wheat.

At what point?

When material and earthly affairs are allowed to take
precedence over our spiritual responsibilities we have
allowed thorns to enter and to choke the wheat. Jesus
said, "But seek ye first his kingdom and his righteousness" (Matthew 6:33). *First* not *last*—Not even second!
This means simply that our duties to God of a spiritual
nature must be given top priority—all else, however
important, must be made secondary and subsidiary.
This means if I have *two* things to do, one of my own
affairs, the other the Lord's, I must take care of the
Lord's affairs first. This means that if I have *two* trips
to make, one of my own interests, the other, the
Lord's, I must make the Lord's trip first. Alas, how
seldom is this really done. Is it not a fact that most
members of the church today have little, or no
hesitancy, in allowing their personal desires to influence their conduct, and their worldly activities to take
percedence over those owed the Lord?

"Let the word of Christ dwell in you richly," Paul
admonished the Colossians (Colossians 3:16). Way's
translation (I quote from memory) runs somewhat like
this: "May the word Messiah speaks unto you have in
your heart in all its wealth its home." I like this
rendering; I believe it to be faithful to the original text.
Does not this passage indicate that our hearts should
overflow with the Word? Should we think, in the light
of this statement, that the Lord is pleased with, and

accepts as proper, little, or no, knowledge of it at all? Does a token examination, a casual reading of the Book for a few moments on Sunday, but wholly neglected otherwise throughout the week, meet the requirements of this passage, or enable one to acquire the knowledge the passage enjoins? To the Corinthians Paul wrote, "Wherefore, my beloved brethren, be ye steadfast, unmovable, always abounding in the work of the Lord, forasmuch as ye know that your labor is not in vain in the Lord" (1 Corinthians 15:58). *Always abounding*—not simply or only always serving. *Abounding!*

Paul's priorities were settled and the goal toward which he struggled was clearly defined. He wrote, "But one thing I do, forgetting the things which are behind, and stretching forward to the things which are before, I press on toward the goal unto the prize of the high calling of God in Christ Jesus" (Philippians 3:14).*

Among the things Paul taught to assure successful completion of the race was to forget "the things which are behind." Fatal to any effort to attain the prize is to look backward along the course one has run, rather than forward. It was clearly the apostle's intent to emphasize that he who would win must ever keep the goal prominently in view. The temptation is great for one who looks back on life's course *to go back!* Lot's wife (Luke 9:62; 17:32), affords a striking example of this fact. We must never forget that he who ceases to struggle against the current will by the current be swept backward!

---

*An allusion to the Grecian games so familiar to the world of the first century. The words, "stretching forward," translate a Greek word (*epekteinomenos*) indicating the intense physical exertion of the runner as he strains every muscle to the uttermost, his body leaning forward as he struggles toward the goal. The words, "I press on toward the goal," (literally, "I run along the line"), is reference to the lines from the starting point to the finish line, within which each runner had to run or be disqualified.

The dangers involved in looking backward are great. Many, in so doing, would see disappointment, discouragement, obstacles they were powerless to overcome, and an awareness of having failed to reach the goal sought. On the other hand, to look back may prompt one to become so satisfied with past achievements as to relax all efforts, and to be content with the goals already reached. The evil effects of looking back are many. To succeed in life we must look to the future.

The goal that awaits the successful completion of the Christian race is not an earthly, temporal garland as was characteristic of the ancient Grecian contests, though exceedingly honorable and prized they were, but a glorious crown of eternal life, and a home forever in a Land where the skies are always blue. The privileges awaiting those who so do involve benefits and blessings infinitely beyond our ability, while on earth, to apprehend; but we may be sure that they are beyond our wildest dreams and our fondest imaginations, and for them we can truly well afford to labor and patiently wait.

Patience is indeed one of the most important and significant requirements of the Christian life. Jesus said, "In your patience ye shall win your souls" (Luke 21:19). There are no shortcuts to success in any field. One can no more bypass God's plan, or possess the blessings of a life of faithfulness, without patient application, than one can cause the flowers to bloom before their time or the petals of the rose to open before its proper season.

I learned a lesson in patience from Paul many years ago that has been of immeasurable benefit to me, and I hope that it will prove to be of equal value to you also. The apostle, on one of his missionary journeys, accompanied by Silas, left Jerusalem, traveled to Derbe and Lystra in Asia Minor, then on through the "region of Phrygia and Galatia, having been forbidden of the

Holy Spirit to speak the word in Asia," and "when
they were come over against Mysia, *they assayed to go
into Bithynia;* and the Spirit of Jesus suffered them
not." Accordingly, having passed by Mysia, they came
to Troas, where Paul had the Macedonian vision, and
thence sailed across the Aegean Sea, landing at
Neapolis, going inland, about nine miles, from the
seacoast town to Philippi (Acts 15:40,41-16:12).

Let it be noted that when Paul and Silas attempted
to enter Bithynia, "the Spirit" forbade them to do so.
This was truly a strange circumstance. Bithynia was a
small province in Asia Minor where, so far as we know,
the gospel had never been preached. Paul's purpose
was to carry the message of salvation to these people
in that Asian province. But, his effort to do so was
thwarted by the Holy Spirit. This was indeed a strange
circumstance. Had I been in the apostle's place, I
would have been perplexed by this; with my lack of
wisdom I might even have argued the point, "Why
not? Why not?"

Be it said to the apostle's credit, he offered no such
demurrer. By the Spirit's behest, he went on to Troas,
where "a vision appeared to Paul in the night: There
was a man of Macedonia standing beseeching him, and
saying, Come over into Macedonia, and help us. And
when he had seen the vision, straightway" he and Silas
set sail and crossed the sea to Neapolis, in Macedonia,
and then traveled to Philippi, having concluded "that
God had called" them "to preach the gospel" in that
area (Acts 16:9,10). There, the jailor and his household
were converted, as were also Lydia and her entourage,
and the Cause of our Lord was established on
European soil. Significantly, Paul's first converts in
Europe were from the area he was instructed by the
Spirit to leave—Asia Minor!

The purpose and plan of the Spirit had now become
clear. Paul's plan, respecting Bithynia, involved the

evangelization of a province, in territory approximat-
ing in size of one of our counties. *God's plan involved
the preaching of the gospel on a continent—the continent of
Europe!* In consequence of this beginning, tens of
thousands, and eventually, hundreds of thousands of
people became obedient to the gospel of Christ. Sadly,
we tend to limit God in our efforts. We see ourselves
converting a few individuals—at most, some people
in a town or city—when God has in mind for us the
conversion of a country or continent.

God has a purpose and plan for us all; and while he
does not speak to us today in a vision as in the instance
before us, he has made known his will in his word for
us, and it is set out there in clear and unmistakable
fashion. We should learn to accept the changing affairs
of life as often providential in nature, and in no
instance should we seek to thwart his plan or to evade
his will. In my own long and eventful life, I have seen
the time when clouds, ominous and heavy, were on
the horizon, and obstacles which, at the moment
seemed to me to be insurmountable; but I have also
seen from beyond the darkened clouds the sun emerge
and shine with greater brilliance than I had ever before
witnessed.

> "I know not where his islands lift
> Their fronded palms in air;
> I only know I cannot drift
> Beyond his love and care."

We are all on a rapid march to the eternal shore, and
soon we shall leave this world to return no more. This
realization ought to prompt us all to reflect seriously
on our relationship to God and to that inevitable
appearance we shall make before the Judge of all. Life
is at best uncertain; and death is the inevitable portion
of the race. The passing, for the righteous, whether
young or old, holds no terrors; and, faithful aged ones,

aware that in the course of nature their sojourn on earth must soon end, await with joy and calm expectation their impending journey.

As older we get it seems hardly possible that a year is ending we seem merely to have begun. And, as the years fly by, to return no more, so we pass through life with equal rapidity and our passing is marked with the same finality as that characteristic of the hurrying years. As one year passes and then dies with its joys and its sorrows, its successes and its failures, into the shadows of the timeless past, so we also pass the time of our sojourning in this life, and move on to other worlds. It is not the quantity but the quality of life that is really significant—not how long one lives but how fully, that actually counts. It was Emerson who said, "We do not count a man's years until he has nothing else to count," and it is noteworthy that the most blessed, the most useful, and the most precious life ever spent on this earth ended after only thirty-three years!

The truly wise do not regret the swift flight of time—they recognize that it is but the working out of the plan of life and an essential step before receiving unending bliss in the world to come. Thus all of us ought to "number our days," and "apply our hearts to wisdom," assured that whatever the future holds it is in the hand that holds the future and through him ultimate triumph.

> "Swift to its close ebbs out life's little day;
> Earth's joys grow dim, its glories pass away;
> Change and decay in all around I see.
> O thou who changest not, abide with me!"

It is of supreme importance that we "redeem the time," literally, *buy up the opportunity*, lest the rapidity with which it passes to return no more should result in our failure to embrace and to claim its benefits

(Colossians 4:5). *Now,* not tomorrow, certainly not next week, nor next year, *now* is "the acceptable time," it is, in reality, the only time we have! It was this that prompted our Lord to say, "We must work the works of Him that sent us while it is day; the night cometh, when no man can work" (John 9:4). The night cometh—indicating the end of opportunity—for us all. In view of this, the immortal words of William Cullen Bryant's beautiful Thanatopsis suggest the aim and end which ought to characterize us in whatever hours and days for us which may lay ahead:

> "So live, that when thy summons comes
> To join the innumerable caravan which moves
> To that mysterious realm where each takes
> His chamber in the silent halls of death,
> Thou go not, like the quarry slave at night
> Scourged to his dungeon, but, sustained and soothed
> By an unfaltering trust, approach thy grave,
> Like one who wraps the drapery of his couch about
>   him,
> And lies down to pleasant dreams."

Death is, indeed, earth's last and greatest adventure and is as insoluble, inscrutable and inexplicable as its concomitant, life. From the occasion of its first tragic occurrence in the race until now, though the wisest, greatest and most thoughtful of men have philosophized, conjectured and speculated regarding it, they have learned nothing, through the exercise of worldly wisdom. The best, indeed, the only reliable and satisfactory definition of death is to be discovered in the affirmation of James, brother of our Lord, the design of which was not really to define it, but to indicate the condition following it. Said he, "The body *without the spirit* is dead" (James 2:26).

Death is the condition existing when the spirit, the immortal nature derived directly from God, is no longer in the body. More than this, regarding the actual process, we cannot, and therefore need not, know. The answers to most questions regarding the transition— and there are many—must await the day of realization. We may, however, from numerous references thereto by the sacred writers determine some things about the nature of the passing from this life to the next; and this we gladly seize and ponder as descriptive of the scenes through which all of us must eventually pass. Word pictures by the apostles allow us to catch a glimpse of what we may expect when it is ours to walk into the gathering twilight as the sun of life sinks for the last time on our horizon.

Paul, greatest of the apostles, aware that life for him would soon be over, wrote: "I am now ready to be offered, and the time of my departure is at hand" (1 Timothy 4:6). The word "departure," as used by Paul translates the Greek word *analusis,* and defined by lexicographers as follows: "An unloosing, (as of things woven), a dissolving (into separate parts). Departure (a metaphor drawn from loosing from moorings preparatory to setting sail) . . . or, according to others, from breaking up an encampment." (Thayer.)

Death is, then,

1. The unraveling of a garment, the separation and disentanglement of the threads of woven cloth. As a piece of cloth, by unraveling, returns to the element out of which it was made, so the individual, in death, undergoes the separation of body and spirit the combination of which is life. Separated, the body goes to the tomb to return to the dust out of which it was made; the spirit wings its way to Hades to await the resurrection day and the judgment, on which occasion the bodies will have been recovered from the dust and made fit for the spirit's eternal habitation.

2. Death is a "dissolving into separate parts," as seen in the abandonment of the body by the spirit. The

figure is quite apposite and fitting in describing the results which attend the flight of the spirit from the body.

3. Death is compared to a departure, as of "the breaking up of a camp," and the "loosing of the ship's moorings" as it prepares to hoist its sails and to launch out into the deep waters. (a) The activities which characterize the taking down of a tent figuratively picture, in impressive fashion, the experience of death. The figure was quite familiar to the Eastern traveler who was accustomed to taking down his tent as he began his journey across the sandy reaches of the desert world in which he lived and moved. Thus, any journey was necessarily preceded by the dismantling of a tent. Paul used this figure when, in 2 Corinthians 5:1, he wrote: "For we know that, if our earthly house of this tabernacle be dissolved, we have a building of God, an house not made with hands, eternal and in the heavens." It is significant that in this instance the word "tabernacle" in our text is translated from the Greek word *skeenee,* the usual Greek word for a tent.

4. Further, it is the loosing of the anchor or ropes which hold a ship to the shore so that it may move out into the deep. This is a common figure of death as a departure from this world to another. Poets, preachers, and painters have often seen in the sailing of a ship a pictorial representation of our final passing from this life. There is something wonderfully impressive in the departure of a giant ocean liner. The bustle of boarding, the tears of parting from friends, the heady excitement of a new adventure, and the throaty roar of the ship's mighty horns announcing departure, kindle interest to thrilling heights. As the great vessel slowly glides out to sea and finally fades from the sight of the watching throng on shore, the shout ascends: "There, she goes!" And, it is not long until other watchers, on another shore, catch a glimpse of her in

the glimmering haze, and cry: "There, she comes!" So it is with those who loose from life's moorings and sail away on the billowing waves of death. Though they pass for a moment from view, others on distant and sun washed shores wait and watch with joy their coming.

> "Twilight and evening bell,
> And after that, the dark!
> And may there be no sadness of farewell,
> When I embark;
> For though from out our bourne of Time and Place
> The flood may bear me far,
> I hope to see my Pilot face to face
> When I have crossed the bar."

5. Death is described, in the sacred writings, as a state of peaceful, dreamless sleep. "But I would not have you to be ignorant, brethren, concerning them which are asleep, that ye sorrow not even as others which have no hope" (1 Thessalonians 4:13). In this passage, the word translated "sleep," is from the Greek term *koimao*, to put to sleep, whence we derive our word "cemetery," from the Greek *koimeterion*, "a sleeping chamber, a burial place." "Sleep" is a euphemism for the word "die," and is often so used in the scriptures. We must not from this assume, however, that death, in all respects, is comparable to sleep; it is not. The cessation of consciousness, characteristic of sleep is not a concomitant of death. Death is like sleep in that it is a ceasing from all activity; a season of rest and repose. In response to the question, "Is death the last sleep?" Walter Scott truly said: "No, it is the last and final awakening!"

Though the "way into the holiest," was not "made manifest" while "the first tabernacle was yet standing" (Hebrews 9:1-9), we may indeed rejoice that the Jewish system, which began at Sinai, and which typified that which would eventually displace it—Christianity with all of its blessings—the historic events which occurred when our Lord died are especially illustrative of this fact. The Holy place—the first compartment of the temple—prefigured the church; the most holy place before which a great Babylonian curtain, woven of fine linen, and embroidered with blue and red and purple, was suspended, represented heaven. This magnificent tapestry separated the inner sanctuary—the most holy place—from the first and beyond which no one save the high priest, and he only once year, might pass. The "way into the holiest" was not yet available and would not be until the Lord, by his death on the cross, removed forevermore the veil separating the two compartments.

The events culminating in this unparalleled action by him were nearing the end, and his triumphant words, "it is finished," uttered in the last hours of earthly life, affirmed the completion of his mission and the termination of his ministry, while in the flesh, to the world. At the moment of his death, the creation, outraged by the depths of depravity characteristic of those who perpetrated the greatest crime of the ages, evidenced its displeasure with a series of events not before, nor since, witnessed by man. Earlier, beginning at midday of the darkest event in all of the world's history, and continuing for three hours, the sun hid her face, and the darkness, like an ominous and angry cloud, swiftly spread over the earth, engulfing it in the gloom of stygian darkness, while the minions of Satan pursued and consummated their evil and hateful work.

Death, at length, mercifully came to the lonely sufferer, as he "let go the spirit," so the Greek text literally asserts, himself choosing the time and manner of his departure. At this moment, all creation, awaiting the signal from its Creator (John 1:2), was convulsed, and the first dread signs of an earthquake gripped and terrified the people of Jerusalem and Judaea. They felt, at first, a slight tremor, heralding its near approach, another and another, each of increasing intensity, until the earth swayed and shuddered and heaved, and broke open into great fissures before the eyes of the fearful and alarmed people. More terrifying than the visible signs of the great quake were the subterranean sounds accompanying it. These, from deep in the earth, began as a faint and distant rumble then quickly increased in volume; they beat again and again on the ears of the inhabitants of Jerusalem with painful intensity; from out of the depths issued a deafening roar which surged over the despairing city, crashed into the mount of Olives, echoed through the valley of Jehoshaphat, and swept like a mighty ocean wave over the land eventually to spend itself and to dissipate its awesome power in the mountains of Judaea and the great plains beyond.

Tombs of the sleeping dead in the holy city broke open under the strains of the reeling earth, and many bodies of the saints there interred arose, "and came out of the graves after his resurrection, and went into the holy city, and appeared unto many" (Matthew 27:52,53).

At the moment of our Lord's death, the great curtain, suspended between the holy place and the most holy compartment of the temple, a great sheet of finely woven material, seventy feet high and four inches thick, ripped suddenly downward—from the top to the bottom, not from the bottom to the top, as if by some earthly effort—in a manner indicative only of divine intervention. It was in the ninth hour of the day—3 p.m., and while the priests were participating in the evening sacrifice in the temple's sacred precincts. They could not have failed to witness these amazing events, nor not to have been profoundly impressed with the unparalleled happenings of that fateful day. Stunned by these displays of divine power, these men may well have been among those of whom it was later affirmed that "many of the priests became obedient to the faith" (Acts 6:7). The Roman centurian, officially in charge of executing the infamous court's decree that condemned to death the Lord of glory, a pagan in religion, was deeply moved, saw in these strange occurrences supernatural confirmation of the Saviour's claims to deity, and bore witness thereto, by saying: "Truly this was the Son of God" (Matthew 27:54).

Of the basic truth of Christianity all men would soon have ample evidence. That which was now so mysterious in this sombre night of sorrow would become clear and simple in the rosy hues of a happy, triumphant and glorious resurrection morning. The gospel story, with its blessed hope and its precious promises, would soon be a reality; from out of the portals of heaven streamed a pure and holy light which illuminated earth's darkest places, swept before it life's deepest shadows, cleansed and purified some of the most defiled of earth's inhabitants and made luminous and bright for the hopeless, the outcast and the despairing, the wonderful way to the heavenly habitations.

When the happy carefree summer of youth has passed into the autumn of age, shadows from the evening sun of our earthly life lengthen, and life itself wears to its eventide, it is comforting, encouraging and reassuring to review the days of our lives and to relish again and again the joys and blessings now seen to be so many throughout our life span. If there were loved ones who shared our joys and our sorrows, and friends who brightened and made glad our existence; if there is an awareness of having served well our generation, and of having striven to be faithful to our Creator, a blessed aura of contentment will surround us, and

peace will pervade our hearts with a holy feeling
freeing us of any fear of the Last Great Adventure.
Greatly blessed and fortunate indeed are those as life
approaches its end whose hearts are free of selfishness
and greed, and whose minds are as pure in thought
as they were in the innocence of their blissful and
happy childhood days.

Preached at the Getwell Church of Christ, Memphis, Tennessee,
December 30, 1984.

AREAS OF CHRISTIAN DUTY

Even the most casual examination of the New Testament reveals that man's duty falls into three distinct categories. These are: (1) his duty to himself; (2) his duty to those round about him, and (3) his duty to God.

With references to the first and to the third of these duties and responsibilities we often teach and preach. We frequently—and quite properly so—emphasize the obligations we sustain to ourselves to grow in grace and in the knowledge of the truth, and in this fashion to fit and prepare ourselves for useful and effective service in the Lord's vineyard. And, we just as often—perhaps more so—address ourselves to those duties we owe to God to obey him faithfully, to serve him acceptably and to worship him pleasingly. But, it seems to me, and it must to all careful observers of the current scene, that we do not place quite the emphasis in our preaching and teaching on the second of these duties—those we owe to one another.

I shall therefore talk to you tonight about our responsibilities toward one another. Quite obviously, I cannot, in the twenty-five minutes or so that I shall speak discuss, in detail, every such duty and responsibility. But, I believe I can in summary and in principle do so, and were I to designate what I regard as basic to them all, I should, without hesitation, say that it is to *love one another*. It is truly amazing how very much the scriptures have to say on this theme.

To determine this for yourselves, take your Bible or New Testament and a concordance and examine the references thereto. Two things, at least, will impress you: the frequency with which such passages appear; and, the emphasis that is given to our obligation therein. As an example, in a passage the reference for which I, for the moment, purposely refrain from giving, our Lord said, *"This my commandment."* You are fully aware that we give much emphasis to keeping the commandments. We frequently recall our Lord's words in the Sermon on the Mount, "Not every one that saith unto me, Lord, Lord, shall enter into the kingdom of heaven; but he that doeth the will of my Father who is in heaven" (Matthew 7:21). We often point to the warning of the beloved apostle, "He that saith, I know him, and keepeth not his commandments, is a liar, and the truth is not in him" (1 John 2:4). And the promise of Revelation 22:14, "Blessed are they that do his commandments, that they may have right to the tree of life, and may enter in through the gates into the city", ought often to be on our lips and always in our hearts.

Before us, and for our consideration, is one of these commandments. *"This is my commandment."* What, Lord? "This is my commandment that you be baptized for the remission of sins?" Were such the statement of the passage, most mature people present could not only quote it, but also supply the reference! "This is my commandment that you meet regularly on the first day of the week?" If these were the words of our Lord here, you know, and I know, they would be quoted much more often than those of the passage under study. "This is my commandment that you give liberally of your means on the first day of the week?" Baptism for the remission of sins, the obligation of the saints to meet on the first day of the week and to give liberally of their means are matters clearly taught and emphasized elsewhere in the scriptures (Mark 16:15, 16; Acts 2:38; 1 Corinthians 16:1,2). But such is not the affirmation of our Lord in the passage under consideration.

"This is my commandment."

What commandment, Lord? "That ye love one another, even as I have loved you." If keeping the commandments is necessary in order to go to heaven, and of course it is, then it follows that this duty stands between us and heaven just as much as faith, repentance, confession and baptism in water stand between the alien sinner and the forgiveness of his sins. Incidentally, the reference I earlier alluded to, and for a few moments withheld, is John 15:12.

In a similar statement, (John 13:35), the Lord said, "By this shall all men know that ye are my disciples . . ." By this *shall all men* know that you are my disciples. This surprises me a bit. I would have expected him to say, "By this God knows you are my disciples;" or, "By this I know you are my disciples;" instead, he said, "By this shall all men know ye are my disciples." It is remarkable that the test here is *human* rather than divine.

By this shall all men know you are my disciples. How shall all men know this? Because we say so? Because we exhibit a pious and positive attitude? Because we engage in religious activity? Because we have been baptized? All of these matters are, of course, necessary, and essential to our ultimate salvation in the sweet by and by. But, such is not the affirmation of our Lord in this passage. How are all men to know that we are his disciples?

Because we have love one for another.

It must follow, therefore, that in the absence of this disposition there is wanting the test by which those about us and the world around us will determine the genuineness of our discipleship.

But, someone may say, "I can see that, and I can appreciate the reasons for it. We are members of the same family. We have a common Father, a common responsibility, a common hope and a common reward. It is characteristic of people thus closely and intimately related to love one another. But, the same book also teaches that we are *to love our enemies.* Now, this is an entirely different thing. Granting that it is possible to love one who is lovable and possessed of winsome, alluring and attractive qualities and characteristics; but, how do you love one not only not lovable but often possessed of attitudes and habits and dispositions which are to you objectionable?"

I am sure that all thoughtful people have wrestled with this problem. I do not hesitate to say to you that if I am expected to entertain the same warmth of feeling for one antagonistic toward me, who actively seeks my ruin and who would, if possible, destroy me, in the same fashion and to the same extent that I would love one near and dear, I'd simply have to be made over! I am certain that the Lord does not expect the impossible. I am also sure that he is much more aware of the difficulty I have submitted than I am. And, I am equally sure that he requires us to love our enemies. How can this possibly be?

I think it unfortunate that some translations of the New Testament do not distinguish between two Greek words both of which are translated by the single English word "love." It is therefore not possible to determine, from the translation alone, which of the Greek words is so rendered, since both words appear in our language as "love." One of these Greek words so translated—*phileo* in various forms, often appears in composition in our language. It is, for example, to be seen in such words as *philosophy*—the love of wisdom; *philology*—the love of words, and *philadelphia*—the love of brethren. Its basic meaning is warmth of affection, emotional love. This is the kind of love that a husband has for a wife, a wife for a husband, parents for children and children for parents. Now, please note this very carefully: this word is never used in any passage in which we are commanded to love our enemies. Never.

There is another word—*agapao*—a more selfless word than the former and which may, but does not necessarily, convey the notion of love flowing out of the emotions. To illustrate: here is a person about whom there may be, to me, nothing attractive. On the contrary, he may be possessed of attitudes, habits and dispositions I find obnoxious and objectionable. But, he is a creature of God, and I am a creature of God. We thus have common origin, and this fact creates a definite relationship between us. My recognition of this relationship, and my willingness to discharge my duty to him in it, is what is involved in this word.*

No. The Lord never told us to love an enemy in the same way we are to love a dear one.

One may at this point say, "I see this distinction; but, out of it another difficulty emerges. We are clearly taught in 1 John 3:15 that he who does not love his brother hates him; one who hates his brother is a murderer; and 'no murderer hath eternal life abiding in him.' Does it necessarily follow that if you do not love one *therefore* you hate him? Why must it be an either/or situation? Granting that you feel no love for some person does this mean that as a necessary consequence you hate the person involved?"

These are matters of great importance to us all and all of us ought clearly to recognize the following fundamental facts: There is no neutral area—no twilight zone—in matters involving basic principles. It

---

*It is of interest to note that *phileo* denotes spontaneous natural affection, often unreasoning in nature, while *agapao* is a deliberate exercise of the will and may properly be required as a Christian duty. The Greek text of John 21:15-17 effectively demonstrates the difference in meaning of these words. To assert, as some have, that *agapao* is a stronger word than *phileo* and that the apostle chose the weaker one in his reply is to lose the significance of the variation. The difference in these words is in their meaning—not in their relative strength. For more detail, see my *Commentary on John*, Gospel Advocate Co., Nashville, TN 1981, pages 441-443.

is simply not possible for you to be in a position where you are neither right nor wrong; the fact that you are not right means you are wrong! It is not possible to be in a situation where you are neither righteous nor unrighteous. The fact that you are not righteous means you are unrighteous. "Unrighteousness" may be properly defined as "the state of not being righteous." It is not possible to be neither in the light nor in the dark spiritually. The fact that you are not in the light means that *you are in the dark!* In like fashion, it is not possible to be in a situation where one, in the sense described moments ago, neither loves nor hates, because the absence of love (described by the word *agapao*) the Lord regards as hate.

These facts make it exceedingly clear that there is absolutely no proper place for compromise in matters of principle for the Lord's faithful people. Though this disposition is by many today regarded as not only permissible but commendable, it will be responsible for leading multitudes of people astray and ultimately to the destruction of their souls in hell. King Saul (1 Samuel 15:1ff), Uzzah (2 Samuel 6:6-8), Nadab and Abihu (Leviticus 10:1,2),—among many others—are striking examples of what happens when men substitute their own wills for the divine. Compromise is the yielding of principle. To illustrate: you are there and I am here. We wish to meet on common ground. However, tolerance suggests that neither of us ought to expect the other to do all the moving! Consequently, you move a bit in my direction and I'll move a bit in yours, and so we find ourselves together.

In matters of expediency; in areas where no basic principle is involved, in situations where there are a half dozen different ways in which a thing may be done *all of which are right* it is indeed proper for the sake of peace to yield since in so doing we merely give up one right way for another. But not in matters of principle. If you are right where you are, I must, under no circumstances, seek to move you from that position. And, if I am right where I am, there I must stand though the heavens fall about me.

No one respects compromisers. People often use them for selfish ends, but while doing so feel contempt for them. A soldier in the Civil War, unwillingly drafted into service, not angry with anybody, not wishing to shoot anybody and especially not to get shot, contrived, so he hoped, to avoid difficulty from either side. He obtained and dressed himself in a Union coat and a pair of Confederate trousers, thinking that this garb would protect him from both sides. His scheme—as all such efforts usually do—failed, and they found him dead on the battlefield. Through the Union coat was a Confederate bullet, and through the Confederate pants a Union bullet! He simply got himself shot at from both sides! It is an obligation of the most solemn nature to adhere undeviatingly to the truth and to maintain a position that is right whatever the consequences. Love of God and respect for his word will allow no other course.

Love is the base on which rests every duty we owe both to God and to man.

A lawyer, not an attorney in the sense we use the term today, but one learned in the law of Moses, and allegedly an authority thereon, came to Jesus about a matter that had been a subject of controversy among Jewish scholars for centuries. Which of the command-ments is the greatest? was a theme about which they argued endlessly. The intent of the lawyer was therefore to elicit from the Lord an expression of opinion on this hotly debated theme. It is of no little interest to note how Jewish traditional law, with its multitudinous duties and responsibilities, arose. The Bible is essentially a book of principles. In the nature of the case it has to be. When I studied law in Texas many years ago and was there admitted to the bar, the civil statutes were in two volumes each about four inches thick, and when to this was added the criminal code, a stack of books eight or ten inches high resulted. This, mind you, involving legislative activity in but a few areas of human relationships over a period of approximately one hundred years.

Suppose the Lord had given us specific and detailed rules governing *every* conceivable circumstance among *all* people in *all* places, in *all* ages. It would be an exceedingly difficult task merely to read through the books in a lifetime, much less to become familiar with all the rules therein. And so the Bible, in large measure, is a book of principles. Of course, there are indeed many specific laws in it; on the other hand, there are numerous principles the application of which must be done in harmony with the varying circumstances under which we live.

It is remarkable that human nature is strangely adverse to the acceptance and application of principles in human conduct. Most of us want specific and detailed legislation, and if the Lord does not supply it we have no difficulty in supplying it for ourselves and especially for our brethren! Most of the controversy and consequent factionalism among the Lord's people through the years has resulted from this persistent and widespread disposition,—of making laws where God made none, and of presuming to speak where He has not spoken.

Far back in the early days of Israel following the giving of the law at Sinai (Exodus 20:1ff), some eminent Rabbi decided that he would take the general principles of the law and from them deduce what he considered to be their proper application. And so he did. As the years passed, some other eminent scholar among them decided that the explanation of the text by the earlier Rabbi needed exposition, so he proceeded to explain the explanation. Of course another—down the line—concluded that the comments on the comments needed commenting on, so he proceeded to comment on the comments of the comments, and so it went. By the time our Lord came to the earth there was a tremendous mass of this traditional material to which the Jews were answerable, it often being regarded by them as equal in authority to, and in some cases superior to the Old Testament scriptures themselves. Jesus said that they made the commandment of God void by these traditions (Matthew 15:1-9).

May I give you a few examples of their amazing rulings? A woman must not look into a mirror on the Sabbath day. Oh! not that there was anything wrong per se in looking into a mirror on the Sabbath day or, for that matter, any other day of the week; but, were she to, she might see a gray hair in her head, and this could tempt her to pluck it out; and since plucking is a form of reaping, and reaping was prohibited on the Sabbath day, a woman must not look in a mirror on the Sabbath day!

A second regulation ran like this: it was wrong, they thought, to eat a chicken on the Sabbath; not wrong, however, to eat an egg on this day. Not only do many people have a penchant for wanting concrete and specific laws, they no sooner get them than they start seeking ways by which to circumvent them. This rule regarding the eating of chicken on the Sabbath day those casuists handled quite effectively. If some Jewish family really wanted to have chicken on that day, they managed to do so by resorting to the following circuitous reasoning: that which they were serving was not really chicken (not permitted on the Sabbath), but only that *which the egg turned out to be*—simply an extension of an egg, which was then held to be acceptable, on the basis of this mode of reasoning, to eat an egg on the Sabbath.

A third instance, and this must suffice for illustration, though they abound in number, involved Sabbath day journeys. The Rabbis taught that it was sinful to travel more than seven-eighths of a mile on that day. But, if some Jew had a trip to make necessitating a greater distance than this, and he wished to do so on the Sabbath, he handled the matter in this fashion: on the day preceding the Sabbath—the day projected for his travels—he carefully covered the route, taking care to deposit bits of food along the way, each portion always within seven-eighths of a mile of another portion, and then "reasoned" like this: "Where your food is there is where you eat; but where you eat is where your home is; therefore so long as you are within seven-eighths of a mile of food, you are never more than seven-eighths of a mile from home!" Remarkable reasoning, was it not? This sounds not unlike some of the specious and fallacious sophistries of our own day!

It was this type of hairsplitting technicality that prompted the Lord to rebuke the Jewish leaders of his own day: "Ye hypocrites," he said, "well did Isaiah prophesy of you, saying, This people honoreth me with their lips; but their heart is far from me. But in vain do they worship me, teaching as their doctrines the precepts of men" (Matthew 15:7-9).

The Jewish teachers agreed that there were six hundred and thirteen precepts and prohibitions to which they were answerable, but differed as to the relative importance of each, and on this theme they often debated. A lawyer, recognizing Jesus as a teacher, and desirous of determining his view on this highly controversial matter, submitted to him the question: "Teacher, which is the great commandment in the law? And he said unto him, Thou shalt love the Lord thy God with all thy heart, and with all thy soul, and with all thy mind. This is the great and first commandment. And a second like unto it is this, Thou shalt love thy neighbor as thyself. On these two commandments the whole law hangeth, and the prophets" (Matthew 22:36-40).

Note, especially, these words: "On these two commandments the whole law hangeth, and the prophets." This is truly an amazing statement. Imagine a peg in the wall, and over it a string draped, the two ends hanging downward. Let one of these ends represent the command to love God with one's whole heart, soul and mind, the other one's neighbor as one's self. Jesus said on these two is suspended the whole of the law of Moses and the teaching of the prophets. These two commands, in principle, involve all that is therein and, it might be correctly added, all of that in the new covenant as well. An eminent Jewish scholar who lived before our Lord came to the earth said, "the law consists of loving God supremely, and your neighbor as yourself. That is all of it. The rest of it is commentary." And, he was right. This is, in effect, what the Lord said. He who loves God with all of his being will seek to do all that the Lord requires; he who loves his neighbor as himself will just as carefully discharge his whole duty to his neighbor. So it is indeed true that the whole of human responsibility is summed up in these two commandments.

Among the duties we often owe to those about us is the obligation to forgive. How great indeed is the need for teaching and further study on this theme! The Jewish teachers had a very limited sense of obligation in this matter. The Rabbis taught that if your forgave someone three times this exhausted all reasonable expectation. If one sinned against you and repented, and you forgave him, and sinned against you again and repented and you forgave him, and sinned a third time and repented and you forgave him, if he sinned a fourth time against you, even though he repented, you were not obligated further. Three times was surely enough they thought.

Peter sensed that there was something too limited about this; but, he, too, fell into the same trap of limitation long characteristic of the Jews. He asked the Saviour, "Lord, how oft shall my brother sin against me, and I forgive him? Until seven times?" He sought to be much more liberal in his view of the matter than were the Jewish leaders; he took their number of three times to forgive, multiplied it by two, and then added one for good measure! "Until seven times?" the fisherman disciple asked, thinking this would surely suffice. But the Lord rejected both concepts. Said he, "I say not unto thee, Until seven times; but, Until seventy times seven," by which he did not mean a multiple of seven and seventy, but to infinity. The number is obviously symbolic; Jesus did not intend to say that we must forgive the penitent person four hundred ninety times, but not four hundred and ninety one! (Matthew 18:21,22). God does not limit his forgiveness for us when we turn to him in penitence; neither should we refuse pardon to those who truly repent of wrongs done to us however difficult it may appear to us to be.*

It is difficult for us to avoid the disposition that when we forgive another we are conferring a favor, and showing unusual tolerance. This impression we sometimes leave when another sins against us, and expresses the desire for our forgiveness. We say, in effect, "Well, if you will act right, and conduct yourself properly, I'll consider it." I must never forget this vital fact: I cannot keep you out of heaven by my

---

*It is of interest to note that the American Standard translators put into the text "until seventy times seven" which would suggest 490 times, and in the margin "seventy times, and seven,", that is, seventy seven times, an action evidently resulting from the mistaken notion that a statement in Genesis 4:24 in some fashion explains our Lord's words here. There is no basis for such a conclusion.

unwillingness to forgive you. You can go to heaven whether I forgive you or not; *but I can't*. I must forgive you, not in order for you to go to heaven, but in order for me to go to heaven; not in order for you to be saved, but in order for me to be saved. The Lord made it a condition precedent to our own forgiveness that we forgive others. He said, "For if ye forgive not men their trespasses, neither will your Father forgive your trespasses." and he also taught us to pray, "And forgive us our debts, as we also have forgiven our debtors" (Matthew 6:12-15).

The tenses of the verbs here, in the American Standard translation, are quite faithful to the text, and are significant in determining the Lord's will. Note: "Forgive as we also have forgiven!" Paul taught us to "Put on, therefore, as God's elect, holy and beloved, a heart of compassion, kindness, lowliness, meekness, long-suffering; forbearing one another, and forgiving each other, if any man have a complaint against any; even as the Lord forgave you, so also do ye" (Colossians 3:12,13). If we are unwilling to do so, we may as well include in our prayers the opposite sentiment, "Lord, if I will not forgive others, then don't forgive me."

Our Lord, in the shadows of Gethsemane, prayed for himself (Luke 22:41), and on the cross for his enemies (Luke 23:34). In that sad and tragic hour he said, "Father, forgive them; for they know not what they do." This earnest plea, in behalf of his tormentors, was far from being a formal petition, uttered for the record; the verb is an imperfect, signifying, *he kept on saying*, "Father, forgive them; for they know not what they do." At each indignity, at every insulting accusation and scornful word, the Lord repeated his prayer in their behalf! He prayed over and over again for his enemies!

Paul enjoined in the Colossian passage just cited two things: (1) forbearance; (2) forgiveness. To "forbear," is to endure, suffer, tolerate; to *put up with!* Prominent among the obligations we sustain to others is to "bear one another's burdens." (Galatians 6:2). It is often easier to *bear* the burdens (share the load) of others than it is to *endure* their weaknesses, peculiarities, and eccentricities. It is, however, our duty both to bear and forbear; it is enjoined upon us both by precept and by example. Paul taught it: Christ practiced it; and he also left us an example that we are to follow (1 Peter 2:21). If we are often by others irritated, let us remember that we doubtless often irritate others; and that the patience we are enabled to develop through the exercise of forbearance will greatly enhance our spiritual stature here, and immensely heighten our happiness hereafter. It is indeed not possible for one to be happy in this life who has not acquired the virtue of forbearance and tolerance of the weaknesses of others. Miserable always is he who harbors in his heart resentment for fancied or even real wrongs; the disposition becomes a cancer which finally eats his own heart out.

Hence, to refuse to forgive others is to compound our own unhappiness in this life and to close the door of heaven against us in the next. Malice, an unforgiving spirit, a heart saturated with resentment, are wholly incompatible with a tranquil life here, and are dispositions certain to force the forfeiture of a blissful life in the world to come. It is interesting to note that the Greek phrase, translated "forgiving each other," (Colossians 3:13), is, literally, *showing favor to yourselves.* Being in the body of Christ—the church—we are members one of another (Ephesians 1:19-22; 1 Corinthians 12:27); and, inasmuch as the brother we forgive is a member of the same body to which we belong, we contribute to our own well being, in restoring him to a proper relationship in that body.

Surely, no higher honour can be conferred upon one, aside from salvation itself, than to do good to, and to be a blessing for others. He who does not utilize the opportunities the ever passing days and the fast flying years provide to be of service to humanity, sins against himself, as well as others and the Lord, because he deprives himself of the blessings which can come only through such service. One who swaps the world for salvation and the privilege of serving his Creator and his fellow men, makes the best bargain he'll ever make in this world, for in so doing, he assures himself of happiness both here and hereafter.

To this end the great and the good of all the ages have borne witness. Hebrews 11 is Inspiration's Hall of Fame. Here, bathed in imperishable light, the truly great of earth appear in solemn array. Sublime characters of the ages, grand old men of prediluvian days, mighty prophets, priests and kings who kept the faith and marched unscathed to glory are exhibited in honored niches. Righteous Abel worships the Most High; Enoch walks with God; Noah, persistent prophet to a skeptical age, unwearily builds an ark to the saving of his house. Moses looks beyond the gilded palace of Pharaoh to the recompense of reward and the Israelites are seen to march with sure steps where moments before the forbidding waters of the Red Sea blocked their path to Canaan.

Honored and revered as were these, there is another who, for sheer faithfulness and devotion to duty, for unwearied service and heroic courage in the face of the most formidable trials, towers over them all like a blue mountain peak, spiraling high in the sky, overshadows every other eminence. Abraham is God's greatest Old Testament example of undaunted faith and undying zeal in every circumstance. Few men in history have been so favored as he, and none has ever been called upon to make the sacrifice which faced him in the lonely heights of Moriah. Between him and the great Jehovah there must have been a bond of sympathy never existing between others; each experienced the anguish of heart in "sparing not his own son" from death; and both found solace in receiving the priceless gifts back again.

At the top of the list of qualities which made Abraham's name great was his unquestioning obedience to his Maker. To his eternal credit is the fact that he never faltered in following the leading of the Most High. When God called he always answered. Even when the command conflicted with his conception of what was proper in the circumstances, he justified God with the calm conviction that the Judge of all the earth will do right. Called to go out into a strange land he turned his back on the comforts of home forever and became a homeless wanderer simply because the Lord commanded it. It may truly be said that the story of his life was one of weary waiting and hope long deferred. The land promises, though of greatest scope for that day, were to be realized only in his posterity; and it was his to dwell in tents while others tilled the soil and ate of its fruits and built and dwelled in its cities. All he ever actually possessed was the tomb where he and his beloved Sarah today sleep in solemn silence awaiting the glorious resurrection from the dead. He was promised descendants as the sands of the seashore but for a hundred years he was childless as to the promise. When at length the blessed promise was realized in Isaac his joy was suddenly cut short by the stern command to offer his son, his only son, the son he loved, in sacrifice. The story of this trial of Abraham's faith is told in Genesis 22, and is utterly without parallel in literature. The preparation for the journey, the weary days of travel, the conflicting emotions tearing at the heart of the anguished father, the innocent wonder of the lad as he observed the wood for the offering, and the knife for the victim, the final preparation and the upraised arm to strike the fatal blow; the sharp cry of the angel which stayed the hand of the father are matters recited with such poignancy that only the hard of heart can refrain from tears at the contemplation thereof. The centuries have not dimmed the light of this event, nor provided a finer example of devotion to duty and unquestioning faith without regard to the cost. When men today wish to speak of faith under trial this historic incident comes first to mind. Nearly two thousand years after it occurred Paul duly recorded it asserting that "by faith Abraham . . . offered up Isaac" (Hebrews 11:17).

His greatness was not in those areas where men of the world usually seek for honor, fame and material rewards. Though he built no city, he sought one "whose builder and maker is God," and his noble example has inspired myriads of others to the same holy quest. He possessed no country here below and wanted none, because his desire was a "better country, that is, an heavenly." He authored no books; he was not a statesman and he lived the life of a nomad; yet, a thousand pens have tried in vain to tell the full story of his radiant faith.

His death is chronicled in quaintness and simplicity. He died full of years, an old man, in a good old age, content with life, and now ready to go to be with him whom he had so long and so devotedly served. This lovely poem, from an unknown author, relates with poignancy and pathos the life of the faithful and illustrious patriarch, and stirs my heart to an extent seldom experienced.

"He knew not the path where he wandered;
   He knew not the journey before,
As the days of his pilgrimage lengthened,
   And life to its eventide wore;
And oft by his tent in the desert
   He dreamed of the way he had trod,
Ere he sought for the beautiful city
   Whose Builder and Maker is God.

"Above were the stars for his compass
   Beneath him the Syrian sands,
And only a promise to lead him
   Through the dreary and desolate lands;
Who doubts his faith must have wavered,
   As he wandered with weariness shod,
In the quest of the glorified city
   Whose Builder and Maker is God.

"He lay by his tent in the even,
   And o'er him night's pageantry rolled;
The stars in their crystalline orbits,
   The moon down a highway of gold;
And ever he heard it, the whisper,
   'Press onward o'er pathways untrod;
There waits you the wonderful city
   Whose Builder and Maker is God.'

"He was broken and aged and weary;
   He longed for the city of rest;
And doubt stood beside him to question:
   'Is the way you have chosen the best?'
Yet still he pressed onward and forward,
   O'er sand and desert and clod,
Still seeking the peace of the city
   Whose Builder and Maker is God.

"One night the great stars in their courses
   Blazed o'er him and glittered and burned,
As he sank by the side of a brooklet,
   And his soul for its heritage yearned.
'I am weary,' he murmured; 'no longer
   May I on my pilgrimage plod;
Yet grant me one glimpse of the city
   Whose Builder and Maker is God.'

"They found him at daybreak; the breezes
  Above him a requiem sung;
One cloud and its shadow crept eastward
  And o'er him a cerement flung;
Yet he smiled as a sleeper who dreameth
  Of fields that the angels have trod
And they knew that he looked on the city,
  Whose Builder and Maker is God.' "

A sermon delivered at the Sharpe, Kentucky Church of Christ, November 29, 1987.

LESSONS FROM THE
BOOK OF JOB

The Old Testament book of Job is one of the most remarkable productions ever penned. The exalted nature of its themes, the depth of its argument, and the ageless character of its teaching give it precedence over every similar human literary effort. Nothing in the *Iliad* of Homer, in the *Aeneid* of Virgil, or in *Paradise Lost* of Milton remotely equals it, and its philosophical concepts far excel anything in the ancient classical writings of the Greek and Roman world of literature.

It is infinitely superior to the best efforts of men because it is not a work of man but a production issuing directly from the hand of God through the agency of the Holy Spirit.

It is the oldest book in the Bible, so most conservative scholars believe—and possibly the oldest complete document in existence. Some ancient writings excavated from Asian tombs antedate it, but these are fragmentary; all fall far short of the minuteness and extent of detail characteristic of this extraordinary work. Its setting is that of the patriarchal period, evidence of which abounds.

Offerings and worship were engaged in by the head of the family precisely as in the days of Abraham, Isaac and Jacob (Job 1:5; 42:8,9). Modes of living, the manners and customs of daily life, are all those of the times of those illustrious patriarchs, and the forms of idolatry mentioned in the book are those known to have existed only in those early ages (31:26-28).

There is in Job no mention of the law of Moses, nor is there any appeal to its edicts—unaccountable if the book were written following the giving of the law at Sinai—and the councils, governing bodies, judges at the gates and forms of legal processes are those long anterior to the promulgation of that legal system which came into being about 1500 B.C. (28:1ff; 29:17,25; 31:28, 35).

There are many allusions in the book of Job to historic events in early biblical history such as the building of the Pyramids, the flood, and the destruction of "the cities of the plain," but no reference to the deliverance of the people from Egypt, the crossing of the Red Sea, or the entrance of the people of Israel into Canaan, the land of promise.

It is incredible and inconceivable that a writer, within the period between the giving of the law at Sinai and the days of the major and minor prophets, would have written a book as lengthy and detailed as Job, yet have omitted all reference to these unparalleled events, and made no mention of the writings of Moses so prominent in Israel's history following the historic revelations at Sinai. The conclusion becomes irresistible in the light of these significant facts that the author did not do so because he wrote long before these events occurred, and before these writings appeared.

The length of life assigned to Job is significant in determining when he lived. While it is not possible to know precisely his age at death, he was certainly more than two hundred years old, since it is clearly stated that he lived for one hundred forty years *following* the tragedies the book details, had begotten seven sons and three daughters and had amassed a considerable store of material possessions *before* they began (1:2,3; 32:6; 42:16). It is interesting to note that the Septuagint Version (Greek Old Testament), has the words "And all the years that Job lived were two hundred forty," in which case he was a hundred years old when his misfortunes began.

It would therefore appear that his age places him in a era long before the days of Jacob and his descendants when the length of life men were privileged to live had been greatly shortened from that of an earlier period of the patriarchal age. Chronological data would make him contemporary with Isaac and in the time frame described in Genesis 22. Eusebius, born about 270 A.D. often alluded to as "the father of church history," says that Job appeared in history about two hundred years before Moses, or about eighteen hundred years before the beginning of the Christian era, thus confirming the correctness of the conclusion we have already drawn.

Job was a real, and not a fictitious person, as most liberal "scholars" allege. Ezekiel, the prophet, identifies him as a righteous man, and mentions him along with Noah and Daniel (Ezekiel 14:14). One might, with as little justification, deny to Noah and Daniel actual existence. James, in a statement that has become proverbial, makes mention of the "patience of Job," and thus provides New Testament proof of the genuineness and authenticity of the book (James 5:11). We shall see later, and with much detail, that Job was a "perfect" (i.e. upright) man who was willing to endure any earthly hardship rather than forsake God (1:1). He exhibited, in clear and striking fashion, the struggles of one who, while he could not understand the reason for his trials, did not blame God for them, and maintained faith in him. He was a native of the "land of Uz," (1:1), a country mentioned also in Jeremiah 25:20 and Lamentations 4:21, and located in an area south and east of the Dead Sea, and in or near the country of Edom not far from Arabia.*

For our purpose in this study, the book of Job is analyzed as follows:

---

*Uz, Job's father, was the son of Nahor, a brother of Abraham (Genesis 22:20,21). Eliphaz descended from Teman, son of Esau and grandson of Abraham (Genesis 36:4, 10-16; 1 Chronicles 1:35,36). Bildad was a descendent of Shuah, a son of Abraham and Keturah (Genesis 25:1,2). Zophar was a Mamathite. There was a city in Judah's territory in the days of Joshua by that name. Thus, traditionally, all of these men had a well defined concept of the one true God as opposed to the idolatry generally prevailing.

I. Historical setting (1-3:26).
II. Job's discussion with his three "friends" (4:1-30:40).
   (1) Was God the author of Job's trials? (4:1-14:22).
   (2) Do the wicked always suffer in this life for their
       sins? (15:1-21:34).
   (3) Was Job guilty of hidden sins? (22:1-31:40).
III. Elihu declares God's justice (32:1-37:24).
IV. God's addresses (38:1-41:34).
V. Job's vindication and recovery (42:1-17).

The "historical section" provides the details which led to the dialogue with which the book is largely composed. Job, an Arabian sheik and an inhabitant of the land of Uz, of great wealth and influence and with a large family and many devoted servants, lived in contentment and honor and enjoyed the approval and approbation of God. Satan, whose name signifies "accuser of the brethren," appeared before God, his purpose being to impeach the character of this great and good man, and to raise doubts regarding his integrity. However, so exemplary and so pure in heart and conduct was he that God did not hesitate to commend his piety unreservedly and to offer him as an example of faithfulness and complete dedication.

Said he to that Evil One, "Hast thou considered my servant Job? for there is none like him in the earth, a perfect and upright man, one that feareth God, and turneth away from evil?" (2:3). Job's piety Satan reluctantly conceded, because he could not deny it, but he sought to impeach it by alleging that it resulted from selfishness because of the blessings God had so abundantly bestowed upon him. Satan therefore proposed a test: "Put forth thy hand now, and touch all that he hath, and he will renounce thee to thy face" (2:5).

To this test of the faithful patriarch God agreed, putting Job in Satan's power, saying only, "Upon himself put not forth thy hand," and disaster quickly came in fourfold fashion. It fell upon Job (1) as a farmer, in the loss of his crops, (2) as a rancher, in the loss of his flocks and herds, (3) as a tradesman, in the loss of his personal possessions, and (4) as a father, in the loss of his children. Despite these personal tragedies, Job "worshipped, and said, Naked came I out of my mother's womb, and naked shall I return thither: Jehovah gave, and Jehovah hath taken away; blessed be the name of Jehovah." And, of him it is affirmed, *"In all of this Job sinned not, nor charged God foolishly"* (2:20-22).

God again directed Satan's attention to Job's faithfulness under severe trial, and to the integrity of his devoted servant Job, despite the unparalleled suffering he had experienced. But Satan was not yet finished. He said, "Skin for skin, yea, all that a man hath will he give for his life. But put forth thy hand now, and touch his bone and his flesh, and he will renounce thee to thy face" (2:4). This test God also agreed to, the only proviso being that Job's life was not to be forfeited.

"So Satan went forth from the presence of Jehovah, and smote Job with sore boils from the sole of his foot unto his crown. And he took him a potsherd to scrape himself therewith; and he sat among the ashes" (2:7) Many Hebraists believe (from this and other references in the book of Job, 7:4,5; 17:1; 19:17-20), that the affliction was *Elephantiais,* one of the most loathsome forms of leprosy known to the ancient world.

Job's wife, who thus far had remained silent in spite of this series of heartbreaking tragedies, following this latest shocking development, lost her faith in God, aligned herself with Satan, and urged Job "to renounce God, and die." Even this crowning act of discouragement, from one from whom he had every right to expect support and encouragement, did not dissuade him from his loyalty to God. Said he, "Thou speakest as one of the foolish women speaketh. What? shall

we receive good at the hand of God, and shall we not
receive evil? In all of this did not Job sin with his lips"
(2:9,10).

His "friends," Eliphaz the Temanite, Bildad the
Shuhite, and Zophar the Naamathite came to console
him, but when they saw that his grief was great and
the misfortunes which had befallen him so pronounced, wept, rent their robes, sprinkled dust on
their heads, and sat with him *seven days without
speaking*. At chapter 3:1, the dialogue, in dramatic form,
the participants of which were Job, Eliphaz, Bildad,
Zophar, and eventually God himself, begins.

The *purpose* of the drama may be gathered from the
themes discussed—questions the answer to which
have occasioned the earnest inquiry and the most
minute scrutiny of the wisest through the ages.

Why do some in this life enjoy great prosperity and
others only privation and endless physical suffering?
Does God have any direct interest in the affairs of
men, or did he create the world and then abandon it
to its own devices? Are human beings motivated solely
by selfish interests? Is there really any such thing as
piety and goodness engaged in for their own sake? If
God does indeed feel an interest in the affairs of men,
and exercises providential care for them, does he do
so on principles of justice and right or by arbitrary
actions only? What is the divine purpose for men in
this world? Is there life beyond the grave? How may
man be just before God? Do disasters and misfortune
result from the sins of those who thus suffer, and do
they evidence God's displeasure with those so afflicted? How may man know God?

First among the many themes discussed in the book
is the question of Job's integrity. This, Satan did not
hesitate to attack. "Doth Job fear God for naught?" he
asked (1:9). Selfishness was really the reason Job
served God the devil alleged—not inherent goodness

and genuine love for his creator—and it was this allegation which prompted him to ask God to take from his servant everything Job held dear except life itself.

God's confidence in Job was fully justified. When calamity came he bore it uncomplainingly; no word of discontent toward God fell from his lips. The loss of his material possessions he accepted without a murmur; bereavement because of the loss of his children laid him low, but he reacted by blessing the name of Jehovah who gave them to him; and when assailed by a terrible and, in that day, incurable disease and challenged by his wife, in the words of Satan himself, to curse God and die, he responded in calm resignation and acceptance of whatever the will of God involved. In all of this, "Job sinned not, nor charged God foolishly." With unwavering confidence in his Creator, he preserved his faith, demonstrated his integrity, and proved that it is possible for one to serve God from no other than unselfish and disinterested reasons. And, what Job did, any other equally faithful and dedicated servant of God can, and would also, do.

We rejoice to know from the subsequent records that God gave the worthy saint "twice as much as he had before," and blessed the "latter end of Job more than his beginning." He was privileged to live a hundred and forty years in happiness and great blessing, saw his sons, and his sons' sons unto four generations, and finally died, "being old and full of days" (42:10-17).

It was inevitable that in the discussion between Job and his "friends" regarding his bitter and painful experiences other issues should arise. Prominent among them was the age-long question of the reasons why some men are prosperous, others suffer adversity; some are happy and contented in life, others are wretched and evermore miserable; some enjoy good health all of their days, others live out their lives in great pain and sorrow.

This controversial and exceedingly complex issue held no difficulties for Job's "friends" whatsoever! They resolved it, at least to their satisfaction, with the observation that inasmuch as God is both righteous and just in his dealings with men, their status—whether prosperous or poor, whether in health or in sickness, whether blessed or cursed—is determined by him solely on the basis of their character and conduct. If they are prosperous, it is because they are good; if they suffer adversity, it is because they are bad.

This view, one long held by many (compare Luke 13:1-5), Job rejected (as our Lord did centuries later) without hesitation; he knew that his difficulties were not occasioned by great guilt or depravity on his own part, though he conceded that the question why many wicked people prosper and many good people suffer in this life was difficult of solution. But, of one thing he was sure: whatever the difficulties, his own integrity and God's inherent goodness and justice made such a conclusion as the three had drawn impossible.

Zophar attempted to cut the Gordian knot by urging the unsearchableness of all of God's actions and the futility of any effort of man in seeking to understand the mystery of any of God's actions. Said he,

"Canst thou by searching find out God?
Canst thou find out the Almighty unto perfection?
It is high as heaven; what canst thou do?
Deeper than Sheol; why canst thou know?
The measure thereof is longer than the earth,
    and broader than the sea." (11:7-9).

Zophar's implication was that Job should accept his calamities without question, even though arbitrary and cruel, solely on the ground of God's sovereignty, and without regard to what is right or wrong. He said,

> If he cut off, and shut up, or gather together, then who can hinder him? (11:10).

Elihu, a later participant in the debates, proposed a possible and partial answer: God suffers hardship and trial upon the good, not for punishment but for chastisement (compare Hebrews 12:1-13), not in vengeance but in love, for their ultimate good and eventual salvation (33:18,28). This premise James, in the first chapter of the book that bears his name, developed at some length: "Count it all joy, my brethren," this fleshly brother of our Lord wrote, "When ye fall into divers temptations (margin, trials); knowing that the proving of your faith worketh patience. And let patience have her perfect work, that ye may be perfect and entire, lacking in nothing . . . Blessed is the man that endureth temptation (trial), for when he hath been approved, he shall receive the crown of life, which the Lord promised to them that love him" (James 1:2,4,12).

This premise, however, we must be careful not to extend beyond that intended by the sacred writers. God is often said to do what he simply allows or suffers to occur; though, in every instance, what does occur will result in great blessing for the dedicated disciple: "And we know that to them that love God all things work together for good, even to them that are called according to his purpose. . . . Who shall separate us from the love of Christ? shall tribulation, or anguish, or persecution, or famine, or nakedness, or peril, or sword? Even as it is written, For thy sake we are killed all the day long; we were accounted as sheep for the slaughter. Nay, in all these things we are more than conquerors through him that loved us" (Romans 8:28, 35-37).

Hope "which springs eternal in the human breast," prompted Job (chapter 3), to look beyond his sufferings to a better day, initially to the end of his earthly trials, but it soon became clear to him that the mere cessation of suffering did not satisfy the desire now stirring in his heart. So, the question arises,

"If a man die shall he live again? (14:14).

In his efforts to find an answer Job saw what at first appeared to him to be an analogy in nature:

"For there is hope of a tree,
If it be cut down, that it will sprout again
And that the tender branch thereof will not cease,
Though the root thereof wax old in the earth,
And the stock thereof die in the ground;
Yet through the scent of water it will bud,
And put forth boughs like a plant.
But man dieth, and is laid low:
Yea, man giveth up the ghost, and where is he?
As the waters fail from the sea,
And the river wasteth and drieth up;
So man lieth down and riseth not:
Till the heavens be no more, they shall not awake,
Nor be aroused out of their sleep." (14:7-12).

But, the analogy did not satisfy and the argument from nature offered no certain proof of a future life. Indeed, the drying up of the waters seemed to suggest a different and unacceptable lesson from that desired. It is through the gospel, by which means life and immortality came to light (2 Timothy 1:10), that we find hope, and not in human reasoning and failing analogies; and it was to the divine relationship Job turned for the hope for which his soul sighed:

"I know that my redeemer liveth,
And at last he will stand upon the earth:
And after my skin, even this body, is destroyed,

Then without my flesh shall I see God;
Whom I, even I, shall see, on my side
And mine eyes shall behold, and not a stranger."
(19:25-27).

It is heartening to know that even in that early age some intimation of a life beyond stirred in the hearts of the faithful, even though it was vague and not clearly defined. Abraham and his contemporaries entertained the hope of "a better country, that is, a heavenly . . ." and in David's day the desire for and the expectation of life beyond the grave had become far more vivid in pious and prayerful hearts. The Psalmist wrote specifically and in detail of a resurrection from the dead (Psalm 16:11; 17:15; Acts 2:25-28); and in the New Testament the fact is repeatedly affirmed and confirmed. Our Lord asserted it (John 5:28,29), Paul proclaimed it (Acts 17:31), Peter proved it both by prophecy and by inspiration and the Lord demonstrated it! (1 Corinthians 15:20).

With what great joy should we claim this immeasurable blessing, and serenely rest in the promise of our Lord, when he said, "I am the resurrection and the life: he that believeth on me, though he die, yet shall he live; and whosoever liveth and believeth on me shall never die" (John 11:25,26). And, how comforting are the words of the great apostle, "For we know that if the earthly house of our tabernacle be dissolved, we have a building from God, a house not made with hands, eternal, in the heavens" (2 Corinthians 5:1). We should evermore rejoice that in the fullness of time God has made known to man, through his infallible word, the riches of his grace, and has given us assurance, "an anchor of the soul, a hope both sure and steadfast and entering into that which is within the veil, whither as a forerunner Jesus entered for us . . ." (Hebrews 6:19,20).

This marvelous blessing is bestowed neither arbitrarily nor unconditionally. Job successfully defended his integrity and moral standing before men, but this did not guarantee his right standing before God. He was well aware that there is a sharp distinction between blamelessness in the sight of men and righteousness in the sight of God! Though wholly free of any crime against humanity, this could not assure Job, or any other, of that righteousness without which there is no escape from the ultimate judgment of God. Hence, the question was raised, vital to the salvation of us all:

"But how can man be just with (before) God?" (9:2).

The question is rhetorical—in this form for emphasis. The obvious answer is, *"In no way."* Man cannot bargain with God. Of this Job was fully aware. No claim of moral purity, no assertion of personal rights, no offer of material things could possibly prevail. He was painfully conscious of the fact that not only was he without bargaining power with God, he could not directly approach him. Said he,

> "For he is not a man as I am, that I should answer him,
> That we should come together in judgment.
> There is no umpire between us,
> That might lay his hand upon us both.
> Let him take his rod away from me,
> And let not his terror make me afraid:
> Then would I speak, and not fear him;
> For I am not so in myself" (9:32-35).

Job, in recognition of the immeasurable inequality existing between himself and God, and his utter inability to approach God directly, longed for an "umpire," an arbiter who would, by agreement by both parties, decide the issue between them. In this remarkable statement the ancient chieftain gave utterance to a need characteristic of us all, and prophetically anticipated the coming of the Savior into the world.

We have all sinned and have come short of the glory of God. Sin alienates us from God, and a right relationship with him may exist only when sinful conduct ends and when the guilt which results from its practice has been absolved. Job saw no immediate solution in his day, and his statement is therefore one of despair.

But, we rejoice to say, not in ours!

An arbiter—umpire—God has given us in the person of his own dear Son (John 3:16). He who knew no sin became sin (a sin-bearer) for us that we might escape its consequences, "and became the righteousness of God in him" (2 Corinthians 5:21). The means of a right relationship with God have been made available to us through the gospel, and by its dynamic powers (Romans 1:16); and all men have the same precious privilege of approach to God. We appropriate these incomparable blessings through our faith in the Lord Jesus Christ and by our obedience to his loving commands (Romans 5:1; 1 John 2:4; Revelation 22:14.

Powerless to explain all the mysteries of sin and suffering in that day, Job and his "friends" ended their dialogues and God spoke to Job out of a whirlwind (38:1). He submitted about forty questions the design of which was to show how little Job—and all other men apart from revelation—really knew of God's works, much less the more profound matters of righteousness and justification in that distant day not fully made known as in ours. Among such matters mentioned here and elsewhere in the book are scientific facts then outside the realm of human knowledge and not discovered and recognized by man until thousands of years later. These include the "empty place in the north," the earth suspended "upon nothing," (26:7), Chlorophyll through photosynthesis (8:16), wind and gravity (28:25), the "springs" of the sea (fresh underwater currents (38:16), the treasures of the snow

(38:22), the color spectrum (38:24), the function of Pleiades, the remarkable phenomenon of Arcturus (38:31,32), and many others.

Out of Job's extraordinary experiences we are led to see what must have been the design of God in giving us the book bearing the patriarch's name: it is, (1) a dependable and reliable source of information clearly reflecting God's will and man's duty to be faithful to his Creator; (2) a revelation of man's destiny and status following death; (3) an assurance of the resurrection of the body; (4) proof of a day of accounting and an impartial and final judgment; (5) a promise of an "umpire"—mediator—to stand between God and man; and (6) an indication of the way of approach to the Father of mercies through him. In view of God's great love for man in the gift of his Son to suffer death on the cross for us, an event this book faintly foreshadows, it is not surprising that the revelation of these great truths should have been included in the first book of the Bible to be written. How greatly blessed are we to have this ancient and precious production!

Highland Church of Christ, McMinnville, Tenn. August 9, 1987.

THE WORTHY NAME

I feel uncomfortable with the phrase, "erring Christian," and long ago ceased to use it in my preaching and teaching. "Erring children of God," yes; for this is what they are, though they err; but not "erring Christians," because the terms are mutually exclusive, and thus involve a contradiction of terms.

The name "Christian" translates the Greek word *Christianos*, a combination of *Christos*, "Christ," and a suffix meaning, *a follower*; hence, a "follower of Christ." It is of interest to note that the three languages with which we principally meet in the New Testament and that were used in the inscription on the Cross—Hebrew, Greek and Latin—meet in this word! "Christos" (Christ), is the Greek translation of the Hebrew word for "Messiah;" the word "Christos" directly derives from the Greek language, and signifying *anointed*, and the suffix, added to produce the term "Christian," is Latin.

A Christian then, is "a follower of Christ." A follower of Christ is one who has acknowledged the Lordship of Christ and seeks earnestly to do his will as set out in the sacred writings. One who turns aside from this divine direction, engages in that which the Lord has not sanctioned, and persists in practices that violate that will cannot, by the wildest stretch of the imagination, be properly styled a follower of Christ—a Christian.

To refer to such a person as an "erring Christian," is the equivalent of saying that one so described is "an apostate who follows Christ," an "unfaithful, faithful person;" "a sinful Christian!"—an absurdity, surely. Sadly, people who have obeyed the gospel do indeed fall from the grace of God and become sinners; but, so long as they persist in this state, they are not followers of the Lord, and ought not to be so described. The disposition to designate those in this capacity as "Christians" does grave injury to the Cause of Christ, and palliates the guilt of the erring by making them to feel that though in sin, they nevertheless have some claim upon the Lord by still *having the right to wear his name!* No such right is theirs, and ought not to be accorded them.

What is involved in this name, and who may properly wear it, is a matter of great importance, and ought, therefore, to occasion the interest and earnest efforts of us all in our search for truth. Pursuant to this end, we shall use the basic formula of the news reporter in seeking out the details of the matter being investigated, and approach the subject in our study as follows: (1) What? (2) When? (3) Where? (4) Why? and (5) Who? Not all of these areas of investigation are of equal importance; nor, may all be determined in the same fashion; but, all are necessary to consider in order to a full and thorough understanding of the significance and proper use of the Christian name.

(1) What?

The Christian name was assigned to the Lord's people, an account of which is recorded in Acts 11:26, for the first time in the history of the world in connection with the work of Barnabas and Saul (Paul) in Antioch. The Spirit's record of it, and the context in which it appears, is as follows: "Then departed Barnabas to Tarsus, to seek Saul: and when he had found him, he brought him unto Antioch. And it came to pass, that a whole year they assembled themselves with the church, and taught much people. And the disciples were called Christians first in Antioch." There are two other instances in which the name *Christian* appears in the New Testament (it does not, of course, occur at all in the Old Testament).

Paul, a prisoner of the Romans, in an appearance before governor Festus and King Agrippa, reasoned so earnestly and eloquently from the scriptures that Jesus is the Christ, that the king, deeply moved, I believe, by Paul's argument, said to the apostle, "Almost thou persuadest me to be a Christian." To this Paul replied, "I would to God that not only thou, but also all that hear me this day, were both almost and altogether such as I am, except these bonds" (Acts 25:1:-26:29).[1]

The third and final instance of the name "Christian" in the New Testament occurs in Peter's first epistle: "But let none of you suffer as a murderer, or as a thief, or as an evildoer, or as a busybody in other men's matters. Yet if any man suffer as a Christian, let him not be ashamed; but let him glorify God on this behalf." (1 Peter 4:15,16). The American Standard Version aptly and, I think, more accurately, renders the final phrase, "let him glorify God *in this name*," i.e., in the name Christian!

James alluded to those in his day who "blaspheme that worthy name" by which the disciples were "called" (James 2:7). We have seen that the name by which they were "called" was the name "Christian."

---

[1]The American Standard translators, thinking that Agrippa was insincere in his response, rendered the statement, "With but little persuasion thou wouldst fain make me a Christian," i.e., "Do you think that with no more effort than this, you can make a Christian of me?" The King James translators, on the assumption that Agrippa was sincere, made the king to say, "Almost thou persuadest me to be a Christian," i.e., "I am almost convinced by what you say to become a Christian myself!"

(2) When?

Any uncertainty with reference to the chronology of that section of Acts which details the origin of the name "Christian" is not of significance in this study, since our interest is to be primarily focused on the relationship of the events mentioned, and not to specific dates.[2]

(3) Where?

The name was assigned to the disciples at Antioch, in Syria, (a place to be carefully distinguished from "Antioch in Pisidia," in the province of Phrygia, Acts 13:14). Antioch, in Syria, was located three hundred miles north of Jerusalem, and destined soon to become a missionary center from which would radiate the gospel, by means of Paul's missionary efforts, to the whole of the middle Eastern world. Jerusalem had the honor of being the city where Christianity began, and from where the gospel first went out to the Jewish world; but, following the dispersion of the disciples, occasioned by persecution of the early church, Antioch soon supplanted that city as the chief seat of missionary effort, especially to the Greek and Roman peoples.

Some of those driven out of Jerusalem (Acts 8:1), "travelled as far as Phenice, and Cyprus, and Antioch, preaching the word to none but unto the Jews only;" however, the gospel was not long limited to the descendants of Jacob; others from Cyprus and Cyrene "spake unto the Grecians, preaching the Lord Jesus." The efforts were immediately and eminently successful; "the hand of the Lord was with them: and a great

---

[2]The date may, however, be determined with a reasonable degree of accuracy. There is historical evidence that the Herod who caused James to be slain and who imprisoned Peter (Acts 12:1-11), died in A.D. 44. Paul and Barnabas had been preaching the word in Antioch about a year prior to that event. It was during their ministry there that the name was assigned the disciples.

number believed and turned to the Lord" (Acts 11:19-21). Thus, in this manner and from that place did the gospel go to the Gentile world.

(4) Why?

Names are identifiers, and in a state of society they are essential. In order to enjoy that unity which the Savior Himself enjoined, there had to be one name equally suited and applicable to all. It ought to be obvious to even the most casual observer that so long as people persist in choosing denominational designations in preference to that intended for the Lord's people, there can never be the perfect family harmony he envisioned. If to this the objection is offered that there are other terms used in the New Testament to identify the followers of Jesus,—disciples, saints, brethren, children of God,—I answer that these designations are not proper names but terms of relationship, character, activity, etc. They were disciples because their relationship to Christ was that of pupil/teacher; saints, because of their consecration to Christ; brethren, as members of the same family; and children of God, as the offspring of the Father.

They were *called* Christians because this was henceforth to be their name. We must be careful and not confuse attributes, relationships, and personal characteristics of the Lord's people with the term which alone distinguishes them before the world. The followers of the Lord, in their relationship to Christ, immediately acquired a relationship with each other; hence, they were called "brethren." Jesus said, "but be not ye called Rabbi; for one is your teacher, and all ye are brethren" (Matthew 23:8). Those who acknowledged allegiance to the Lord soon acquired a reputation for holiness and godly conduct; hence, were "saints," i.e., consecrated persons. Ananias, the gospel preacher

who baptized Paul, is the first to have used it, so far
as our record goes when, reluctant to approach a man
who had thus far exhibited the greatest violence
toward the faithful, responded to the Lord's bidding
to go to Paul by saying, "Lord, I have heard by many
of this man, how much evil he hath done to thy saints
at Jerusalem" (Acts 9:13). These saints, having been
born into the family of God were his "children,' and
are often so identified.

Let it be carefully noted that all of these terms—
disciples, brethren, saints, children of God—evidence
relationships, the recognition of which required and
presupposed earlier acquaintance with them. With the
possible exception of the last—children of God—the
other terms do not clearly identify the movement to
which they belonged. Disciples of whom? Whose
brethren? For what reason, saints? It was necessary,
therefore, that a term should come into use which
would enable all who heard of them to know
immediately whose servants they were. *No other name
could so effectively achieve this, and so on the verge of the
world wide proclamation of the gospel, the name "Christian,"
by divine edict, was given to the Lord's followers.* It is the
sum of all the rest.

(5) Who?

By whom, and under whose authority, was the
name *Christian* given? (1) The name was assigned
derisively and in reproach by the enemies of Christianity, so most liberal "scholars" allege. But if such had
been the case, and the name was given for the purpose
of reflecting unfavorably on those to whom it was
assigned, the attempt miserably failed; far from being
embarrassed or feeling belittled by it, the early
Christians regarded its assignment as an honor of the
highest order, and they henceforth wore it proudly,
happily and gladly, and many of them died rather than

to renounce it. It was not given to them by their enemies.

(2) Others, remarkably, have thought that the disciples themselves assumed the name "Christian" as the natural and normal consequence of being followers of Christ. Among those holding this view was brother J. W. McGarvey, and expressed by him in these words: "It (i.e., the name Christian) is just such a name as a number of grave and dignified friends of the cause, had they been sitting in council on the subject, may have adopted" (New Commentary on Acts, page 228). True, he followed the foregoing comment with these words, "For its divine approval, we need no other assurance than that found in its acceptance by the apostle." This affirmation and the foregoing one from that eminent scholar appear to be inconsistent; his implication is that the early disciples choose the title without divine authorization, but in an action sanctioned by the Lord! This, we shall see is in clear conflict with the text of Acts 11:26, and is one of the exceedingly few instances when I have been unable to accept a conclusion of one of the most profound Bible students in the world. I think he held this position because his teacher, Alexander Campbell, whom he admired greatly, attempted to influence the brotherhood to accept the designation, "Disciples of Christ," rather than the name "Christian," as the proper "name" for God's children.

Campbell, in an article in his paper, the Millennial Harbinger of 1839, pages 401-403, under the title *Our Name*, advanced the following reasons in support of his position that the phrase "Disciples of Christ" is a more appropriate term for children of God to wear than "Christian:

"1. It is more ancient; it was a designation known to the church from the beginning; whereas, the name 'Christian' was not assigned until several years following the establishment of the church on the day of Pentecost (Acts 2:1ff).

"2. It is more descriptive; people are often named after their leaders, parties, principles, nations, when they have no intention by so doing to indicate that they are students of the one or ones whose names they bear.

"3. It appears more often; 'the disciples' are so designated more than thirty times as such, but only three times as Christians in the scriptures.

"4. It is more appropriate; other groups style themselves 'Christians;' 'Disciples of Christ' is thus a more unique name for the people of God to wear."

Brethren of that day were not greatly impressed with these views of the scholarly Campbell and, for the most part, rejected them. 1. If the age of a title is the only determining factor, there are those which antedate both "Disciples of Christ," and "Christians." Among these are "men of Israel," (Acts 3:12), "children of the prophets," (Acts 3:25), "believers" and others equally sacred (Acts 5:14). There was, as we shall later see, special reasons why the name "Christian" was not earlier assigned. 2. Though the former was by him regarded as the more descriptive, the latter is, in reality, far more so, inasmuch as one may be a pupil, student, or disciple and admirer of Christ, yet fall far short of meeting the requirements of a Christian. 3. His third reason is especially weak; the scripturalness of a matter is not to be settled on the basis of the number of times it appears in the scriptures; the word "scriptural" does not admit of degrees of comparison; a thing is just as true though but once mentioned in the Bible as if referred to therein a thousand times! Moreover, Campbell accepted as irrevocably binding many matters mentioned no more often than the name "Christian." 4. Were we to reject every religious act previously appropriated, we would find ourselves without any item of the Christian faith since all religious bodies teach some truth and correctly identify some scriptural practices.

(3) A third and, I think, the only correct view is that the name was divinely given by inspiration through Paul and Barnabas, and that the passage, properly construed, fully supports this conclusion, and no other. This I shall seek to sustain by two specific arguments, the first of which is philological, the second, by direct statements from the scriptures.

1. Philological Proofs

That portion of the verse especially relevant to our studies in this area, as it appears in the King James' Version, reads: "And it came to pass, that a whole year they assembled themselves with the church, and taught much people. And the disciples were called Christians first in Antioch." So also is the rendering of the American Standard Version with only slight variation and that of no significance. Three verbs that are of primary importance should be noted at this juncture. 1. "They assembled" (sunachthenai); 2. (they) "taught;" (didaxai); 3. the disciples "were called" (chrematisai) "Christians . . ." *Sunachthenai* is aorist, infinitive passive of *sunago*, to bring or gather together; *didaxai* is aorist, infinitive active of *didasko*, to teach; and, *chrematisai*, is aorist, infinitive active of *chrematidzo*, "in the NT to utter a divine communication, to be divinely instructed, receive a revelation or warning from God, to receive an appellation, to be styled" (Bagster's Analytical Lexicon).

It will be seen, from this analysis of the Greek text, that the first verb under consideration (assembled) is passive voice—the two following ones, active. Amazingly, the translators reversed the Holy Spirit's order; they rendered the first verb, which is passive, by an active one, the second verb, which is active, by an active one, and the third verb, which is an active verb, as a passive one! Why this variation? Why did those men resort to a device that obscures the clear and unmistakable meaning of the Greek text, in their translation?

These men all believed in the propriety of wearing human names in religion as identifiers; was this a calculated effort on their part to justify this common denominational practice? In order to do this, they fragmented one sentence into two, changed the active voice into the passive, an infinitive into an indicative, and the accusative case into the nominative! I can see no reason whatsoever for this unwarranted mishandling of the text. Had they translated the verbs properly, it is likely that most people, who regard the scriptures as an infallible guide would be wearing the name "Christian," today.

That portion of the passage, especially pertinent to our present study, properly rendered, reads: "And it came to pass that . . . they taught many people and they called the disciples Christians first in Antioch."

"They taught . . ."

"They called . . ."

Those who "taught" were Paul and Barnabas.

Those who "called" were those who taught.

Paul and Barnabas "taught".

Therefore, Paul and Barnabas both "taught" and "called" the disciples Christians. This, they did by inspiration. The name thus came by divine direction through the medium of the Holy Spirit by whose infallible powers they were guided.

This rendering is in complete and perfect harmony with the syntax of the Greek language; it meets the requirements of the text and is a proper translation. I am well aware that brother McGarvey, in his New Commentary on Acts (page 228), wrote, "The new name which here and now originated proved the most potent name that has ever been applied to a body of men. The question, who originated it, whether Barnabas and Saul, or the disciples of Antioch, or the unbelievers of Antioch, has occasioned more discus-

sion than its importance justifies. To an untrained
reader of the Greek it might appear that the passage
should be rendered, 'they were gathered together with
the church, and taught much people, and called the
disciples Christians first at Antioch,' thus representing
Barnabas and Saul as the authors of the name; but this
rendering is condemned, and that of our text is
justified by almost unanimous judgment of scholars."

The case he offers in defense of the rendering he
sought to support in his commentary is far less weighty
than his words suggest. 1. These "scholars," to whom
he refers were, with the rarest exception, devotees of
denominational bodies who believed and taught that
the name *Christian* was given in derision and by the
enemies of Christ to the early disciples—a view which
McGarvey rejected. Though he appealed to them in
support of his view that the verb "chrematizo" should
be rendered intransitively, he was unable and unwilling to follow them to the conclusion they drew
touching its origin. 2. Every Greek lexicon I consulted
touching this matter—and this included Arndt &
Gingrich, Thayer, Robinson, Bagster, and Abbott-
Smith and these authorities might be greatly extended—
gives the basic and root meaning of the word under
study as a divine calling. It is alleged, however, that
Acts 11:26 is an exception and signifies merely to call
or style. This is an unwarranted and unjustified
conclusion.[3]

A simple induction of its New Testament usage is
highly instructive regarding the word *chrematizo*. It
appears nine times, in the King James' version, and is

[3] Romans 7:3, sometimes offered as an instance where the active voice
must be rendered passively in English, is not an exception. It is not the
community, but God, who originates the description there given. "She"
(the woman under consideration), shall act the "adulteress," or, to coin a
word, she shall adulterize! Adultery is "voluntary sexual intercourse
between a married man and some one other than his wife, or between a
married woman and some one other than her husband." (Webster's New
Collegiate Dictionary.)

rendered seven times as a transitive verb, six times passively, and once in the active voice. The passive form was used in Matthew 2:12-22, Luke 2:36, Acts 10:22, Hebrews 8:5 and Hebrews 9:7; in all of which it is rendered in passive form and with passive meaning, and in Hebrews 12:25, where it is in the active form and with active meaning. This demonstrates clearly that the verb is transitive and that in all the other passages, excepting Acts 11:26, the translators rendered the term in perfect harmony with its meaning.

Moses E. Lard, in a direct response to McGarvey on this theme, effectively refuted the view that the passive rendering of the verb is the proper one in Acts 11:26. In his Quarterly for 1864, pages 263, 264, he wrote, "Further, that *chrematizo* has its regular active passive voice, and that it is found in both these in the New Testament, is a simple well known fact incapable of being denied. Now that the Holy Spirit had a reason for using the one of these instead of the other, where it has used either, will not be questioned. In the passage in hand it has used the active. It then had a reason for it—what was it? Had it used the passive, it must have remained forever uncertain whether the disciples were called Christians first by Saul and Barnabas or by others: using the active, all is clear—Saul and Barnabas certainly gave the name. How shall the active be rendered into English? Passively says brother Campbell—passively says Dr. Hackett—passively says brother McGarvey. Are these authors right? *We think not.* Why, if the passive form is necessary in English, and if the subject of the infinitive is to be left uncertain—why, we repeat, was not the corresponding form used in Greek and a corresponding uncertainty thereby created? This is a tough question for those that render passively. They will never answer it."

Thus, the meaning clearly appears: Saul and Barnabas, speaking by inspiration, called the disciples *Christians!* We shall now see that the giving of this name was a part of a divine plan determined hundreds of years earlier.

2. Direct Biblical Proofs

Approximately seven hundred years before the Lord came to the earth, the great Jehovah, through the prophet Isaiah, promised his people a "new name:" "The Gentiles shall see thy righteousness, and all the kings thy glory: and thou shalt be called by a new name, which the mouth of the Lord shall name" (Isaiah 62:2). It was to be given following the end of the Jewish system: "And ye" (that is, the Jews) "shall leave your name for a curse unto my chosen: for the Lord shall slay thee, and call his servants by another name" (Isaiah 65:15). It was to be given in God's house which can only refer to the church: "Even unto them will I give in mine house and within my walls a place and a name better than of sons and daughters: I will give them an everlasting name, that shall not be cut off" (Isaiah 56:5).

An induction of these passages will make clear what that name was:

1. It would not be given until after the Jewish system ended; hence, it could not be any term, title or other appellation in use prior to the death of Christ on the cross.
2. It would be given only after the church was established; this occurred on the first Pentecost following the Lord's death.
3. It would be given only after the Gentles had become heirs—along with the Jews—of the blessings of the Kingdom. The first Gentiles admitted were those of

the house of Cornelius about A.D. 41, and resulting
from Peter's mission to Caesarea (Acts 10:1ff).
4. It was to be a "new name;" hence, it could not have
been given prior to the events recorded in Acts 10.
5. It is significant that in the chapter immediately
following the calling of the Gentiles to the blessings
of the gospel the "new name"—*Christian*—was first
used (Acts 11:26).

No other name, however ancient, honorable and
distinguished, can meet the demands of these prophe-
cies. It follows, with all the force of a demonstration,
that the name given at Antioch was that which the
Lord's people were to wear henceforth and forever. It
is the sum of all others; to wear it properly is to be
accorded by the Lord himself the highest honors and
the most exalted privileges. The great and good of the
ages, when faced with torture and certain death unless
they renounced it, gladly gave up all in order that they
might be deemed worthy of suffering shame for the
name of Christ.

It is sometimes said that "there is nothing in a
name!" but, no one really believes this. The next time
you hear this said, inform the person who so affirms
that hereafter you will address him as the devil. See
how quickly he resents and renounces such a designation. If there is "nothing in a name," why is not this
name as good as any?

Jack Womack has been a friend of mine for well over
a third of a century. I have never known a finer
Christian, a more dedicated follower of the Lord. With
unswerving fidelity to the Cause and often with great
sacrifice, he has served his Master longer than many
of those who will read these lines have lived. Some
years ago, a denominational preacher came into
brother Womack's furniture store and asked for a
donation to their church building fund. "Certainly,"
brother Womack responded. He wrote out a check for

$1,000 and handed it to the preacher, who was overwhelmed by this liberal "contribution." He had reached the door before he discovered that the check was not signed. Moments later, he returned to brother Womack's desk with the observation that the check was without a signature. "Quite so," brother Womack answered. "You preach that one name is as good as another; put any name you like on the check!" He thereupon explained to the misguided man the vital importance of speaking where the Bible speaks, of being silent where the Bible is silent; of calling Bible things by Bible names; and of adhering to the scriptures in all matters of faith and practice.

It is significant, and the fact ought to be especially impressive to all those who wear any name except Christ's, that many of their own leaders have renounced human names and titles, and have urged their followers to accept the name Christian. Charles Spurgeon, greatest of all Baptist preachers, once said, "I look forward with pleasure to the day when there will not be a Baptist living. I hope they will soon be gone. I hope the Baptist name will soon perish; but let Christ's name last forever." (Spurgeon Memorial Library, Vol. 1, page 168.)

Martin Luther, founder of the Lutheran denomination and world famed religious reformer, said: "I pray you to leave my name alone, and call not yourselves Lutherans, but Christians. Who is Luther? My doctrine is not mine. I have not been crucified for any one. St. Paul, (1 Corinthians 1:13), would not that any should call themselves of Paul, nor of Peter, but of Christ. How then does it befit me, a miserable bag of dust and ashes, to give my name to the children of Christ? Cease, my dear friends, to cling to these party names and distinctions; away with them all; and let us call ourselves only Christians after Him from whom our doctrine comes." (Stork, Life of Luther, page 289.) May we who live today never discredit it, or dishonor the memory of those who gave up so much for it.

John Wesley, the acknowledged head and founder of the Methodist church, once wrote: "Would to God that all party names and unscriptural phrases and forms which have divided the Christian world were forgot; that we might all agree to sit down together as humble, loving disciples at the feet of the common Master, to hear His word, to imbibe His spirit, and to transcribe His life into our own." Albert Barnes, whose commentaries on the Bible have been a blessing to me for a half century, said: "Should not, and will not, all these divisions be merged into the high and holy name 'Christian?'"

The great slogans which moved and motivated those noble men of an earlier age who loved the truth and were determined to preach it, and it alone, are as relevant today as ever: "Nothing ought to be received into the faith or worship of the church, or be made a term of communion among Christians, that is not as old as the New Testament." "Rejecting human opinions and the inventions of men as authority, or as having any place in the church of God, we might forever cease from further contentions about such things; returning to, and holding fast by the original standard; taking the divine Word alone as our rule; the Holy Spirit as our teacher and guide; and Christ alone, as exhibited in the Word, for our salvation; that, by so doing, we may be at peace among ourselves, follow peace with all men, and holiness, without which no man shall see the Lord. Let it be a constant reminder to us of our obligation to serve faithfully and worthily Him whose we are, and whose name we are privileged to wear."

"Jesus calls us o'er the tumult
Of our life's wild, restless sea,
Day by day His sweet voice soundeth,
Saying, 'Christian, follow me.'
"Jesus calls us from the worship
Of the vain world's golden store;
From each idol that would keep us,
Saying, 'Christian, love me more.'
"In our joys and in our sorrows,
Days of toil, and hours of ease;
Still He calls, in cares and pleasures,
'Christian, love me more than these.' "

Hundreds of years before the events predicted occurred, and in full anticipation of the worldwide scope and proclamation of the gospel, Amos prophesied: "In that day will I raise up the tabernacle of David that is fallen, and close up the breaches thereof; and I will raise up his ruins, and I will build it as in the days of old: that they may possess the remnant of Edom, and of all the heathen, *which are called by my name* said the Lord." Let it be carefully noted that it was David's dynasty—not the Jewish temple—that was to be rebuilt. Those who were to occupy this building (the church) were to be called by the Lord's name—the name Christian. By reference to Acts 15:13-17, it will be seen that this was in the process of being done at the time of the events there described occurred. Jesus, lineal descendent of David, had already been made Lord and Christ and raised up to sit on the throne of his illustrious ancestor (Acts 2:30-36), and thus David's "house" had been rebuilt. Through it the gospel was being preached to "the heathen," (the Gentiles), and the new name had been given. (Acts 11:26.) This honored title we are privileged to wear. Let us ever glorify God in this name (1 Peter 4:16).

What is in a name? Our salvation, our hope of heaven, the glorification of the Lord and the honor of

His cause. May we never forget that the name "Christian" keeps alive in the hearts of true believers the sufferings of our Lord on the cross, enshrines the struggles of the faithful of all the ages, and is the record of countless imprisonments, of indescribable suffering, of sorrow, of pain, of heartache, of hope, of joy, of glorious expectation, of ultimate and eventual deliverance and our final salvation.

Those who would become Christians must believe the gospel (Mark 16:15,16), repent of their sins (Luke 13:3), confess their faith in the Lord (Romans 10:10), and be baptized into Christ for the remission of sins (Romans 6:3,4; Acts 2:38). Those who thus do, the Lord saves, adds to the church (Acts 2:47), and makes of them Christians.

Preached in Woodbridge, VA., September, 1987

WHO, OR WHAT, IS GOD?

The remarkably fine audiences we are having in this meeting, the absorbing manner in which you listen to what I have to say, and the concern you feel for spiritual matters as evidenced by your coming in such large numbers, all please me greatly and prompt me to make the best effort I can in the presentation of these vital matters. I am aware that there are many visitors in the audience tonight, and that numerous area congregations are represented. Moments ago, brother Colley whispered to me that there must be twenty-five gospel preachers present. For all of this we are deeply grateful; and I should like for you to know that in coming you have made a definite and substantial contribution to the success of our meeting.

By announcement earlier made, I am to speak to you tonight on the theme, Who, or What, is God? How does Deity manifest himself in our world? What is the mode, or manner, of his operations? You will agree that these are matters both vital and interesting, matters indeed all of us, at one time or another, must have pondered, and often with no little perplexity.

Were I to ask you, "How many Gods are there?" You would, of course, quite properly say, "There is but one God, and the scriptures often so affirm." The Shema of Israel reads: "Hear, O Israel, the Lord our God is one" (Deuteronomy 6:4). We are also told therein of the "Godhead," consisting of three persons, the Father, the Son and the Holy Spirit (Colossians 2:9). How is it possible that there is but one God, yet three persons in the Godhead? The answer is that the word **God** is the name of the divine nature, and since there is but one divine nature, there is but one God.

However, there are three persons possessing this one divine nature; and by a figure of speech which

121

grammarians call the synecdoche—where a part is put for the whole or the whole for a part—each person of the Godhead is called **God** in the scriptures.

The Father is often so designated, one example of which is in the familiar passage, John 3:16: "God so loved the world that he gave his only begotten Son . . ." Here, the Father is distinguished from the Son, and the Father is called **God;** sometimes, however, the Son is distinguished from the Father, and the Son is called **God.** An instance of this is seen in John 1:1: "In the beginning was the Word, and the Word was with God, and the Word was God," and identified in the context as the one who "became flesh and *dwelt* among us," literally, "pitched his tent among us," for so the Greek verb translated "dwelt" (*skeenoosen*), signifies (John 1:14).

The Holy Spirit is in similar fashion so indicated. When Ananias and Sapphira sought to deceive the early church, Peter charged them with lying to the Holy Spirit; and, in the same context, said that in so doing they had "lied unto God" (Acts 5:3,4). Thus, the Holy Spirit is also called God. It is, therefore, quite in harmony with biblical phraseology to speak of God the Father; God the Son; and God the Holy Spirit—one God, since there is but one divine nature, with three persons possessed of this one nature.

Evidence of plurality in the Godhead abounds in the sacred writings. This fact clearly appears in the earliest portions of the Bible in the use of plural pronouns in references to the Godhead: "And God said, Let *us* make man in our image, after *our* likeness . . ." (Genesis 1:26). Note that it was **God** who thus spoke, but who is alluded to by the plural pronouns *us* and *our*. All the members of the Godhead are included in the word **God** of this passage.

It is remarkable that this concept of deity is introduced to us in the first verse of the first chapter of the Bible: "In the beginning God created the heavens and the earth." The word **God** translates the Hebrew word "Elohim," plural form of "El," one of the names of Deity in the Old Testament. The verb of the passage, "created," is from the Hebrew "bara," and singular in number. We have the interesting circumstance in this verse of a plural substantive or subject, and a singular predicate or verb. In English, the verb must agree with the subject in number and person; but, not in Hebrew; and there is here clear proof of the Godhead in the plural subject, and the concept of unity in the singular form of the predicate—a plural substantive to indicate plurality in the Godhead; a singular predicate to guard us against accepting any form of polytheism, and at the same time to teach us the unity of the divine nature.

The first Person of the Godhead—the Father—is to sinful man unseen and unapproachable. "No man hath seen God at any time . . . ," so said John, the apostle (John 1:18), and Paul described him as " . . . dwelling in light unapproachable; whom no man hath seen, nor can see . . ." (1 Timothy 6:16). From the moment of the tragic events in Eden and the sin of Adam and Eve in that primeval paradise, God has not allowed sinful man to approach him directly; always, since that event, there has been a sinless intermediary between God and man as mediator. Under former dispensations, it was a lamb without spot or blemish; it is still a Lamb, the Lamb of God, Christ Jesus our Lord, who serves as our Mediator between God and man, and who, as the Redeemer, takes away the sins of the world (1 Timothy 2:5; John 1:29).

When the Israelites were encamped about Sinai, awaiting the giving of the law, they were forbidden to approach the mount, down into which the holy presence of God had come, or to touch it, the penalty for which was sudden and certain death (Exodus 19:20-25).

Had there been no additional revelation of God to man, the impression that God is both unknowable and unapproachable would most likely have prevailed. How can you really know a Being whom you can neither see nor draw near? Consequently, in the fullness of time, God sent his Son into the world, among other reasons, for the purpose of revealing God to man. He who came is first identified for us as the Word. "In the beginning was the Word, and the Word was with God, and the Word was God" (John 1:1). Have we wondered why the second Person of the Godhead is called the Word? Why was this the term by which he was known prior to his advent into the world?

Bear in mind that a word is an expression of an idea—the vehicle which carries the idea we wish to express. Jesus exhibited the nature of God in his own Person; he brought into the world a clear demonstration of Deity, since he possessed every attribute of the Father. He was, therefore, the total embodiment of the idea of God and which, through him, was made known to the world. He is said to have "declared" the Father, (the Greek is, literally, *interpreted* him (John 1:18). No ordinary man was ever close enough to the Father to see him and to come to know him in all of his fullness; but Jesus, being the "only begotten Son of the Father," and so close to him as figuratively to have been said to be "in the bosom of the Father," and in consequence of his vast knowledge of God, is fully able to make him known to us.

Hence, the Word—the expression and revelation of God to man. In him dwells the fullness of the Godhead "bodily" (Colossians 2:9); he is "the express image," (the replica, as for example, the imprint of the rubber stamp on the white page), of the Father (Hebrews

1:1-3), and possessed of the same "form" (literally, *divine essence*) of the Father (Philippians 2:5-11).

I have long thought that most of us do not make the effort we should in acquiring a greater and more detailed knowledge of the second Person of the Godhead as revealed in the scriptures. Should I do no more in this sermon this evening than to deepen your understanding of this Wonderful Person, and to broaden your concept of him to whom we are so infinitely obligated, it would surely be worth a hundred such meetings as this. Usually, when people think of Christ, his historic mission and work, they have in mind largely, if not entirely, his earthly sojourn. Books, on the life of our Lord are most often of the same limited scope. Lesson material regarding him deals, for the most part, with his earthly ministry; sermons on the life of Christ frequently embrace no more than the period between his birth of the virgin Mary and his ascension. But these areas involve only the tiniest portion of the revealed life of him whose we are, and whom we must serve if ever we are privileged to enter into eternal life.

Any proper approach to this study must include not one, but five, different periods of activity clearly revealed to us in the Bible regarding him, and his mission to this planet. Let us examine them carefully.

1. Christ, in his pre-existent state
2. Christ, in the Old Testament
3. Christ, in the flesh
4. Christ, glorified, at God's right hand
5. Christ, in the ages to come

1. Christ, in his pre-existent state.

The eternal nature of our Lord is repeatedly taught and emphasized in the Bible. John's grand prologue begins with the sublime affirmation, "In the beginning was the Word . . ." (John 1:1). We have already observed that our Lord is designated as "the Word," because he came into the world for the purpose of revealing God to man. The verb "was" asserts his eternity, meaning, "evermore existing." In one of our Lord's clashes with unbelieving Jews, he said, "Before Abraham was I am" (John 8:58). Here, the verb "was," means *came to be;* The words, "I am," signify, *evermore existing.* There was a time when Abraham was not; he was born, i.e., he came to be; but, our Lord, possessing an eternal nature, has evermore existed. Being of the same "form," literally, *essence* of the Father, he is as eternal as the Father (Philippians 2:5-11). Indeed, he and not the Father, was the actual Creator of the Worlds and all things therein (John 1:2; 2 Timothy 1:9).[1]

2. Christ, in the Old Testament

The birth of our Lord of the Virgin Mary occurred at a definite time and place, and it is easy to assume that if he existed before this historic event it must have always been in heaven, and that his earthly sojourn began in Bethlehem. This concept, though a popular one, is incorrect; there are many references in Old Testament writings to the second Person of the Godhead which place him on this planet long before his fleshly birth at the beginning of the Christian era.

He who is referred to in the King James' Version of the Old Testament as **Lord** and in the American Standard Version as **Jehovah,** is often the second Person of the Godhead, and not the first Person—the Father. Indisputable evidence of this will be seen in the well-known prophecy of Isaiah regarding the Harbinger— the forerunner—of Christ. "The voice of one that crieth, Prepare ye in the wilderness the way of Jehovah; make level in the desert a highway for our God." This is the rendering of the American Standard Version, edition of 1901. The more familiar verbiage of the King James' Version is, "The voice of him that crieth in the wilderness, Prepare ye the way of the Lord, make straight in the desert a highway for God" (Isaiah 40:3). Matthew, in chronicling the fulfillment of this prophecy, applied it to the work of John the Baptist in introducing Jesus to the world and in preparing a people for him. Thus the "Lord" of the King James' Version, and the "Jehovah" of the American Standard Version, is the Christ of the New Testament! The name "Jehovah" occurs many times in the Bible and it signifies, "He who was, and is, and is to come, the Almighty," words our Lord applied to himself in Revelation 1:8. There is much other evidence that often the name "Jehovah," in the Old Testament, alludes to the Messiah long promised.

Men often saw "the Lord," (Jehovah) and conversed with him "face to face," in the Old Testament period (Exodus 33:11; Deuteronomy 5:4; 34:10; Psalm 27:8; and often elsewhere.) But, "No man hath seen God at any time . . ." (John 1:18). It must follow, therefore, that he whom men could, and did, see, was not the One they could not see! The Lord (Jehovah) appeared to Abraham "by the Oaks of Mamre," (Genesis 18:1), to Isaac, forbidding him to go into Egypt (Genesis 26:2), and to Jacob in Paddan-aram (35:9). John said that the vision which Isaiah saw of Jehovah, "high and lifted up" and "sitting on a throne," was Jesus, himself: "These things said Isaiah, because he saw his glory; and he spake of him" (Isaiah 6:1; John 12:41). The "rock" that followed the Israelites in the wilderness en route to Canaan was Christ (1 Corinthians 10:4). Christ, on earth, with the Israelites in the trackless wastelands of the wilderness of wanderings fifteen hundred years before his entrance into human flesh in the first century of this era!

These are but a few of the many instances of the foreshadowing of the second Person of the Godhead in the Old Testament.

3. Christ, in the flesh.

In type and antitype, in symbols and in ceremonies, in prophecy and in preparatory work, the descent of Deity into human flesh is vividly and unmistakably taught in the Old Testament. From the first faint glimmer of redemption, expressed in the promise of Genesis 3:15, until the full-orbed revelation through the prophets, the purpose and plan of God in sending the Redeemer into the world is evident. Abraham saw his day "and was glad," (John 8:56); to that great patriarch he was the "Seed," through whom all the families of the earth would be blessed (Genesis 12:1-3), to Jacob, the Deliverer; to David, the King; and to all the prophets, the Messiah, who would bring salvation and deliverance to his people.

The plan of the ages necessitated his incarnation, his ministry to men, and his death on the cross: "Wherefore when he cometh into the world he saith, Sacrifice and offering Thou wouldest not, But a body didst Thou prepare for me . . ." (Hebrews 10:5). The humiliation involved in the surrender of his heavenly position was voluntarily, freely and gladly accepted. "Then said I," (the Hebrew writer quotes him as saying), "Lo, I am come . . . to do Thy will O God" (Verse 7). His assumption of flesh, in being born into the human race, was essential to the atonement he would make thus enabling man to be saved; but, his ministry to men has continued through the ages, and began with the beginning of the race.

In one tremendous affirmation Paul describes our Lord's acceptance of his humiliation: "Have this mind in you, which was also in Christ Jesus: who, existing in the form (essence) of God, counted not the being on an equality with God a thing to be grasped, but emptied himself, taking the form of a servant, being made in the likeness of men; and being found in fashion as a man, he humbled himself, becoming

obedient even unto death, yea, the death of the cross."
(Philippians 2:5-8). From this, we learn among many
other things, that he (1) was of the same nature as the
Father; (2) he was equal to God; he (3) "emptied
himself," i.e., he voluntarily accepted the state of
humiliation into which he must enter in coming into
human flesh; (4) he assumed the role and work of a
servant, which accounts for the inferiority of position,
compared to his Father, ascribed to him in the New
Testament; (5) he gave up the glory he had through
the ages possessed. This, for him was not easy; this is
evidenced in the fact that when his work was nearly
done, he looked backward to the position he had once
held, but gladly surrendered and prayed, "And now,
Father, glorify Thou me with Thine own self with the
glory which I had with Thee before the world was"
(John 17:5).

4. Christ, glorified.

The glory which he once possessed, gladly relin-
quished, and asked his Father to restore to him, in the
shadows of Gethsemane, became his, when he was
crowned King of kings and Lord of lords, having led
captivity captive and given gifts to men, on the first
Pentecost following his resurrection (Ephesians 4:8).
It was then that he was "set" at the Father's "right
hand in the heavenly places, far above all rule, and
authority, and power, and dominion, and every name
that is named, not only in this world, but also in that
which is to come", and God "put all things in
subjection under his feet, and gave him to be head
over all things to the church, which is his body, the
fullness of him that filleth all in all" (Ephesians
1:20-23).

One of the most thrilling and exciting statements in
all of the Old Testament, to me, is David's marvelous
description, seen prophetically by the Psalmist, hundreds of years before it occurred, of the Lord's

approach to, and entrance into the heavenly city on the occasion of his ascension. When he came near the gates of heaven, his journey to glory now nearing its end, the announcement was made, "Lift up your heads, O ye gates; and be ye lifted up, ye everlasting doors: and the King of glory will come in." From inside the Holy City came the inquiry, "Who is the King of glory?" The answer was given, "Jehovah, strong and mighty, Jehovah mighty in battle" (Psalm 24:7,8). The gates were opened. The Lord had returned to his home, his mission of redemption and atonement, accomplished, and his triumph over death and the grave secured. From subsequent revelation we learn that on the occasion of his coronation, he began his reign and assumed his regal powers over his kingdom, and that his sovereignty and authority continue to this hour.

5. *Christ, in the ages to come.*

The eternal future begins when this, the Christian age, ends. Its termination will mark the end of our Lord's reign and the subsequent abdication of his throne to his Father. This event, we have certain and unmistakable knowledge of, in the words of the greatest of the apostles. In describing the events that are to transpire in the consummation of these matters, the apostle wrote, "But each in his own order: Christ the firstfruits; then they that are Christ's, at his coming. Then cometh the end, when he shall deliver up the kingdom to God, even the Father; when he shall have abolished all rule and all authority and power. For he must reign, till he hath put all his enemies under his feet. The last enemy that shall be abolished is death" (1 Corinthians 15:23-26).

Thus, the events of the last days are clearly designated and outlined. (1) Our Lord is now reigning; (2) he will continue his reign until his enemies are destroyed; (3) his last enemy is death; (4) he must reign, then, until death is destroyed. (5) Death will be destroyed in the resurrection at the Last Great Day. Hence, Christ must reign until the resurrection. (6) Then, the last of his enemies having been subdued, he will have returned the Kingdom to the Father. Then, "the tabernacle of God" shall indeed be with men, "and he shall dwell with them, and they shall be his peoples, and God himself shall be with them, and be their God: and he shall wipe away every tear from their eyes; and death shall be no more; neither shall there be mourning, nor crying, nor pain, any more: the first things are passed away" (Revelation 21:3,4). How we should rejoice to know that we shall be "like him, for we shall see him as he is" and to have him in warm, loving fellowship as our elder brother, through endless ages!

It is indeed a thrilling and exciting experience to look into these various aspects of our Redeemer and Lord and to see him as (1) the pre-existent Christ; (2) the Christ of the Old Testament; (3) Christ in the flesh; (4) Christ glorified and now in heaven; and (5) Christ in the ages to come—our elder brother and Saviour forever!

Our studies of the nature of Deity and of the Godhead in this sermon have thus far involved the first Person—the Father—and the second Person—the Son. There remains to be considered the third Person of the Godhead—the Holy Spirit. It is unfortunate that an aura of mystery has been suffered to envelop this vital theme, and that many people today think it not only impossible, but improper, to attempt to discover his nature and mode of operation. In consequence of this long standing aversion to any real investigation of the subject, much misunderstanding exists touching his Person and work. We shall, therefore, in some detail, within the limits of time remaining for this speech carefully examine the teaching of the Scriptures

regarding the matter and, for those who will follow
us closely, strip away much of the misapprehension,
in the church and out of it, of the Holy Spirit's mission
and work in the world.

(1) The Holy Spirit is a Person.

He is no less a person than is God, the Father, or
Christ, the Son. It is simply not possible to overemphasize this fact. Indeed, it is because of a failure to
recognize this fundamental and vital truth that so
much confusion prevails today regarding the subject.
An awareness of this simple, scriptural, and clearly
affirmed fact effectively guards one against many
erroneous and hurtful theories prevalent about the
matter. Were it possible to induce people to see that
the Holy Spirit is a Person, just as the Father is a
Person, and the Son is a Person, it would be much
easier to convince them that the idea of a literal, actual,
personal, bodily indwelling is not taught in the sacred
writings. A thoughtful person will have no difficulty
in seeing that one literal person does not literally dwell
in another literal person!

Sadly, as has been the case with much other biblical,
basic and fundamental teaching we have done through
the years, this concept has become beclouded and
often displaced by the denominational view that the
Spirit operates independently on the heart in subjective and mysterious fashion, apart from the Word,
somewhat on the order of the "better-felt-than-told"
fantasy long in vogue, and still being taught, in
sectarian circles.

2. The Holy Spirit is a masculine Person.

The Holy Spirit is not only a Person, not only
possesses distinct personality—he is a masculine
personality, and is so identified in the scriptures. Let
us observe with care the personal pronouns regarding
him in John 16:13: "Howbeit when HE, the Spirit of

truth, is come, HE shall guide you into all the truth: for HE shall not speak from HIMSELF; but what things soever HE shall hear, these shall HE speak: and HE shall declare unto you the things that are to come." The coming of the Holy Spirit to the apostles was to guide them into all the truth, and to declare to them things that were to come. Thus did our Lord reveal to the twelve the manner in which divine revelation would come to them, when he had returned to heaven and was no longer with them. Again, and with great emphasis, the Holy Spirit is revealed in this passage not only as a distinct person, but also as a masculine person. The reiteration of the pronoun "he," in John 16:13, clearly evidences that it was our Lord's intent in this statement to emphasize especially this fact.

(3) *The Holy Spirit communicates by words or their equivalents.*

There is no other way by which communications can occur—ideas be transmitted—except by the use of words, signs of ideas, vehicles of thought. Impressions are received by the brain through the medium of the five senses (seeing, hearing, smelling, feeling, and tasting), and in no other way; and, since we can neither smell truth, taste it, or experience sensible evidence of it through our fingertips, we must either hear or see it on one of the modes by which ideas are transmitted. Words are either heard by the ears or seen with the eyes; in no other fashion may intelligible communication be achieved. Fortunately, we have clear and convincing evidence of the manner in which communication was accomplished. David said, "The Spirit of Jehovah spake by me, and his word was upon my tongue" (2 Samuel 23:2). The Spirit, with David, made intelligible contact, and by this means communication was effected. How? By *speaking*. What was the medium or instrumentality of that communication? *Language.*

How was intelligence conveyed? *By words.* There simply is no other way!

Paul, in his first letter to his son in the gospel, Timothy, wrote: "But the Spirit saith expressly, that in later times some shall fall away from the faith, giving heed to seducing spirits and doctrines of demons" (1 Timothy 4:1). Of an impending apostasy the apostle in this manner warned the young evangelist. This, he did by using words. He is said to have done so, "expressly;" that is, plainly and clearly. Here, again, both the message and the manner of its transference are indicated. How was the communication accomplished? By words. Through what method? Language. I again emphasize: there is no other way.

An understanding of, and appreciation for the Spirit's mode and manner of operation is absolutely vital to a proper apprehension of the teaching of the scriptures regarding the Spirit's work. When one is brought to the realization that the only way in which the Holy Spirit ever influenced people involved the use of words and the medium of language, no longer will one fall into the grievous error so common today, both in and out of the church, of thinking that the Spirit leads, guides and directs through intuition, inner leadings, hunches, etc. How does the Holy Spirit communicate? Through words: "He that hath an *ear*, let him *hear* what the Spirit *saith* to the churches" (Revelation 2:11).

3. How was the Spirit's Communication with Man done?

The revelation of the Spirit was accomplished through men selected by the Lord and directed by the Holy Spirit. A passage from the pen of Paul which all of us should thoroughly study and fully master makes absolutely clear the manner in which this was accomplished. "But unto us God revealed them through the Spirit: for the Spirit searcheth all things, yea, the deep things of God. For who among men

knoweth the things of a man, save the spirit of the
man, which is in him? even so the things of God none
knoweth, save the Spirit of God. But we received, not
the spirit of the world, but the spirit which is from
God; that we might know the things that were freely
given to us of God. Which things also we speak, not
in words which man's wisdom teacheth, but which the
Spirit teacheth; combining spiritual things with spiritual words" (1 Corinthians 10:13). From this remarkable statement we are able to gather the following facts:
(a) A revelation from God to man has been made; (b)
this revelation was made "by the Spirit;" (c) just as one
man cannot know what is in the mind of another man
until it is revealed by words, so we cannot know what
has been in God's mind until he reveals it to us through
words; (d) Paul and other inspired men were the
instruments through whom the Spirit, by means of
their writings, made known to us what was in "the
mind of God," that he desired to reveal to us; (e) the
words by which the revelation was thus made were the
words of the Holy Spirit—not those of men.

It ought already to be apparent what we shall now
clearly see that, contrary to popular views often today
offered, it was never the Holy Spirit's function to
originate truth—only to *reveal* it! A passage, already
before us in this study, makes this crystal clear: "The
Spirit . . . shall not speak from himself; but things
whatsoever he shall hear, that shall he speak . . ."
(John 16:13). We have earlier seen in this study, this
evening, that these were the words of our Lord to his
apostles, chosen by him to receive, through the
inspiration of the Holy Spirit, the message of life and
salvation they were, therefore, to deliver to men. Let
it be carefully noted that the Spirit was to speak only
that which had been delivered to him by the Lord and
which, in turn, he was to pass on to the inspired

writers. Thus, it was never the function of the Holy Spirit to originate truth, only to reveal it.

(4) Where is this message today to be found that the Holy Spirit received and passed on to the world?

The answer to this vital question is easily and quickly determined and is decisive of the matter: "Every scripture inspired of God is also profitable for teaching, for reproof, for correction, for instruction which is in righteousness: that the man of God may be complete, furnished completely unto every good work." (2 Timothy 3:16,17). The scriptures are thus the sole source of our information regarding the will of God and our duty to him. It should be observed that the word is said to (a) make us "complete;" and (b) to furnish us "completely unto every good work." There are thus two things the word is said to do for us: (1) It makes us complete; that is, it meets our every need, supplying all the information necessary in order to the full and complete discharge of our duties to God; and (2) it put into our hands an instrument totally adequate to the discharge of every duty owed to all others. It thus both *fits* and *outfits us* supplying, as it does, our every need. In view of the change in the covenants and the law (Hebrews 8:6-13), the message of the Spirit to us today is that set out in the New Testament (Hebrews 1:1).

It is of interest and importance to note that the words, "inspired of God," in 2 Timothy 3:16, translate a Greek word meaning "God breathed." By this it is meant that these words, containing the message of salvation, set out in these wonderful writings, are directly from God as much so as one's breath comes from one's body. The phrase, "every scripture inspired of God," must not be interpreted to mean, "only such scriptures as are inspired of God," implying that some scripture is not inspired; the word "scripture" is never used in the New Testament other than as inspired matter. The meaning is, "Every part of the scriptures," that is, the whole of them, issues from God, who gave them. They are, therefore a revelation of God to man, informing us fully of our duty to him. Implied in this is, of course, the fact that the message thus given is within the mental reach of all accountable persons. "If any man willeth to do his will, he shall know the teaching, whether it is of God . . ." (John 7:17). This ought forevermore to settle the matter whether the gospel of Christ—by which alone salvation is possible (Romans 1:13-16)—is sufficiently clear and complete to provide us with the knowledge of salvation, and to guide us to heaven!

It would be well for us, at this point, to pause briefly, and to summarize that which we have thus far noted. Of whom are we speaking? The Holy Spirit—third Person of the Godhead. What are his characteristics? He is a Person; he possesses distinct personality; he is a masculine Person. What was his function in God's plan in relation to man's salvation? To reveal the details—not to originate, modify, or, on his own, to supplement them. In performing this function, how did he communicate with man? By words. Through whom? Inspired men. Where is this communication, as it applies to us today, to be found? In the New Testament. To what extent does it meet our need? Fully, "completely, unto every good work."

Let us, for the moment, suppose that someone, in spite of these infallible affirmations, inspired comments, and incontrovertible facts, claims divine guidance by the Holy Spirit, apart from and independent of the Word of truth, the gospel. What harm can result from holding such a view? Is there anything seriously wrong with thinking that one's intuition, heart promptings, and hunches are leadings of the Holy Spirit? (a) It is gross error so to believe; the position, that the Holy Spirit operates apart from and in addition to the word, is positively, palpably and unmistakably false, being opposed to the plainest teaching of the scriptures, as we have clearly shown earlier in this speech. It is the TRUTH, not ERROR that frees us from the bondage and misery of sin (John 8:32).

(b) The view, that the Spirit must illuminate the scriptures before we can understand them, is an impeachment of Paul's claim that the scriptures "furnish" unto "every good work;" if there are influences wrought upon us, apart from, and in addition to, the word, it follows *that the word is not enough;* but, it says that it is; *is it?* If it is, we have no need of additional influences; if it is not, its claims are false. If we are unable to trust the word of God in its affirmation to sufficiency here, how can we rely on its declarations in other matters involving our well being and needs? Must the Spirit illuminate his own writings? If we cannot understand the original message of the Spirit without illumination, how do we know that we can understand the "illumination?" Do we need an illumination of the illumination in order to understand??? The idea is preposterous, and a serious reflection on the Spirit that in revealing the mind of God he had to resort to additional revelations in order to remedy his original defect.

Are we not led by the Spirit, and do not the scriptures so affirm? "For as many as are led by the Spirit of God, they are the sons of God" (Romans 8:14). The sum of our information on how to live the Christian life is contained in the New Testament. When we follow this teaching we are faithful children of the Father. It was, as we have earlier seen, through the Spirit's agency in directing the writers of the Bible to the knowledge of the truth, and their commitment of this revelation to the pages of the New Testament, that we are privileged to have available to us the way of salvation. It must follow, therefore, that one who yields to the teaching of the New Testament is being led by the Spirit; one who rejects this teaching, rejects the Spirit who gave it. To obey it, is to be in obedience to the Spirit; to reject it, is to reject the Spirit who gave it. We are therefore "led" by the Spirit when we follow the teaching of the Spirit set out in the scriptures.

Are there not passages which assert that the Spirit is in us? There are, indeed; and I am not aware of any one who questions this. Of the **fact** there is no doubt; but, the fact must not be confused with the **mode** or **manner** of "indwelling." Paul wrote, ". . . His Spirit . . . dwelleth in you" (Romans 8:11). From this we learn that there is a sense in which the Spirit is in us. It should be noted, however, that this passage does not say *how* this occurs. Does the passage declare that the Spirit dwells in us literally? No. Personally? No. Bodily? No. Abstractly? No. So to assert, then is to add to what the verse says; it is to inject into it a claim it does not make. God, the Father, is as plainly said to be "in" us (1 John 4:15); Christ, the Son, is also said to be "in" us (Colossians 1:27); but, we do not from this conclude that the Father and/or the Son are in us literally, personally, bodily or abstractly, but representatively. The Spirit dwells in us in precisely the same fashion as each of the other members of the Godhead. The Father, the Son, and the Holy Spirit are in us as their wills are allowed to direct, control and influence our lives. This they do through the moral influence they exercise upon us through the teaching which they gave us. Such is the extent, and the only extent in which deity, whether the Father, the Son, or the Holy Spirit, "indwells" us!

The Holy Spirit strengthens us (Ephesians 3:16), but he does it by means of the word of truth which he gave us (Psalm 119:50). He sanctifies (2 Thessalonians 2:13), but he does so by the truth, which is God's word (John 17:17); he saves (Titus 3:5), justifies (1 Timothy

3:16), and directs us (Romans 8:14), but he does this with the "engrafted word" (James 1:21). We must never forget that every influence wrought upon us, all the moral suasion necessary to keep us in the right path, every spiritual need necessary to our happiness here, and our eternal salvation hereafter, derive directly from the scriptures which the Holy Spirit, through inspired men, gave us.

If the Spirit acts by means of the word of truth—the scriptures—and the Spirit intercedes for us, how can the word do this? This question, not infrequently raised, always distresses me, because it evidences gross misapprehension of a magnificent passage of scripture which, properly understood, offers us one of the most blessed privileges of the Christian life. The passage (Romans 8:26,27), from the pen of Paul, reads: "And in like manner the Spirit also helpeth our infirmity: for we know not how to pray as we ought; but the Spirit himself maketh intercession for us with groanings which cannot be uttered; and he that searcheth the hearts knoweth what is the mind of the Spirit, because he maketh intercession for the saints according to the will of God."

There are three movements, or propositions, in this marvelous statement. 1. The Spirit helps us in our infirmity; (2) we know not how to pray as we ought; (3) the Spirit makes intercession for us with groanings which cannot be expressed. Let us examine each of these wonderful statements carefully. (a) *The Spirit comes to our aid in our infirmities.* The word "infirmity" means weakness; so the Spirit "helps" us in our weaknesses. The Greek word translated "helpeth," in the verse before us, occurs only once more elsewhere in the original text, and the other instance is when Martha asked Jesus to have Mary to "help" her (Luke 10:38-42).

The literal picture of the Greek verb is of one who stands on the other side, and asks for assistance. It is very possible that when Martha made this request of Jesus, she stood before a heavy table or some other object and wanted Jesus to tell Mary to get on the other side and help her. Such, at least, is the literal picture of the Greek verb involved. Figuratively used here, of course, it represents the Holy Spirit standing on the other side of our difficulty and lifting with us. He does not do all the lifting; he does not leave it to us to do it unaided and alone; he lifts with us.

(b) *We do not know how to pray as we ought.* How painfully conscious surely all of us are of this fact. Often, when the troubles of the world are on our shoulders; when clouds, ominous and heavy, are on our horizon; bewildered, confused, agitated, incoherent— unable even to put in words of our need—it is then that our needs are often greatest. And, it is then this precious and wonderful passage assures us that deity is not unmindful of our needs and promises to come to our aid.

(c) *The Spirit makes intercession for us with groanings which cannot be uttered.* Whose "groanings?" Strangely, there are those who insist that these "groanings" (Greek, *unutterable sighs*) are those of the Holy Spirit, but those who thus do are faced with the impossible task of explaining why the Holy Spirit should ever groan or sigh, or find difficulty in expressing himself! It is not the Spirit who groans, but the burdened Christian, struggling under the loads of life, vainly seeking to put in word his many needs.

The Holy Spirit assists us by bearing to the throne of grace our needs. He is fully able to do so because he knows the innermost thoughts of our hearts we are unable to express. Simply put, the Holy Spirit makes known to the Father that which we are unable to express in word in our prayers. This is clearly stated in verse 27. God, the great heartsearcher, sees in the mind of the Spirit our needs, and makes provision for them. We must carefully distinguish between mediation and intercession. Only Christ can mediate for us (1 Timothy 2:5), but to intercede for another is simply to plead in another's behalf, and this the Spirit can, and does, do. This influence is wrought by the Spirit on the mind of God—not man; and, in heaven—not on earth! Thus, the passage has no bearing on, and ought not to be cited in any study, of the work of the Holy Spirit on earth. To do so confuses, not edifies.

A is hopelessly bankrupt, completely insolvent—broke, if you please. B has money to loan, but will not let A have it on A's unsupported word. C appears on the scene and B, on the strength of C's name, lets A have the money. A represents man, morally and spiritually bankrupt. B represents God, against whom man has sinned, and who is therefore under no obligation to hear and answer his prayers. C represents Christ, who stands good for man; and God, on the strength of Christ's name, hears and responds to man's petitions. A, in borrowing money from B, on C's name, does not know how to draw up the note. So, A calls in the help of D, who assists in preparing the note. D, then, represents the Holy Spirit—who helps us fix up the note! This "fixing", it is important to see, is in heaven—not on earth; the influence thus wrought is on the mind of God—not that of man.

East Main Street Church of Christ,
Murfreesboro, Tennessee, April, 1986

GRACE AND LAW

It is indeed heartening and gratifying to me to be privileged to appear on the Freed-Hardeman College Lectureship again this year (1987), as I have done, in one fashion or another, with but one year's absence, for more than a third of a century. I appreciate, far, far beyond my ability to express these multiplied opportunities to share with you the warm fellowship and delightful Christian association characteristic of these delightful days; and I think all of us will agree that the passing years have brought many blessings to multitudes of us from having participated in these annual gatherings of thousands of people on this campus. For many of us these hallowed halls echo with the voices of great and good individuals, long since gone, we confidently believe, to be with the Lord, who influenced us so wonderfully in the long ago, and whose memories we rejoice always to hold in reverence. These precious people live in honored and perpetual remembrance in our hearts and for them we shall evermore be thankful.

I would like to compliment the lectureship committee for having selected a general theme so relevant to brotherhood needs of our day. Beyond doubt, the subject of Grace and Law, assigned to me for discussion before this great audience tonight, involves one of the most vital and fundamental matters claiming our attention in our time. It is my opinion, based on wide brotherhood observation, that there is a great and pressing need—a critical need—for much teaching on a subject much too neglected by all of us in recent years. It pains me that more and more brethren are tilting toward the theology of denominationalism on the subject of Grace and Law, and the unmistakable concept of Calvinism is becoming increasingly discernible in the preaching and writing of many these days. This, I think, will become obvious as we proceed with this lesson tonight.

May I, in the outset, direct your attention to the following terse and significant statement dealing directly with the theme of the evening: "For the law was given by Moses, but grace and truth came by Jesus Christ" (John 1:17). The sacred writer makes clear that by "the law" he meant those edicts issuing from Sinai when the Israelites, encamped about the holy mount, received through Moses, the commandments of God (Deuteronomy 5:2). "Grace" and "truth" are said to have come "by Jesus Christ," because it was he who authored the New Covenant wherein the system of redemption embraced in the phrase "grace and truth" is embodied. Thus the "law", on the one hand, and "grace and truth," on the other are put in contrast *as to their origin* and the manner in which they were vouchsafed to those for whom intended.

There are those who think that all of the Old Testament is to be classified as "law," and all of the New Testament as "grace," and that the two are mutually exclusive. Where there is law, we are told, there is no grace; where there is grace there is no law. Those who so do are wrong—grievously wrong—on both counts. John's affirmation, "The law came by Moses, but grace and truth came by Jesus Christ," denotes the manner and means by which the respective systems came to man; it was wholly foreign to the writer's purpose, and a gross and hurtful misapprehension of his intent, to exclude *all* law from grace and *all* grace from law, as many among us do. The clear and obvious conclusion of the premise advanced is unacceptable even to those who so contend: if there was no grace in the Old Testament, *there was no truth either!* The most avid proponent of the concept that law and grace cannot exist side by side is unwilling to affirm that John's statement, "The law came by Moses, but grace and truth came by Jesus Christ," eliminates "truth" from the law. Why then contend that grace is no part of it, if truth—which, along with grace, "came by Jesus Christ"—is included?

It is far from correct to contend that there was no grace manifested on the part of God toward man in the Old Testament period. Every page of that portion of the holy volume provides either direct or indirect evidence thereof, and not infrequently it is so affirmed. Moses said that Noah "found grace in the eyes of the Lord," and the Hebrew word (chen) translated "grace" in the passage (Genesis 6:8) often occurs in the Old Testament books. Though a flaming sword was erected at the gates of the Edenic paradise from which man, because of his sin, was excluded, in order to bar his return to that Garden of delight, there were also cherubim placed there, symbolic of the mercy and redemption through grace which would ultimately be made available to the fallen race, the first faint evidence of which was in the promise to the woman that the heel of her seed would crush the serpent's head (Genesis 3:15). That the death which the first pair in Paradise suffered was not eternal, and mercy and another chance was given them, was a clear manifestation of God's grace in the outworking of his plan to provide mercy and ultimate redemption to man.

God's promise to the faithful Abraham even more vividly evidences this characteristic of the grace of God to be extended to all of the race (Titus 2:11,12), when he said to that illustrious patriarch, "Get thee out of thy country, and from thy kindred, and from thy father's house, unto a land that I will shew thee: and I will make of thee a great nation, and I will bless thee, and make thy name great; and thou shalt be a blessing: and I will bless them that bless thee, and curse him that curseth thee: and in thee shall all families of the earth be blessed" (Genesis 12:1-3). This promise of many centuries ago, during Abraham's early sojourn in the land of Canaan—to bless all the families of the earth—extends to all of us "who also walk in the steps of that faith of our father Abraham . . ." (Romans 4:12). The covenant, originally made with Abraham, and reasserted to each of the heads of the families of his descendants (Genesis 26:1-4; 35:9-12), speaks eloquently of the grace of God which comes down to us today.

Thus early in the history of the race was the gospel—the good news of redemption—declared and plans for its implementation begun: "The scripture, foreseeing that God would justify the heathen through faith, preached before the gospel unto Abraham, saying, In thee shall all nations be blessed" (Galatians 3:8). Here, too, is positive proof of God's intention to make salvation available to all the sons and daughters of men, the message, the motivation and the means themselves being exhibitions of his grace and goodness toward men. The gospel is the embodiment of grace, and that it was preached to Abraham, evidences the existence of grace in that distant day. It involves grave error therefore, to contend, as some among us do, that law and grace are antagonistic toward each other and mutually exclusive.

It is helpful, in this study, to have a clear perception of what both "grace," and "law" are. A simple, but nonetheless full definition of "grace," is *unmerited favor*. I emphasize the adjective *unmerited*. It is not enough to say that grace is favor. It is indeed that, but more—much more. Genuine grace is favor of a special kind—that which is undeserved, unmerited, and freely bestowed by the Lord. You may, for example, do something nice for me, and I, because of your kindness, react in gratitude and "return the favor," and do something nice for you! This is not the case in the favor God does for us in providing salvation. His grace toward us—his favor in our behalf—is wholly unmerited. "But God commendeth his love toward us, in that, while we were yet sinners, Christ died for us" (Romans 5:8). We did not deserve it, we cannot earn it and, of course, we cannot obligate God for it. Let this definition of grace impress itself indelibly upon our hearts: grace is the unmerited favor of God.

It would, at this point, be well for us to fix firmly in our minds what *law* is. Strangely, those who often speak and write about law and grace almost always exhibit a vague and inadequate understanding of what law really is. This is especially true of those who aver that there is absolutely no place for "law" in God's plan for man today, because of their erroneous assumption that grace excludes law—all law, every law, any law from God's plan to save. What then is "law?"

Law "is a rule of action." A rule of action imposed by a superior—in this case, of course—God. To say, therefore, that there is "no law" in God's plan for our salvation today as set out in the New Testament is simply to say that there are no rules of action, no standard of conduct therein to which we are to conform in order to appropriate salvation. This is basic Calvinism—the pure and unadulterated sort—right out of Calvin's Institutes. It is no less false because it is advocated by some we style brethren today. The truth is, the Bible abounds with rules of conduct; there are scores of specific rules in the New Testament regulating conduct, as even the most casual examination thereof will immediately show. It is absurd to say that Christians are without law ("rules of conduct") in determining their actions, and yet this is precisely what is done when it is claimed that Christians are not under law, in this, the gospel age.

To allege that one is saved without compliance with any law is the equivalent of saying that it is not necessary to do the will of God in order to be saved! Those who so affirm will deny this, of course; but, it nonetheless follows if there are no rules (laws) regarding one's response to God. Jesus said, "Not every one that saith unto me, Lord, Lord, shall enter into the kingdom of heaven; but he that doeth the will of my Father which is in heaven" (Matthew 7:21). The "will" of the Father involves "rules" with which we must all comply in order to be saved. The "rules" of God, and the "laws" of God are precisely the same. Therefore, God's law requires compliance with his laws in order for us to be saved.

But, did not Paul plainly say that "by grace are ye saved through faith; and that not of yourselves: it is the gift of God: not of works, lest any man should boast?" (Ephesians 2:8,9). One of the most elementary rules of exegesis is that words appearing in a passage of scripture must be understood in the sense that the writer intended. To disregard this simple and obvious principle of interpretation is to involve oneself in hopeless and fatal confusion in the study of the scriptures. If we conclude that by the word "works" in this passage it was the apostle's design to exclude all work, any work, every work of whatever nature, from the plan of salvation, Paul is made to contradict himself in this very passage since he makes "faith," a condition of salvation by saying, "by grace are ye saved *through faith,* since faith itself is a work! "Then said they unto him," (that is, to Christ), "What shall we do that we might work the work of God? Jesus answered and said unto them, **This is the work of God, that ye believe on him whom he hath sent**" (John 6:28,29). Obviously Paul is not in conflict with himself in the passage and, consequently, any interpretation of this verse which excludes any action on the part of man is false.

Moreover, such an interpretation puts two inspired writers in conflict with each other. James wrote, "But wilt thou know, O vain man, that faith without works is dead? Was not Abraham our father justified by works, when he had offered Isaac his son upon his altar? Seest thou how faith wrought with his works, and by works was faith made perfect? And the scripture was fulfilled which saith, Abraham believed God, and it was imputed unto for righteousness: and he was called the Friend of God. Ye see then how that by works a man is justified, and not by faith only" (James 2:20-24). James says it is by "works." Paul says it is not by "works." Both spoke by direct inspiration of the Holy Spirit. Both are therefore right. How may the apparent contradiction be resolved?

It is clear from the passages involved that these writers used the word "works" in two different senses. This difference is more than implied—it is asserted. One excludes "works," the other includes "works." The "works" Paul excludes are those of which one might *boast*. The "works" that James includes are those that *perfect* faith. Works that "perfect" faith, i.e., bring it to maturity and to the point of blessing one, are the commandments of God. One evidences one's faith in God by simply doing what God says—no more, no less, no other. This is the only real test of faith. John wrote, "He that saith, I know him, and keepeth not his commandments, is a liar, and the truth is not in him. But whoso keepeth his word, in him verily is the love of God perfected: hereby know we that we are in him" (1 John 2:4,5).

The objection is occasionally offered that Paul, in Ephesians 2:8,9, has in mind the justification of the alien sinner; whereas, James, in chapter 2, has reference to "works" characteristic of children of God.

This attempt fails since Paul and James refer to the same scripture (Genesis 15:6): Paul, to prove that justification is by faith, and James to prove that justification is by works! Rahab, "the harlot," is offered by James as an example of one justified by works (James 2:25). She was far—very far— from being a child of God when she "received the messengers and had sent them another way." Neither here, nor anywhere else in the scriptures, is it taught that one is justified, saved, pardoned and redeemed by faith alone. The truth is, as we have already very clearly seen, the two inspired writers, Paul and James, used the word "works" in two different senses, the former with reference to meritorious works man might design to save himself, and the latter with reference to working "the work" of God, that is, the keeping of God's commandments.

Faith blesses only when it prompts its possessor to obedience. Said James, "Ye see then how that by works a man is justified, and not by faith only. . . . For as the body without the spirit is dead, so faith without works is dead also" (James 2:24,26). When the spirit leaves the body death results; life is dependent on their union, death is inevitable and occurs at the moment of their separation. This indeed, is the best brief definition of death I can offer. What is life? The union of body and spirit. What is death? The resulting condition when the spirit leaves the body. Thus, the determining factor in whether life exists is whether the spirit is yet in the body. In similar fashion, according to James, that which validates faith is works—the keeping of God's commandments—and that which evidences faith's impotency, indeed, whether it is alive—is that which exists when faith is not followed by "works" i.e., the keeping of the commandments of God.

The "works" that Paul *excludes* are those of which one might boast. What type or kind of "works" fall into this category? Were it possible, on the basis of our activity in the Lord's service, to obligate God, and thus earn salvation, we might well boast of our achievement! Salvation is by grace—the unmerited favor of God—and can never be earned nor deserved by man. It is appropriated through compliance with the conditions the Lord himself set out—obedience to his will and humble submission to his commandments. It is no less a free gift because of such appropriation. When you invite me to move from the living room to the dining room for a meal you are graciously providing, I do not obligate you to furnish the food simply because I have brought myself to the place where it is available. The meal is nonetheless an expression of your kindness and generosity and, in no sense, earned by me! Keeping the commandments brings those who thus do to him who provides the feast of salvation. Only those who comply therewith are saved by his grace!

I have earlier alluded to an effort often made today to equate law—any law, every law, all law—with obedience, and then to insist that since Paul asserts that we are not under law "but under grace" (Romans 6:14), to maintain that one must comply with conditions— even those conditions which the Lord himself set out—in order to be saved, is *legalism*. Legalistic to insist that one must do what the Lord said must be done in order to be saved? Is not this surely the ultimate in absurdity? The extent of the deception characteristic of those who thus affirm is staggering, and results from drinking too deeply from the polluted streams of denominationalism which long since diverged from the apostolic river of truth flowing down from the Lord to us today.

Paul's affirmation, "For ye are not under the law, but under grace," is either limited by the context in which it appears, or it is not. If it is not, then Christians, being without law of any kind, are *a lawless people!* It is ridiculous to say in one breath the children of God are under no law whatsoever, and in the next to deny that they are lawless. These conclusions inevitably follow: (a) if we are not under law, then we are not answerable for our actions; if we are under no law, then we, as children of God, cannot commit sin, because sin "is the transgression of the law" (1 John 3:4). Hence, no law, then no restraint; no restraint, no disobedience; no disobedience, no sin! Calvinists, aware that these conclusions follow from the foregoing premises, and are therefore logical and proper, readily concede them and attempt to support them; they are at least consistent in their error. Those among us who urge that law and grace are always and everywhere antithetical, and shrink from the conclusion to which the premise inevitably leads, are neither logical or right!

I cannot overemphasize the fact that if we would know the truth on any theme, we must use biblical terms in the sense in which the original writers used them, and in no other. Paul's statement to the Romans, "For ye are not under the law, but under grace," cannot mean that we are under *no law of any kind* today, since it was the same apostle who wrote, "There is therefore now no condemnation to them which are in Christ Jesus, who walk not after the flesh, but after the Spirit. For the law of the spirit of life in Christ Jesus hath made me free from the law of sin and death" (Romans 8:1,2). There is, then, "the law of the spirit of life" to which children of God are answerable today. Gentiles, never under the law of Moses, were nevertheless answerable to, and therefore under "the law" to God, and to Christ, the apostle declared in one of his letters to the church in Corinth (1 Corinthians 9:21). There is "the royal law of liberty" (James 1:25), the "law of Christ" (Galatians 6:2), and, as we have already seen, the law of the spirit of life in Christ Jesus" (Romans 8:1,2).

It is right and far from being legalistic to do, as conditions precedent to salvation, that which the Holy Spirit commands. The Bible abounds with clear and unmistakable evidence of this fact. These appear on almost every page. They cannot, they must not, be dispensed with if we desire the approval of the Lord here, and salvation in heaven hereafter. Merely to list them would extend this sermon indefinitely; but, here are a few, gathered at random from the sacred writings. "Be ye followers of me, even as I also am of Christ." "Keep the ordinances as I delivered them unto you . . ." Let a man examine himself, and so let him eat of that bread, and drink of that cup . . ." These are from the eleventh chapter of 1 Corinthians.

Note these excerpts from the book of Ephesians: "Walk worthy of the vocation wherewith ye are called." "Keep the unity of the Spirit in the bond of peace." "Wherefore putting away lying, speak every man truth with his neighbor." "Be ye angry and sin not: let not the sun go down upon your wrath." "Let him that stole, steal no more . . ." "Let no corrupt communication proceed out of your mouth." "Grieve not the Holy Spirit of God . . ." "Let all bitterness, and wrath, and anger, and clamour, and evil speaking, be put away from you, with all malice: and be kind one to another, tenderhearted, forgiving one another, even as God for Christ's sake hath forgiven you."

There are hundreds of others. These are "rules of action." Law is "a rule of action;" therefore, these are laws. How dare one say that it is legalistic to insist that these and similar rules are not conditions precedent to our salvation! These codes of conduct with which

the scriptures abound are both preceptive and pro-
hibitory; some actions are commanded, others forbidden; but, both fall into the category of the "law of the
spirit of life in Christ Jesus," and thus effectively refute
the absurd claim that the Christian is under no law
whatsoever.

The usual response by those immeshed in this error
of grace excluding all law is to point to Paul's statement
in Romans 6:14, "For ye are not under the law, but
under grace." It should be observed, first of all, that
Paul, in this passage, *does not say* that the Christian is
not under *law*. The definite article must not be
disregarded. That which the child of God in this, the
Christian age, is not under, the apostle asserts, is THE
law. A special law, to which the Christian is not
answerable, is involved. What law?

In the next chapter is the answer: "Wherefore, my
brethren, ye also are become dead to the law by the
body of Christ; that ye should be married to another,
even to him who is raised from the dead that we should
bring forth fruit unto God" (Romans 7:4). What law
was this? As if he anticipated the error to which we are
responding and took especial care to refute it, he
rhetorically inquired, "What shall we say then? Is the
law sin? God forbid. Nay, I had not known sin, but
by the law, for I had not known lust, except the law
had said, THOU SHALT NOT COVET" (Verse 7).
What law said, "Thou shalt not covet?" This was the
law of Moses, given at Mount Sinai. This law, to which
the Jews were formerly answerable, was nailed to the
cross by the Lord (Colossians 2:14), and was replaced
by "the perfect law of liberty" (James 1:25). That law
under which the Romans were not then ̣ swerable,
was the law of Moses. Paul's purpose was not to
contrast law, all law, every law with grace in Romans
6:14, but only that law which the Judaizers (false
teachers who had appeared among the early Chris-

tians) were erroneously insisting was still in force and necessary to be kept in order to salvation.

The theme of the book of Romans—in many respects the most profound volume in the New Testament—is that justification is by means of a system of faith—the gospel of Christ—and not by the edicts handed to Moses in the mountain (Exodus 20:1ff; Deuteronomy 5:1ff). And, the "law," in Romans may, by a simple induction, be seen to be the law of Moses under which the Israelites lived for fifteen hundred years—from Sinai to the cross—and which law the Lord took out of the way, nailing it to his cross (Colossians 2:14). Let us, at this point, note a few of the many instances therein appearing. The law, which the Gentiles did not have, since the oracles of God were given through the Jews, was the law of Moses (Romans 2:12-16). The law, upon which the Jew rested, in which he found instruction, gloried in, and often violated, was the law of Moses (2:17-24). The ordinances to which the apostle alluded in 2:25-28, were those incorporated in the law of Moses. The works of the law, which could not justify, were the works of the law of Moses (3:19,20). The righteousness in Christ, apart from the law, was that which was apart from the law of Moses (2:21-26). The law of works, contrasted with the law of faith, was the law of Moses (Romans 3:27,28).

The blessing, pronounced upon the illustrious patriarch Abraham and cited by Paul to prove that Abraham was not justified by the law, (because it was extended to him before the giving of the law, and therefore could not have operated in Abraham's case), was the law of Moses (4:9-14). The law, from which the Jews had been severed by virtue of a death having occurred, and to which they were no longer joined, was the law of Moses (Romans 7:1-6). The commandment, which Paul discovered to produce death in him was the law of Moses (7:7-25). The law which was

"weak through the flesh," and could not justify was
the law of Moses (8:2). There are many similar allusions
elsewhere in the sacred writings between the law of
Moses and the law of faith. These are more than
sufficient to show that the law, which the apostle puts
in contrasts with "faith," (i.e., the gospel system of
faith), was the law of Moses. It is, therefore, poor
exegesis, and the effort leads to grave error, to array
grace against all law, by citing passages that deal
specifically with the law of Moses, and thus were not
intended to involve all law.

This is far from saying that salvation results from law
keeping, or that one may, by human effort, merit it.
The Lord saves us by his grace, but he does so *only
when we comply with the conditions he sets out as necessary
to the appropriation of it. These conditions are faith (Hebrews
11:6), repentance (Luke 13:3), confession (Romans 10:10),
and baptism in water for the remission of sins (Acts 2:38),
followed by a life of godliness and Christian service.* Any
doctrine regarding grace which eliminates these conditions is false, because their essentiality is asserted by
inspired writers, as well as by the Lord himself.

Current concepts regarding the doctrine of grace is
either to reject these conditions in totality, or to regard
them with indifference; and those who thus do charge
that we who believe that these commands, and all
other conditions set out by the Holy Spirit, are essential
to salvation are legalists! It is not legalism to do what
God said do, in the way that God said do it, and for
the reasons that God said do it; and humble, obedient
servants of the Lord will not be disturbed by such wild
and senseless charges. No amount of theological
jargon can cover up the fact that only those who fear
God and keep his commandments gain his approval.
Peter said, "Of a truth I perceive that God is no
respecter of persons: but in every nation he that feareth

him, and worketh righteousness, is acceptable to him"
(Acts 10:34,35).

Closely associated with the doctrine that grace rules
out obedience is the equally false theory of "imputed
righteousness," as today being taught by some among
us. Righteousness denotes that state or condition
wherein one is in a "right" relationship with God. The
word "righteousness" derives from the word "right,"
and this suggests that which is straight (not crooked);
so, a righteous person is one who is straight, i.e., *lined
up perfectly with God.* I have long thought that the best,
brief definition of righteousness is simply "right-
doing." He who is righteous is such because he does
right. "He that doeth righteousness is righteous, even
as he is righteous" (1 John 3:7). It is here affirmed that
a certain type of character is righteous. Of whom is
this asserted? He who does righteousness. No other
is. But righteousness is simply doing right. Therefore,
he who does right—keeps God's commandments—is
righteous, and no other is. "All thy comandments are
righteousness" (Psalm 119:172).

The doctrine of "imputed righteousness" as today
being taught is that at the point the Lord saves us, he
also transfers to us his righteousness, and we are
thenceforth possessed of "Christ"s righteousness,"
and therefore as righteous as he! There are at least two
grave errors involved in such teaching. (1) It starts with
the assumption that the phrase "righteousness of
Christ," means the personal righteousness of Christ,
i.e., the righteousness he himself exhibits. This is
wrong. The "righteousness of Christ," is the righteousness of which he is the author, and that which he
requires of his followers—not his own personal
righteousness. It should not be difficult to perceive the
utter falsity of the doctrine of transferred righteousness. Were it so, the sinner becomes as pure and good
as Christ; Christ, not guilty of sin, will, of course, never

stand in judgment. Why, then, should any one, as
good as he, be judged? Of what should such be
judged?

The contention some make on this is repugnant both
to reason and to revelation. Goodness is a personal
characteristic which can never be transferred. It is truly
the height of absurdity to contend that because one
person is good, another is! It is, of course, quite true
that in consequence of our Lord's vicarious death, we
are released from the bondage of sin, and absolved of
its guilt, but this is far from saying that we are thereby
made positively good in the absence of any *good works*
on our part. When the governor of the state pardons
a felon and restores to him his citizenship, the
pardoned person is no longer considered by the state
to be guilty of the crimes charged, but this is far from
making of him a valuable citizen with a long record of
civic usefulness and responsibility simply because he
has been pardoned. This record the free man must
achieve for himself.

(2) There is infinite difference between *not imputing
guilt* (this the Lord does to a sinner in saving him), and
in *conferring merit* (this the Lord does not do when he
forgives the sinner). The word "impute" (reckon, in
the American Standard Version), does not mean to
make good, but simply to justify; to regard as
righteous; there is no instance in classical Greek
literature where the word is ever used to mean that
one, in the act, has had merit conferred upon him. The
primary import of the word is to denote change in
position with reference to him who confers it, and not
bestowal of virtue.

In response to this it may be said that Abraham's
faith was imputed (reckoned, counted) to him "for
righteousness" (Romans 4:9). "For righteousness."
Indeed, so. *FOR* righteousness, i.e., the act of believing
was, by the Lord, regarded as an act of obedience—in

the absence of further duties at the moment—and so credited (imputed) to him. The Lord simply accepted Abraham's faith as an act of righteousness. To this end, James speaks plainly, clearly, unmistakably: "Was not Abraham our father justified by works, when he had offered Isaac his son upon the altar? Seest thou how faith wrought with his works, and by works was faith made perfect? And the scripture was fulfilled which saith, *Abraham believed God, and it was imputed unto him for righteousness:* and he was called the Friend of God. Ye see then how that by works a man is justified, and not by faith only" (James 2:21-24).

If we wish to believe and to teach the truth, we must sharply distinguish between a righteousness imputed (credited, reckoned, counted) to one because such an one is in a right relationship to God, through obedience to his will, and the righteousness which Christ himself owns, and which is alleged to be transferred to the sinner. The former is clearly taught in the scriptures; the latter originated with Augustine and Calvin, and is wholly false. If to this it is objected that Christ is said to have been made "righteousness' for us (1 Corinthians 1:30), it should be noted that this means no more than that he became the *means* of righteousness for us, i.e., it is through him that we are privileged to attain to righteousness through the sacrifice he made in our behalf. But for this fact there would be no righteousness of any kind available. It should never be forgotten that it is only through the doing of his will that we lay hold of this blessing. It was he himself who said, "Not every one that saith unto me, Lord, Lord, shall enter into the kingdom of heaven; but he that doeth the will of my Father which is in heaven. Many will say to me in that day, Lord, Lord, have we not prophesied in thy name? and in thy name have cast out devils? and in thy name done many wonderful works? And then will I profess unto them, I never knew you: depart from me, ye that work iniquity" (Matthew 7:21-23).

Salvation is attributable to many things in the scriptures. God saves; Christ saves; we are saved by the revelation of truth made by the Holy Spirit; we are saved by grace, by faith, by works, by baptism—by ourselves! (Acts 2:40). God saves us by having given us a plan whereby we may be saved; Christ saves us by having executed this plan, and the Holy Spirit saves us by having revealed this plan. We are saved by grace, because of God's love for us; by faith, since it is the motivation which leads us to accept the plan; by works, because through keeping God's commandments we appropriate salvation; by baptism, because it is the final and consummating act of salvation. To select one of these—baptism, for example—and to insist that because it is said that "baptism doth also now save us" (1 Peter 3:21), we are therefore saved by baptism *alone* is to be guilty of grave and fatal error, but error no more grave, nor less fatal, than to assert, as some among us today do, that we are saved by grace apart from, and independent of, the conditions on which the Lord bestows salvation.

We must be careful that we do not minimize one doctrine of scripture by overextending another one. This is an ever present threat to proper exegesis, and one against which all of us need ever to be on guard. Men often do this and thus greatly mislead others, even in those instances where the doctrine they emphasize, when considered in relation to other teaching of scripture, is true. Predestination (the doctrine that God predetermines events) is clearly taught in the Bible; there are those who, having recognized this fact, go on to contend that such predetermination extends to an arbitrary selection of some and the passing by of others, and that this is so fixed that the number of those thus arbitrarily selected (or, as the case may be, rejected), can neither be increased nor diminished. Of the former it is affirmed that their salvation is certain and they cannot lose it, of the latter that their damnation is inevitable, and they cannot—however much they might desire— escape it.

It is quite true, of course, that the Lord has predetermined some to salvation, but this relates to those who do his will—a choice all may freely make. This, the scriptures plainly assert: "But we are bound to give thanks always to God for you, brethren beloved of the Lord, because God hath from the beginning chosen you to salvation through sanctification of the Spirit and belief of the truth: whereunto he called you by our gospel to the obtaining of the glory of our Lord Jesus Christ" (2 Thessalonians 2:13,14). All are called by the gospel (Mark 16:15,16); thus, all are privileged to be among the predestined to salvation. Many, tragically, will be lost; but not because they could not, but because they chose not, through rejection of the gospel, to be saved.

God's love for the race is clearly taught, and often affirmed in the sacred writings (John 3:16). There are those who insist, by overextending this characteristic of God, that since he gave his Son to die for the world, all the world will eventually be saved—regardless of any response it may, or may not make—and thus they argue for universal salvation. God did indeed love, and so love, the world that he gave his only begotten Son to die in our stead, and on our behalf, but only those who believe in him—a belief that validates itself through obedience (James 2:24-26), will escape perdition. Salvation is by grace, but not by grace alone; salvation is by faith, but not by faith alone; salvation is by works, but not by works alone; salvation is by baptism, but not by baptism alone. May we never forget that "He that saith, I know him, and keepeth

not his commandments, is a liar and the truth is not
in him" (1 John 2:4).

"Now of the things which I have spoken," to
paraphrase Paul (Hebrews 8:1), "this is the sum."

How are we saved? It depends on what viewpoint
is ours as we contemplate this question. God saves.
Man cannot save himself. We are all lost in a sense in
which it is impossible for us to save ourselves. Our
friends cannot save us. If saved at all, God must do it.
He "is the Saviour of all men, speciallly of them that
believe" (1 Timothy 4:10).

There is, however, another sense in which we can
save ourselves. "And with many other words he
testified, and exhorted them, saying, Save yourselves
from this crooked generation" (Acts 2:40). We are lost
in a sense in which we can save ourselves and the Lord
will not save us. "And to you that are afflicted rest
with us, at the revelation of the Lord Jesus from heaven
with the angels of his power in flaming fire, rendering
vengeance to them that know not God, and to them
that obey not the gospel of our Lord Jesus: who shall
suffer punishment, even eternal destruction from the
face of the Lord and from the glory of his might" (2
Thessalonians 1:7-9). God saves in providing a plan
man could never have devised. Man saves himself by
complying humbly and fully with this plan. *It is a fatal
mistake for man to attempt to do only that which God can
do for him, or to leave for him to do that which he must do
for himself!*

1. *Grace* is the *principle* upon which man is saved.
Man, in his state of alienation, is lost and under
sentence of condemnation. He cannot plead that the
sentence should be annulled on the ground of justice.
Sinful man is a violator of God's law, and justice
demands exaction of the penalty. He cannot come into
court and plead that the penalty is too severe and ask
for mitigation. He *deserves* its full exaction. He cannot

plead his own worth or merit. Moreover, there is not enough animal blood in the world to wash away his sins, nor money to purchase his salvation. *Grace,* unmerited by works, undemanded by justice, and unpurchased by worth, is the principle of salvation.

2. The *blood* of Christ makes salvation possible. "It is not possible that the blood of bulls and of goats should take away sins" (Hebrews 10:1-4). The sacrifices of former dispensations were typical and derived their efficacy only as they prefigured and foreshadowed the shedding of his blood on the cross. From the tragic fall in Eden till now God has never allowed man to approach him save through an innocent being. "But Christ having come a high priest of the good things to come, through the greater and more perfect tabernacle, not made with hands, that is to say, not of this creation, nor yet through the blood of goats and calves, but through his own blood, entered in once for all into the holy place, having obtained eternal redemption" (Hebrews 9:11,12).

3. The *agent* by which the way of salvation has been provided is the Holy Spirit. Were it not for the revelation he made, man would have no knowledge of the provisions that are his for salvation. "Howbeit when he who is the Spirit of the truth is come, he shall guide you into all the truth" (John 16:13). This revelation was made to the apostles (John 14:16,17).

4. The *motive* of salvation is the love of God. "For God so loved the world that he gave his only begotten Son, that whosoever believeth on him should not perish, but have eternal life" (John 3:16). Contrary to the doctrine of the creeds, which allege that it was necessary for Christ to die the shameful and ignominious death of the cross in order to appease the wrath of an angry God, the truth is that Christ's coming was a manifestation of that love and a result of it instead of a condition precedent to it. "But God commendeth

his love toward us, in that, while we were yet sinners, Christ died for us" (Romans 5:8). God gave his Son, and Christ came to die for us *because* he loved us, and not that he might love us later.

5. The *power* by which salvation is effected is the *gospel*. "For I am not ashamed of the gospel: for it is the power of God unto salvation to every one that believeth; to the Jew first, and also to the Greek? (Romans 1:16). The word "power" in this passage is translated from the Greek term *dunamis*, from which is derived our English words "dynamic," "dynamo," "dynamite." The gospel is thus God's dynamite to save! For this reason one never reads of a case of conversion in the New Testament except in connection with the preaching of the gospel. "It pleased God by the foolishness of preaching to save them that believe" (1 Corinthians 1:21). Thus, notwithstanding the fact that grace is the principle of salvation, love the motive, the blood of Christ the procuring cause, the Holy Spirit the agent, unless the gospel—God's power to save—is preached, believed, and obeyed, salvation will not result.

6. The *place* of salvation is the body of Christ, the church. "The husband is the head of the wife, as Christ also is the head of the church, being himself the saviour of the body" (Ephesians 5:23). Christ is "the *saviour of the body!*" But what is the body? "And gave him to be head over all things to the church, which is his body" (Ephesians 1:22,23). The church, *which is his body!* The church is his body, but he is the saviour of his body; therefore, he is the savior of the church! But forgiveness of sins is only in the body of Christ. "In whom we have our redemption, the forgiveness of our sins" (Colossians 1:14). The body of Christ is the church (Ephesians 1:22). Therefore, forgiveness of sins *is only in the church!* What church? Its *name:* "the churches of Christ" (Romans 16:16). The name of its members:

"Christians" (Acts 11:26). Its *practice:* a regular meeting on the first day of the week (1 Corinthians 16:1,2). The Lord's Supper observed each first day of the week (Acts 20:7).

7. The *conditions* of salvation are: (1) *faith:* "Without faith it is impossible to please him" (Hebrews 11:6). (2) *Repentance:* "But except ye repent, ye shall all likewise perish" (Luke 13:3). (3) *Confession:* "And with the mouth confession is made unto salvation" (Romans 10:10). (4) *Baptism:* "And now why tarriest thou? arise, and be baptized, and wash away thy sins, calling on his name" (Acts 22:16). Nothing less than complete compliance with all of these conditions will enable one to claim the blessing of salvation. Faith, in order to produce a blessing, must prompt to obedience. The Pharisees believed, but would not confess him, hence were not saved (John 12:42). Faith without works is dead. The moment one attempts to separate faith and works, *faith dies!* (James 2:26). Faith is the wholehearted acceptance of the gospel of Christ and a willingness to trust its conditions for salvation. Repentance is a change of mind, resulting in a change of life. Confession is a public acknowledgment of one's faith in the Lord. Baptism is a burial in water, into the name of the Father, the Son, and the Holy Spirit (Romans 6:3,4; Matthew 28:18-20). Those who thus do are saved (Mark 16:16; Acts 2:38). In the process of salvation the Lord adds to the church (Acts 2:47). We may be assured that he will make no mistake.

More than this one need not do to be forgiven of past, or alien, sins. *Less than this one cannot do and be forgiven.* This and this alone, without addition, without subtraction, without modification, is the *way of salvation* for the alien sinner.

Freed-Hardeman College Lectureship
February 1987

WHAT IS INVOLVED IN OBEDIENCE TO GOD?

Do you regard yourself as an accountable person who will one day die and eventually stand in judgment before him who created you? (Romans 14:12; John 5:28,29; Heb. 9:27). Does it concern you that your manner of life on earth and your response—or lack of it—to the will of God as expressed in the New Testament will determine your destiny through endless ages? (Revelation 22:13,14). Have you realistically faced up to the fact that whether your ultimate destination is heaven or hell, your enjoyment of the former, or your endless torment in the latter, is directly related to your improvement of opportunity in the one, or neglect in the other, while here on earth you live? In view of these incontrovertible facts, is it not simply good sense and the exercise of practical wisdom to determine what those duties are, and to make sure that you have truly embraced and discharged them? (Hebrews 9:27).

Even occasional readers of the scriptures soon become aware that the Bible abounds with passages emphasizing the obligation of all responsible persons to submit to the will of the Lord as a condition precedent to salvation.

Paul, greatest of the apostles, warned that the Creator will render "vengeance to them that know not God, and to them that obey not the gospel of our Lord Jesus: who shall suffer punishment, even eternal destruction from the face of the Lord and from the glory of his might" (2 Thessalonians 1:8,9); and our Saviour said, "Not every one that saith unto me, Lord, Lord, shall enter into the kingdom of heaven; but he that doeth the will of my Father which is in heaven (Matthew 7:21). To this he later added, "And why call

ye me, Lord, Lord, and do not the things which I say?"
(Luke 6:46). When certain Jews exhibited interest in
him and his teaching but evidenced shallowness of
conviction, Jesus said to them, "If ye continue in my
word, then are ye my disciples indeed; and ye shall
know the truth, and the truth shall make you free"
(John 8:31,32).

What was the nature of the truth of which he spoke?
Did he intend from this to convey the idea that the
blessings he would bestow were dependent on
conformity to the gospel by which means salvation in
the scriptures is promised? (Romans 1:13-17). What
does it mean to "obey" God? Does one obey God
who, ignorantly or otherwise, substitutes human
reasons for divine ones in approaching him?

Many in the denominational world and some in the
church today think so.

The scriptures teach—and I shall engage to show
this by the most irrefutable evidence—that those who
so do are wrong, seriously wrong, tragically wrong in
the advocacy of this view, and that the consequences
are disastrous and destructive of the souls of those
who accept and follow these dangerous doctrines.

It cannot be seriously denied that edicts, when
enacted by properly constituted authority, may not be
disregarded with impunity; and when such enact-
ments issue from divine sources clearly reflecting the
will of the Judge of all the earth, loyalty, love and fealty
demand and require full and unreserved submission
thereto. The rejection of this principle in the govern-
ments of men produces criminals, in the government
of God, sinners. To this fundamental and basic rule of
law there are, and can be, no exceptions.

There are three requisites to obedience, any one of
which omitted renders invalid the other two.

   (1) We must do what the Lord *said do.*

(2) We must do what the Lord said do *in the way and manner in which the Lord said do it.*

(3) We must do what the Lord said do, in the way and manner in which the Lord said do it *for the reason or reasons that the Lord said do it.*

A simple illustration will make clear these basic and fundamental facts: (1) Were the Lord to command us to go west and we go east, we have disobeyed him. (2) Were he to bid us go west to work in the fields, and we go west but work in a factory, we have disobeyed him. (3) Were he to tell us to go west and work in the fields to earn money to buy a house in which to live, and we go west and work in the fields to earn money with which to purchase an automobile, we have disobeyed him. To *obey* is "to follow the commands" of another (Webster's New Collegiate Dictionary.) We thus "obey" God only when we do what he says, in the way or manner he designates, and for the reason or reasons he specifies. Any other action on our part in such a situation is not obedience but disobedience, and involves not submission of will but the substitution of the human will for the divine—an action often shown in the scriptures both by precept and example to be alike presumptuous and fatal.

The conditions essential to salvation set out in the New Testament are simple, clear and unmistakable. In order to become a Christian, one must exercise faith in the Lord and in his word (Hebrews 11:6; Mark 16:16), repent of one's sins (Luke 13:3), confess one's faith in Christ (Romans 10:10), and be baptized in water unto (for, in order to) the remission of sins (Acts 2:38; 1 Peter 3:21). Those who thus do are saved from past (alien) sins and are by the Lord added to his church (Mark 16:15,16; Acts 2:38), which he built (Matthew 16:18), and wherein are all spiritual blessings (Ephesians 1:3). It is in this fashion that one becomes a Christian (Acts 11:26; 1 Peter 4:16), a member of the body of Christ (Ephesians 1:19-21), and possessed of the promise of eternal life (1 John 2:25). Luke, inspired historian of the early church, has shown us that those who thus did met regularly on the first day of the week for worship (Acts 20:7), an action which involved singing the praises of God (unaccompanied by instruments of music), the teaching of the word, prayer, the contribution, and communion and fellowship of the saints in the regular observance of the Lord's supper every first day of the week (Acts 2:42; 1 Corinthians 16:1,2).

It will be observed that I have noted that there is set out in the New Testament *four* steps—faith, repentance, confession and baptism in water for the remission of sins—as conditions precedent to salvation from past, or alien, sins. There are those in great numbers about us—in fact, most of the denominational world—who have no serious objection to the first three, indeed, themselves urge these conditions on those they would influence, but who strenuously object to the fourth, baptism in water, as a condition essential to this end. And they do this in spite of, and despite the fact that the scriptures clearly assert that baptism, when preceded by faith, repentance, and confession, is "for" (in order to) the remission of sins (Acts 2:38), puts one into Christ (Romans 6:3,4), and is the consummating act in God's plan to save (Mark 16:15,16; 1 Peter 3:21).

This conclusion, that these requirements must all be met in order to obtain the forgiveness promised, not only irresistibly follows—as all know who are informed in what the Bible teaches on this superlatively important theme, and who really respect the Lord and the authority of his word—but it also may be easily and convincingly shown from other considerations in the sacred writings. There is proof that Paul, the apostle to the Gentiles, wrote First Corinthians in the early part of A.D. 57, and near the conclusion of a lengthy period of labors in Ephesus. He had established the church in Corinth about five years earlier. The immediate occasion of the writing of this epistle was the arrival of a family, or some portion thereof, consisting of a Christian woman of Corinth whose name was Chloe. From her, or other members of her household, Paul learned of unseemly behavior and improper conditions prevailing in the church in Corinth, and requiring his immediate attention.

"It hath been signified unto me concerning you, my brethren, by them that are of the household of Chloe", he wrote, "that there are contentions among you. Now this I mean, that each one of you saith, I am of Paul; and I of Apollos; and I of Cephas; and I of Christ. Is Christ divided? was Paul crucified for you? or were ye baptized into the name of Paul?" (1 Corinthians 1:11-13). From this we learn that dissension had arisen in Corinth; contentions prevailed produced by partyism— factionalism resulting from extreme favoritism toward preachers! So pronounced were these preferences, factions appeared in the congregation and alienations followed. Paul was among those thus "honored," an "honor" which he unhesitatingly declined, rejected and repudiated, since the disposition to engage in this type of favoritism by the Corinthians, or any others presuming to be faithful followers of the Lord, was wholly foreign to the spirit of New Testament Christianity (Romans 12:3,10).

Among the questions pointedly asked by the apostle to bring the people to realize the sinfulness of their attitude and conduct in promoting factionalism in the congregation in Corinth was this: "Is Christ divided?" more literally, *"Is Christ parceled out in small portions?"* Did the Corinthians think that it is possible to rend the body of Christ into small bits and divide it among several different groups, and each "bit" (faction) have a small portion of Christ? This is the implication which obtains wherever division occurs. It is remarkable in the light of this sharp rebuke by the apostle that some religious groups not only promote this type of division, but also in it rejoice and boast of it, sometimes actually thanking God for existence of the different denominations!

Though Paul was one of those elevated to the head of a party by some members of the church in Corinth, he refused to accept the assignment asking, "Was Paul crucified for you?" Had the apostle died on the cross for those who sought in this fashion to follow him, there would be some appropriateness in the situation there obtaining; but, he was not crucified for them and they were therefore in grave error in seeking to identify themselves by his name. He inquired further, "Were ye baptized into the name of Paul?" The implication is clear and obvious. Had they been baptized into Paul's name, they might, with propriety, wear his name. Into his name they had not been baptized; hence, they had no right to wear his name; they had been baptized "into the name of Christ" (Matthew 28:18-20); only Christ's name—the name *Christian*—might they therefore properly wear!

Lessons of great present and practical value emerge from this highly interesting and significant statement. In addition to teaching us the sinfulness of division, and the impropriety of wearing the names of men as religious designations, we are by it plainly taught that baptism in water, "into the name of the Father, and of the Son, and of the Holy Spirit," (Matthew 28:18-20), is absolutely essential to submit to in order to become a Christian.

The pattern and procedure, as well as the thrust, of the apostle's argument is this: "Had you been baptized into the name of Paul, you would, in consequence, be a Paulite; had you been baptized into the name of Cephas, you would thereby become a Cephasite; had you been baptized into the name of Apollos, you would be an Apollosite. But, you were not baptized into Paul's name, therefore, you are not a Paulite; you were not baptized into the name of Cephas; therefore, you are not a Cephasite; you were not baptized into Apollos' name; therefore, you are not an Apollosite. You were, however, baptized into the name of Christ, and in consequence, you became a *Christian,* and so may properly and correctly wear Christ's name."

There is one step more in the apostle's logical chain of reasoning, inspired analysis and conclusive deduction:

IF YOU HAVE NOT BEEN BAPTIZED AT ALL, YOU HAVE NO RIGHT TO WEAR ANY NAME RELIGIOUSLY—NOT PAUL'S, NOT CEPHAS', NOT APOLLOS', NOT LUTHER'S, NOT CALVIN'S, NOT EVEN CHRIST'S NAME!

Here, also, is clear and irrefutable evidence of the fact that the disciples of the first century church were taught not only to accept Christ as their only Head and Redeemer religiously, but to reflect this fact to all others by wearing only his name. Luke, in his record of the events of the early church, wrote that the disciples "were called Christians first in Antioch" (Acts 11:26). It is significant that these disciples, who were privileged to have the guidance of men inspired and divinely directed by the Holy Spirit, not only claimed to be Christians, it was by this divinely given name they were known. There are those of our day who claim to be Christians, but who choose to wear, and to be identified, by some other name—usually in honor of some man or human institution. We should not ever lose sight of the fact that these of whom we read in the New Testament not only claimed to be Christians, *this is the name by which they were called.*

Ought we not today to show the same honor to our Saviour that characterized the early Christians?

We have already seen that our Lord, in the simplest, plainest possible fashion made baptism, in water, a condition of salvation from sin, and instructed his disciples both to preach and to practice it (Mark 16:15,16). Every allusion thereto in the New Testament either asserts or implies this fact. It must inevitably follow that any action not in harmony with this relationship invalidates the act divinely designated. Invalidation of any act of deity is not obedience—it is disobedience. A command to perform an act authorizes no more, no less, no other, than that commanded. Were this not so, exactness and definiteness in contracts, legislative acts and judicial decrees would be impossible, and such documents rendered meaningless and without validity. The Bible, the source of man's only hope in this world and in that to come, would henceforth be worthless, no longer able to supply us with the assurance of eternal salvation for which the hearts of us all deeply yearn.

Again and again, in the inspired writings, this principle of definiteness is shown, in no instance more clearly than in that of the interesting and informative case of Naaman (2 Kings 5:1-14). That leprous officer was instructed to dip, to dip seven times, to dip seven times "in Jordan," in order to be healed of his loathsome disease. Suppose that instead of conforming to the command to "dip," he had applied to the swollen nodules which disfigured him the balm of Gilead; or, if he dipped, to have done so six times; or, if he dipped, dipped seven times in the clear waters of Damascus rather than in the Jordan; or, if he dipped, dipped seven times, in Jordan, but without faith in the act, and to please his servants, would he have received the marvelous blessing of healing and restoration he so desperately needed?

The first observance of the Jewish feast of the Passover on the final night of the sojourn of Israel in Egypt affords us with an equally interesting and edifying illustration of this principle (Exodus 2:2-24). A lamb (not a yearling) was to be offered; it was to be offered on the tenth day of the month (not the ninth or eleventh); the lamb was to be killed in the evening (not in the morning); it was to be of the first year (not some succeeding one); it was to be a male (not a female); the blood thereof was to be sprinkled on "the lintel" and on "the two side posts," of the house (not on the roof); the people were to eat unleavened bread seven days (not six) during the festival. Can it be possible that any person possessed of even ordinary reasoning powers would conclude that the Israelites, in performing the generic command to offer a lamb, could have altered, at will, the specifications of that ancient memorial feast without incurring the divine displeasure? Or, that such deviation from the Lord's command would have been regarded by Jehovah as acceptable and obedient acts?*

Despite the only proper conclusion to which these premises lead, it is nonetheless alleged that it is possible for one to "obey" God in baptism, though wholly in error regarding its divinely designed purpose, and under the mistaken notion that one is in possession of salvation before and with it. More specifically, there are those who contend that one may consider oneself to be already saved **before and**

---

*The Israelites were not told *not* to offer a calf; or, if they offered a lamb, not to do so on the ninth or eleventh day; or, if they offered a lamb and did so on the tenth day, not to slay the animal in the morning, and so on, but these conclusions (indicated in the parentheses) necessarily follow. If they had offered a calf, instead of a lamb, or a lamb two years old, or offered the sacrifice on the ninth day, or sprinkled the blood on the roof and ate unleavened bread for only six days, would this have been in compliance with the will of him who thus legislated?

without the baptismal act,—may indeed submit thereto for some non-biblical reason, apart from, and even in conflict with the design set out by inspired men in Acts 2:38, Romans 6:3 and 1 Peter 3:21, and still receive every blessing available to and intended for the obedient believer.

Our Saviour said, "And ye shall know the truth, and the truth shall make you free" (John 8:32). The clear and obvious import of this statement is that the only way accountable persons may escape the bondage of sin is by and through obedience to the truth. But, if it is possible to obtain full and complete pardon from sin by disregarding truth and following error, does this not mean that error is fully as efficacious in producing salvation as the truth and should, therefore, be as fully valued? In which case, is it not just as well to "know error," as it is "know the truth" in order to have the freedom from sin we seek, since in that event it would be as effective? Jesus said that only those who do his will shall enjoy the benefits and blessings of the kingdom (Matthew 7:21). Do those who not only do not conform to his will, but who oppose it, and who urge others to disregard it, qualify for all the blessings it offers? Then, truth has no advantage over error, and falsehood is equally efficacious in producing deliverance from the power and presence of sin. This conclusion necessarily follows from the premises we are asked to embrace.

It is said that remission of sins (Acts 2:38) is not the only design of water baptism taught in the Bible, and that it is impractical and unrealistic to insist that all who respond to the invitation should be familiar with each of them. This objection is without merit, since all references thereto imply the design given in Acts 2:38. Acts 22:16, ("wash away thy sins"), Romans 6:3, ("baptized into Christ,") 1 Peter 3:21, ("baptism doth also now save us") Moreover, the only thing baptism is said to be *for* in the scriptures is *remission of sins!* In any event, there is not the slenderest support for the assumption that one may deliberately disregard the purpose and design of water baptism which the Holy Spirit specified, and at the same time "obey" the Lord.

The scriptures make it exceedingly clear that salvation on the one hand, and damnation on the other, are matters dependent on whether one obeys, or disobeys, God (2 Thessalonians 1:7-9). This principle, demonstrable both by precept and by example in the divine revelation, is wholly at variance with the current view that the "intent" to obey God, in lieu of actual obedience, is acceptable to him, though that which is engaged in is in conflict with what he has commanded. He who submits to sprinkling or pouring for baptism has, as his intent, to "obey God," i.e., he is motivated to such action in his response to what he has been erroneously led to believe is acceptable baptism. But, neither desire nor intent will transform a disobedient act into an obedient one. Only when we wholly yield our wills to the Lord, only when we do what he said, only when we do what he said do, in the way he said do it, and for the reason, or reasons that he said to do it, do we *obey* him and qualify on his terms for the salvation he offers.

It is insisted that those who hold to error touching the design of water baptism have certainly been misled, but that any response by them to God, so long as it issued from a vague feeling that inasmuch as baptism is the "door" into "the church," and that it symbolizes the salvation believed already attained, there is some obligation to submit thereto; and that those who are thus influenced render acceptable obedience to God, though admittedly in error touching its purpose and design. Are we prepared to extend this type of reasoning to other areas? Let us see.

We are taught, both through direct statement and by apostolic example to observe the Lord's Supper each first day of the week (Acts 20:7), in commemoration of the suffering and death of our Lord. The emblems, the bread representative of his body, and the fruit of the vine which portrays his shed blood, are the elements of the Supper. *May one, ignorant of the divine design of the Lord's Supper, nonetheless partake of it acceptably, sincerely believing that the elements have been miraculously changed into the actual body and blood of the Lord* as Catholics teach? These in this ecclesiasticism very definitely "intend" to "obey God," and they think they are doing so, though in fact they are grossly disregarding the true design, and in grave error touching the proper significance of the elements. But, if one may render suitable and acceptable obedience to God in water baptism while disregarding its true design, why not also in the Supper of the Lord? Those who think that God accepts the "intent" for the scriptural act should have no problem in fellowshipping those who subscribe to, and practice, the Romish doctrine of transubstantiation!

Error, like leaven, influences all with whom it is in contact, and once embraced, moves its adherents on and on to other areas, each such move involving further abandonment of truth and deeper involvement in error. The view, that there are devout and knowledgeable "Christians" in all the denominations, on the assumption that God has accepted their baptism on the ground that the "intent" which motivated them was to "obey God," leads on to additional grave errors, among them the following:

(1) The rejection of the confession as one of the conditions of salvation. If an immersion, preceded by the statement, "I believe that God, for Christ's sake, has pardoned my sins", and this before and without baptism, and also without the "good confession"

(Romans 10:9,10), is acceptable to God, then one of the four conditions in order to salvation—the confession, "I believe with all of my heart that Jesus is the Christ, the Son of God" (Acts 8:37), may be omitted and disregarded with impunity. If the "formal confession" is unauthorized, it not only may be excluded from our teaching on what one must do to be saved, *it must be!* We cannot have it both ways. if it is authorized, it must be **included,** if it is unauthorized it must be **excluded.** *If authorized, it is wrong to omit it, if unauthorized, it is wrong to include it.* It is, however, said to be "unto" (*eis* "in order to" salvation (Romans 10:10), as are also belief (Romans 10:10), and repentance (Acts 11:18). If one is at liberty to reject one of the conditions (the confession), said to be (*eis*) in order to salvation, why not, with equal impunity, exclude belief (for the heathen) and repentance (for the impenitent), of which conditions no more is affirmed?

(2) Acceptance of the "invisible church" concept, and assignment of a denominational character to the church. The view under review is little more than a sophisticated form of that concept long advocated by denominational churches which have always sharply distinguished between that which is styled "the body of Christ," alleged to contain all the saved, in contradistinction to the visible church bodies (denominations) one of which we are alleged to be. We have, in the process, even acquired a distinctive designation—the "Yellow Pages Churches of Christ"—by which our separation into a distinct denominational organization is revealed. We thus take our place—in the religious world—as one of the visible denominations, sharing with all others the salvation the great invisible body affords and in fellowship with all others whose "intent" is to "obey God," however far removed, in fact, and in act, that may be—in that one Great, Invisible church which, according to the position being

examined, is the only true church of Christ and inclusive of all "knowledgeable" and "devout" Christians, of all denominations but, unfortunately, today divided into various sectarian groups which divisions current unity meetings are seeking to eliminate!

(3) The abandonment of any logical reason for those in denominational churches to obey the gospel. If the "intent" to obey God is equivalent to the act, and God accepts the "intent" as the act, though admittedly not done in harmony with New Testament teaching, these "knowledgeable" and "devout Christians" said to be in "all" denominational churches are not lost; hence, need no salvation; are in the kingdom, therefore, do not need to be born again; are in Christ, therefore, do not need to be baptized into him; are in the church, therefore, do not need to be added to it! Why, then, should any effort be made to induce them to be baptized at all? Is there not great inconsistency in advocating the doctrine of "intent" and then urging those who can be persuaded to leave their communions and come to us to be baptized? Are they in Christ? If yes, they have no need of baptism; have they been born again, they cannot again be born of water and the Spirit. Why, we insist, is baptism even suggested to any one in the denominational world if the premises herein being examined are true? If their original response was to "obey God," on entering the denominational fellowship, and this suffices to win God's approval (as is now being taught), why require at all this superfluous and repetitive action? Do not the greater number of those who identify with the various religious organizations of the land do so under the conviction that in so doing they "obey God?" Is not the prevailing practice of those who contend for the foregoing premises grossly inconsistent in urging baptism upon these people at all?

Faced with this obvious conflict between the teaching of the doctrine of intent which renders such response unnecessary, and the practice of it which implies its necessity, there are those who abandon the original concept of "intent," and insist that it is possible for people to become and be New Testament Christians in a spiritual atmosphere admittedly alien to the teaching and practice of genuine Christianity. Plainly put, it is insisted that people, desirous of learning the truth, may do so independently of their religious surroundings and while participating in them. But, is this really reasonable? May one be subjected week after week to the presentation of the doctrine that salvation is "by faith only," and before and without water baptism, yet learn that it is not by faith alone but only through a full response to the commands of the Lord in order to be justified? (James 2:24). May one regularly hear some of the Lord's edicts deprecated, denied and denounced as nonessential, but nonetheless conclude that baptism, to the penitent believer, is for (in order to) the remission of past, or alien, sins?

In the unlikely event that, in spite of teaching to the contrary, through independent study one does indeed come to a full knowledge of the truth respecting salvation in such a setting, is it at all likely that an earnest, honest and sincere searcher for truth would be content to continue in such a communion, and support with his presence and by his financial means that which he now believes to be contrary to the teaching of the holy scriptures and opposed to the best interests of mankind?

The reason for religious dissension and diversion is not because of any ambiguity or obscurity of teaching in the scriptures; the way is so plain that "wayfaring men, though fools, shall not err therein" (Isaiah 35:8), and "If any man will do his will, he shall know the teaching . . ." (John 7:17). The problem is not properly attributable to any difficulty in the divine revelation, but results from a deep-seated unwillingness on the part of many people to bring their wills into subjection to the will of God.

Denominational theologians do not teach the obvious import of the scriptures touching the plan of salvation because they have difficulty in understanding it; it is because they do not think that the matters taught in Acts 2:38, Mark 16:15,16 and many other similar passages, are important! The problem is not one of interpretation, but of faith, and it will not be resolved so long as human judgment is allowed to take precedence over the divine. The plan of salvation is indeed simple and easily understood; but, not more so than many other matters essential to our salvation here and hereafter. The name, the doctrine, and the practice of the New Testament church are all plainly and clearly taught in the New Testament; is it likely that one, who through independent study has learned the truth on what to do to be saved, would not have as easily and as quickly determined the truth on these matters as well? Could one, having so done, be content to remain indefinitely in an institution which disregarded them?

Our obligation to all lost people is exceedingly great. It is neither narrow nor sectarian to urge that in order to enjoy the approval of our Lord here, and the bliss of heaven hereafter, we must abide in his teaching, and do his will (Matthew 7:21; 2 John 9). We do not serve the cause of the Saviour, nor do we contribute to the well-being of those in error, by minimizing the importance of a full and faithful response to the Lord's commands.

Sunday, October 4, 1987
Edgewood Church of Christ
Columbus, GA

PROFILE OF APOSTASY

It is indeed a thrilling and exciting privilege to me to be associated with you in the work we love, to enjoy your warm and Christian fellowship in our efforts to proclaim the primitively pure gospel, and to note the excellent interest which continues to characterize the meeting. It is my earnest desire, in this service, as in all of our meetings, to teach the truth and to preach the word in such fashion that only those impressions that are good will be made, and that the Lord will be pleased and happy with our efforts.

We have been greatly blessed by having been put in trust with the sacred truths of God's Word, and we are truly privileged to be representatives in behalf of the cause we love and for which our Saviour died. For this glorious, and at the same time, awesome honor, we ought to be exceedingly grateful and thankful, and we should demonstrate this gratitude and thanksgiving in the manner he approves. Inherent in this is a continuing responsibility on the part of us all to maintain stedfast and unwavering devotion to him, and unswerving loyalty to his word; and we must never cease to exhibit a pure faith and a faultless practice in all matters religious, however great the cost may be and whatever the consequences which follow. Anything less than this is not enough; anything more than this is too much; this, and this alone, without addition, without subtraction, without modification is the solemn obligation of us all, and from it may we never waver nor turn aside.

There is a statement in Judges 2:6-14, that has long impressed me, and though penned with reference to matters in the long, long ago nonetheless speaks to our day with a relevancy with which we ought, each one of us, especially to be aware.

"Now when Joshua had sent the people away, the children of Israel went every man unto his inheritance to possess the land. And the people served Jehovah all the days of Joshua, and all the days of the elders that outlived Joshua, who had seen all the great work of Jehovah that he had wrought for Israel. And Joshua, the son of Nun, the servant of Jehovah, died, being a hundred and ten years old. . . . And also all that generation were gathered unto their fathers: *and there arose another generation after them, that knew not Jehovah,* nor yet the work which he had wrought for Israel. And *the children of Israel did that which was evil in the sight of Jehovah,* and served the Baalim; and they forsook Jehovah, the God of their fathers, who brought them out of the land of Egypt, and followed other gods, of the gods of the peoples that were round about them, and bowed themselves down unto them: and they provoked Jehovah to anger . . and he delivered them into the hands of spoilers."

The far-reaching influence of a godly man, neither afraid nor ashamed to teach the truth, is clearly seen in the life of Joshua. While he and the elders he had directly influenced were yet alive, the people were loyal to Jehovah and faithful to his cause. Apostasy came when "there arose another generation which knew not Jehovah, nor yet the work which he had wrought for Israel." Let it not be overlooked that had the previous generation properly trained its children in the right ways of the Lord, they would not have been beset by the ignorance which led to their downfall. May those who love God, who wish to see his will preserved in the earth and their offspring saved, never forget that children do not, by biological succession, inherit religion; they acquire it through teaching and in this way alone. Whether the religion they thus acquire is true or false depends solely on the type of teaching they receive. Is it not truly shocking that so many parents today—many of them members of the church—are disregarding this obvious fact?

Sadly, the love of ease and the desire to enjoy these bountiful blessings led ultimately to the downfall and eventual destruction of the people of Israel. The command of Jehovah to drive out the idolatrous peoples of the land and to maintain that separateness essential to the preservation of purity of doctrine and life were soon forgotten as they settled down to enjoy their rich inheritance. In direct contravention of God's purpose and plan for them, they launched their own "unity summit," established social and fraternal relationships with the peoples round about, married into their families, and easily and readily accepted their modes of worship and the idols they reverenced. Jehovah, who had given them the land and provided them with the blessings in which they revelled, was first ignored and finally forgotten.

Three things, at least, were responsible for their downfall. (1) The compromise they effected with the heathen peoples—the Canaanites; (2) their covetousness and love of ease; (3) Their tolerance of and loss of any detestation for the wickedness and idolatry about them. Had they obeyed the voice of the Lord, avoided all fraternal relationships and expelled from the land the people responsible for these evil influences, later temptations would not have faced them, nor would they have succumbed to the influences which led them inevitably into apostasy.

These actions led easily and quickly to the second thing responsible for their departure: their willingness to tolerate, and finally to accept the ungodliness of their neighbors, which, in turn, led to the third reason for their fall: the loss of any revulsion or objection to doctrines and practices contrary to the will of Jehovah. Plainly put, their failure to obey the voice of the Lord, and their acceptance of limited fellowship with the

heathen propelled them, step by step, to their own
destruction. The status quo was more alluring and
attractive to them than doing the will of God.

The grave dangers involved in countenancing false
doctrines and unauthorized practices and the disastrous results attending them are nowhere better
evidenced than in this ancient historic event. Inhibi-
tions, resulting from a knowledge of, and a dedication
to the truth, eventually wear down through association
with, and tolerance of those who have no intention of
renouncing their unscriptural actions, and eventually
disappear. We are, alas, seeing this happen in our own
day.

> "Vice is a monster of such frightful mien,
> As to be hated needs but to be seen;
> But seen too oft, familiar with its face,
> We first endure, then pity, them embrace!"

The fatal pattern, so often characteristic of religious
people, quickly appeared in Israel's case. (1) Unwavering faithfulness of Joshua and of his generation; (2) a
second generation which, though it did not apostatize,
lacked the zeal and enthusiasm of the preceding one;
(3) a third generation which slipped easily and quickly
into apostasy. While the second generation did not
apostatize, the *second* generation did not transmit the
truth to the *third* generation with the zeal, emphasis
and fervor with which the first generation transmitted
it to the second, so apostasy came in the third
generation. We are undoubtedly in the second generation here this evening.

How vividly and in stark detail do we see the
contemporary religious scene in the churches of Christ
today exemplified and mirrored in these remarkable
words from that ancient historian. The chilling consequences, resulting from a failure to continue the
message and methods as evidenced in these words,

ought especially to rest upon our hearts, evermore abide in our consciences and prompt us to greater and more intensive efforts in behalf of the "Old Paths."

Note it carefully: so powerful was the impact of truth which Joshua taught on the people of Israel, no apostasy was seen and no departures were observed in that day and generation—nor in the generation which followed. Joshua's contemporaries listened with respect and appreciation to his stirring appeals to maintain faithfulness and loyalty; they witnessed the power of God in the deliverances they had enjoyed from their dangerous and powerful neighbors—the Canaanites—and they saw ample evidence of God's goodness in a land of great bounty and blessing. They were indeed the favored people of Jehovah. They lived in houses they did not build, they drank water from wells they did not dig, they ate the fruit of vineyards they did not plant. Theirs was a goodly land—one the Bible describes as flowing with milk and honey. Nonetheless, they yielded to the evil influences about them, imbibed the sinful practices of their neighbors, and ignored the will and way of the God of their fathers.

Many of us have been at the feet of great and good men of the past who loved the truth and who shunned not to teach and preach the whole counsel of God; and we are therefore fully conversant with the differences between truth and error. Many of us would die rather than to renounce the faith and to turn to denomination-alism. But, while we of the second generation will not forsake the truth for decadent denominationalism, there is the frightening possibility that we are not teaching the truth to the *third* generation with sufficient clarity and emphasis to guard it against eventual apostasy, in which case the imposing meeting houses our brethren have erected at much expense and with great sacrifice will one day serve as temples in which their own grandchildren will do homage to a false and apostate religion. Whether intended or not, those who do not instruct their children in the right way and teach them the truth of the gospel, as set out in the New Testament, will inevitably and eventually face this alternative.

It is fatal to forget that every generation must have all the truth taught to it all over again, or departure and apostasy are the inevitable results. This is easy to overlook and to disregard. Matters, so familiar to us, are by no means so to those who have never heard them; and, the consequences of such neglect is abandonment of those things most dear to the faithful. Some time ago, I heard brother Franklin Camp— faithful, able and dedicated gospel preacher— comment that, in his opinion, the next ten years are especially critical ones for the churches of Christ. I would agree, modifying the statement only to point out that *every* ten years' period is a critical one for the churches of Christ, since this is approximately the period in which each generation receives and formulates those views later to influence and direct its course. An untaught generation, when it moves to maturity and assumes responsibility, lacking in loyalty and conviction, has no hesitancy in abandoning the "Old Paths," and advancing into uncharted areas more palatable to materialistic minds. Like Israel of old, they then do that which is evil in his sight and shall, as Israel was, by him be rejected.

A view rapidly gaining credence among us is that the basic and fundamental facts of Christianity are of only comparative significance—at best are elementary and of minor importance—and may, therefore, be passed over with little, or no emphasis and without danger. Some indeed, do not hesitate to exhibit contempt for them, and for those of us who choose to adhere tenaciously to that which is written. "Why," it is asked, "should the church be concerned about elementary matters when great social and economic ills beset the race?" Such a disposition disregards the fact that a house is no more secure than the foundation that underlies it, and that men build safely only when they build soundly (Matthew 7:24-27). It is as reasonable and as sensible to argue that because geometry and calculus are important in mathematics, addition and subtraction, division and multiplication are not, and may, therefore, without loss, be disregarded. The simple fact is that only by doing our Lord's will here are we assured of salvation and a habitation, "not made with hands," in the heavens, hereafter (Matthew 7:21; 1 John 2:4).

Any generation, which does not respect and cherish its heritage, eventually loses it. Those who do not learn from history the mistakes of earlier generations are destined to repeat them. The Lord has not left us without witness regarding these matters; the Bible abounds with the tragic records of those who, through apostasy, failed their Creator. "For whatsoever things were written aforetime were written for our learning, that through patience and through comfort of the scriptures we might have hope" (Romans 15:4). "Now these things happened unto them by way of example; and they were written for our admonition, upon whom the ends of the ages are come" (1 Corinthians 10:11). "Behold then the goodness and severity of God: toward them that fell, severity; but toward thee, God's goodness: otherwise thou also shalt be cut off" (Romans 11:22).

A half century ago, from our pulpits throughout the land, with rarest exception, a message of power and purity rang out sharply and clearly, and members of the church were traditionally famous for knowing the Book and for their readiness to defend and uphold it. Basic and fundamental teaching was the order of the day; no uncertain sound was tolerated and false teachers were quickly exposed and rejected. Sadly, this is far from the case in our day. How often do you hear sermons these days on the distinctive characteristics of the churches of Christ; the differences which obtain between truth and error; and the sinfulness of denominationalism? When have you listened to a stirring discourse on What must I do to be saved? The identity of the New Testament church, the Work of the Holy Spirit in conviction, conversion and sanctification, the New Birth, and the many other thrilling themes which characterized our preaching a generation gone by?

Not only were those the days of plain and powerful preaching, debates were often conducted with those about us, with the result that multitudes of people learned the truth and obeyed it. Some time ago, a Baptist preacher, who often in days past debated us, was asked why such debates were no longer held. His response was that in those days the type of preaching done by those whom he styled, "Church of Christ preachers," constituted a definite threat to the Baptists and it was therefore necessary to oppose us, and to counteract such teaching. He added that this is no longer so, since most preachers of the church of Christ today seldom, if ever, make any attempt to distinguish between the teaching of the Baptists and that of the churches of Christ.

It is my observation that the Baptist preacher was correct in his analysis of the situation. Many among us are without conviction; often, those of this number resent, rather than support, the plain and uncompromising presentation of the gospel. The preaching they prefer and applaud moves nobody; they want it done in such fashion that people will discover that they are Christians without really knowing how it all happened. The preaching those of this category prefer the preacher to do is weak, insipid, and follows this pattern, "You must believe, as it were; and repent in a measure; or, you'll be lost to some extent!" One of the laments I hear from faithful brethren with increasing regularity over the land where I go is that one so infrequently hears the gospel preached with the power and potency of former days.

I am often told of preachers who seldom (sometimes, never) set out the plan of salvation in their sermons, and in many instances extend no invitation at all. The phraseology often heard is, "If you have a feeling of need, come forward and let us help you." But, it is the solemn and sacred duty of the preacher to *create* a sense of need, by opening the hearts of people so that they will "give heed" to the gospel, as Paul did in Philippi for Lydia and her household (Acts 16:13-15). It is inconceivable that one who styles himself a *gospel* preacher would omit that which is the chief purpose of our preaching—to induce people to obey the gospel, and thus be saved. When brethren protested that in a certain meeting, the design of which was to reach the lost with the gospel, the conditions of salvation were not being mentioned, much less emphasized, the preacher answered, "You think one who does not preach baptism does not preach the gospel." While, of course, baptism is not the whole of the gospel, it is certainly a part of it, and to omit it in one's preaching is to proclaim a mutilated and powerless gospel. Said Paul, "Though we, or an angel from heaven, should preach unto you any gospel other than that which we preached unto you, let him be anathema" (Galatians 1:8).

Evidence of how far men may move away from that which, through the years, has been our finest and best appeal to a lost world, is seen in the fact that there are those among us, in ever increasing numbers, who not only do not feel deep commitment to the Word of truth—the gospel, but who exhibit contempt for those of us who still teach it and insist upon total adherence to it. We are "Bible thumpers," with a "chapter and verse mentality," they like to describe us!

This disposition, to minimize the Word of God, and to regard it as "a dead letter," has long been characteristic of the denominational world, and of those who profess no religion whatsoever, and all of us have had contact with those thus influenced. It is, therefore, doubly sad when men among us show disrespect for the divine volume. Some time ago, one of "our" preachers published a statement in his bulletin saying it would be good for churches of Christ if the *Bible were put out of them for a period of six months*. It is incredible that one posing as a gospel preacher, would make such a statement, and even more incredible that an eldership and congregation would, for one moment, tolerate one who did! Many years ago, brother G.C. Brewer, who went to be with the Lord in the late fifties, a dear friend of mine and, in many respects, an intellectual giant, wrote, "It would be a glorious thing if all so-called members of the churches over the country were forced to sit at the feet of a gospel preacher for a series of six weeks' preaching each year. Gospel preaching would stave off any departures and would create and educate some real Christians to carry on the work of the Lord. There is no substitute for gospel preaching."

When Garland Elkins, whose knowledge of, and ability to aptly quote the Word on any occasion and subject is phenomenal, ably defended the truth on a national talk show, frustrated unbelievers, as unable as were the rebellious Jews of old to withstand the wisdom with which Stephen spoke, said that Elkins was blinded by the Bible! *Blinded* by the Bible. When men call darkness light, and light darkness, how great indeed is the darkness!

Love of the truth and dedication to every basic
principle of New Testament teaching are the distin-
guishing marks of the true children of God; and any
preacher, elder, deacon, Bible school teacher or other
person who will not confess full and unwavering
allegiance to the Word of God, in word and in life,
ought to be rejected. John, beloved disciple of the Lord,
wrote: "And hereby we do know that we know him,
if we keep his commandments. He that saith, I know
him, and keepeth not his commandments, is a liar, and
the truth is not in him. But whoso keepeth his word,
in him verily is the love of God perfected: hereby know
we that we are in him" (1 John 2:3-5). These divine
declarations cannot be disregarded with impunity.
They clearly and unmistakably evidence the fact that
only as we obey the Lord's will and conform to his way
as is taught in his word do we enjoy his approbation
in this life, and have the assurance of salvation in the
life to come.

Jesus said to certain Jews that believed on him, "If
ye continue in my word, then are ye my disciples
indeed; and ye shall know the truth, and the truth
shall make you free" (John 8:31,32). Paul wrote, "But
we are sure that the judgment of God is according to
truth." (Romans 2:2). Error is as basic to the operations
of the devil as the truth is to the cause of our Lord,
who is himself the embodiment of truth. By error Satan
seeks to induce all of those he possibly can to remain
under his control, and subject to his whims, and in
this he is successful so long as they reject, and treat
with contempt, the truth. His schemes are both
numerous and devious; those he cannot ensnare in
one fashion, he seeks to entrap in another. His bait is
often enticing and his methods effective. The basic
principles of Satan have not been altered since the fall
in Eden; they have simply been made more sophisticated, and thus more deceptive and effective. The

devil's goal remains the same: to turn as many of the Lord's people from light to darkness as he possibly can!

He attempts to achieve his purpose either by persuading them to reject the will of God for his own—a direct approach—or, by influencing them to regard the will of God as indicated in the sacred writings as of comparative unimportance, and which may be disregarded at will. The first he attempts to accomplish by prompting people to measure all religious matters by a subjective standard—what they think or feel—regardless of what the Bible says; and the second he effectively operates by inducing people to think that they are at liberty to do *anything they choose in religious matters* provided the Lord has not specifically forbidden these actions! The former effort impeaches divine authority; the latter, its sufficiency. The first says, in effect: "I'll decide, not the Lord, what commands should be obeyed;" the second proposes, "In the absence of a specific prohibition I'll determine what pleases him."

False doctrine is as essential to the operations of the devil as truth is to those of our Lord, who is himself the embodiment of truth. By error Satan seeks to seduce the saints, and to persuade all he can to rebel against the Saviour through whom alone is salvation obtainable. His efforts, in this respect, have been tragically successful; and today millions bow before him having accepted his delusions, and thus put themselves outside the blessings of the faithful.

Whether people prefer to follow their own concepts; or to presume to speak where he has not spoken, either attitude is one of rebellion; and is, in the last analysis, a repudiation of God himself. The first of these has served Satan well in the denominational world by prompting the people therein to reject New Testament teaching regarding what one must do to be saved, the identity of the church, and its manner and mode of worship. In my boyhood days I knew an elderly lady, committed wholly to what was then described as "heartfelt religion," (which was nothing other than the more sophisticated subjectivism which today leads its devotees to follow their feelings in preference to any affirmation of the word), unable to justify by the word of God her views, would exclaim: "I don't care what the fetched old Bible says; I know how I feel." Though most people would shrink from using such phraseology today, many have reached the same conclusion, and for the same reason.

The second—the idea that the scriptures must specifically forbid an act before it is wrong—continues to divide people over unauthorized practices, one of which is the use of a mechanical instrument in connection with the worship of God. Those who thus do now readily concede that it is not taught in the scriptures either by command, precept or example; nevertheless they persist in the practice under the umbrella of an euphemistic phrase, "the hermeneutical principle," by which they really mean, "I can do anything I choose in worship, provided the Lord has not specifically prohibited it." Those who thus do ought to accept, without question, (being logically bound to do so) similarly unauthorized items such as the counting of beads, the sprinkling of babies and dancing in worship, none of these actions being *specifically* forbidden in the New Testament! Any inferential argument they would offer against these and other unspecified acts they are estopped from offering, since the same inferences lead to the rejection of instrumental music in worship, as well. Those who truly respect God's word spurn such liberties with the divine will, determined to operate solely on the premise that **he** *knows best what* **he** *wants us to do in worship to* **him,** *and has so indicated in* **his** *word!*

Consider carefully these words: Moses, the first writer of the Bible warned, "Ye shall not add unto the word which I command you, neither shall ye diminish from it, that ye may keep the commandments of Jehovah your God" (Deuteronomy 4:2). Near the middle of the sacred volume Solomon wrote: "Add thou not unto his words, lest he reprove thee, and thou be found a liar" (Proverbs 30:6). And, just before the curtain of inspiration was finally drawn—as if to provide a final warning of any tampering with the will of God as set out in the scriptures,—in the last book, the last chapter, and near its end, John said, "I testify unto every man that heareth the words of the prophecy of this book, if any man shall add unto them, God shall add unto him the plagues which are written in this book: and if any man shall take away from the words of the book of this prophecy, God shall take away his part from the tree of life, and out of the holy city, which are written in this book" (Revelation 22:18,19).

The slogan, "We speak where the scriptures speak; we are silent where the scriptures are silent; we call Bible things by Bible names, and do Bible things in Bible ways; and, we may properly act only when there is either a direct command, an apostolic example or a necessary inference for the act, or acts, involved," has been abandoned, if it ever was to those who so do a viable and acceptable rule. That there are those among us, in ever increasing numbers, who are not offended by this officious intermeddling with the will of God, who seek fellowship with them, exchange pulpits, have them appear on our lectureships and to write for our papers, evidences how far removed they are from the practices and positions of earlier days. NO compromise involved? This, the Lord will ultimately decide, and the future status of the church reflect.

If we are to maintain a pure faith and a faultless practice, there are certain sacrifices which accompany

it. Unity is indeed an admirable goal; but, it may not
be properly sought and enjoyed at the expense of
compromise or abandonment of truth. "Compromise"
is an ugly word, and describes a detestable practice. It
is possible only when those who thus do have suffered
loss of that deep and abiding belief that the Word of
God is inviolate and that we dare not add to, take from,
or otherwise modify it. Pilate may not have been
among the first to exhibit disrespect for *truth*, but he
was by no means the last, and he *has* had, and
continues to have, many imitators. Some, indeed,
insist that truth is really unattainable, and that the
effort to discover it a useless and unnecessary exercise.
Others—and these have occasionally made themselves
heard among "us"—have advanced the notion that to
urge that "we" have the truth, in contrast to "others,"
is arrogant in spirit, sectarian in disposition, and
dogmatic in doctrine. There are those who actually
affirm that because some of us *claim* to be right, and
to be identified with the New Testament church, and
to it alone, turns us into bigoted sectarians!

It is not unheard of these days for some to say that
"we may be wrong" in doctrine and in practice
ourselves, and therefore there ought never to have
been division and alienation over such matters as
instrumental music, premillennialism, marriage and
divorce, and other issues that have occasioned division
in the past. Was Pilate right, when he airily dismissed
the notion that there is such a thing as truth, after all?
Is it no more than a delusion, a figment of the
imagination? Have we turned mountains into mole-
hills, and resorted to legalism, by an unjustified
insistence that we ought to do only what God has said,
no more, no less, no other? Would we have been better
off if the giants of the faith who fought so vigorously
for a pure faith and biblical practice to insure the
immeasurably rich heritage we now may claim, had

been theological weaklings and religious cowards and such issues would, in consequence, have never appeared? But, what of the alternative? No purity of faith; no loyalty to truth; no commitment to biblical principle? How thankful ought we to be, who are the inheritors of the priceless heritage now ours, that those men, and countless thousands of others from Joshua's day to the present hour, did not think that we may be wrong about what the Book teaches!

If the truth exists; if it is available; if it is within our capability to receive it, why should we not seek it out and, having determined what it is, claim it as our own? Are we sectarians simply because we want to be right, and believe that we are right? Surely, somewhere, sometime, some of the Lord's people must have been right and members of the true church, nothing more, nothing less. If so, may not those who attained to this status be privileged to say so without being liable to the charge that they are narrow-minded bigots and conscienceless sectarians? For several years there have been those among us who see little that is good in the churches of Christ and scarcely anything that is bad in the denominational world. Those of this category often say that we should give up our traditions for the sake of peace, harmony and unity in the religious world. What are these traditions, alleged to be a barrier to the unity we all enjoy seeing?

Those who offer these allegations never specify what they are. They like to tell us that we are so wedded to tradition that we can never harmonize with others in the community; and that we should, for the sake of unity, give them up. Give up what? We may be sure that those characteristics, peculiar to us, which have developed through the years, are not formidable obstacles in uniting with other religious groups; we are not opposed and rejected by the religious community because of the design of our church buildings, hours of assembly on the first day of the week, or the number of songs we sing in worship.

The truth is, they reject us because of basic and fundamental differences over the name, the doctrine, and the practice of the New Testament church: whether men may properly honor the Lord Jesus Christ by wearing human names (Acts 11:26), whether salvation is by faith only (James 2:24-26), whether one may apostatize and fall away from the grace of God and be lost (Galatians 5:4), whether sprinkling and/or pouring are acceptable substitutes for baptism (Romans 6:4), whether baptism in water is for (in order to) the remission of sins (Acts 2:38), whether the Lord's Supper is to be served every first day of the week (Acts 20:7), whether God's praises may be sung to mechanical accompaniment, and many others. These are non-negotiable characteristics of the Lord's church, clearly taught in the scriptures, that separate us from the world around us. Which of these items of truth may we acceptably surrender and give up in order to enjoy fellowship with the denominations, *and still maintain fellowship with the Father, and his Son, Jesus Christ?* (John 14:12; 1 John 1:1-4)

These are matters clearly, plainly and emphatically taught in the Bible. To insist that the church about which we read therein is without distinctive characteristics is absurd; to argue that though they exist, they may be ignored, is unbelief. If we may be in error regarding some, or all, of these matters, it follows, and to the same extent, that the denominations may be right about them—a conclusion those influenced by this reasoning soon reach. This inevitably leads to deterioration of conviction, and a consequent weakening of opposition to any of the doctrines of men. We have, alas, seen this happen, questions raised as to the validity of our plea, hesitancy on the part of those who so do to avow confidence in it, and sharp criticism of those of us who seek to maintain it. It is far from surprising that those who thus do no longer preach with conviction and power the principles and precepts of undenominational Christianity, and that their converts are equally unstable in the faith and without real commitment. "For if the trumpet give an uncertain voice, who shall prepare himself for war?" (1 Corinthians 14:8)

The men responsible for the original proclamation of the gospel entertained no such weakness and uncertainty regarding the message they bore. When efforts were made to silence Peter and John, those courageous disciples, in the face of imprisonment and possible death, responded: "Whether it is right in the sight of God to hearken unto you rather than unto God, judge ye: for we cannot but speak the things which we saw and heard" (Acts 4:13-21). It is edifying and refreshing to note how often boldness is attributed to the first evangelists of the gospel. The Jewish council "beheld the boldness of Peter and John" (Acts 4:13). The disciples prayed that the Lord would look upon the threatening of their opposers and grant until "thy servants to speak thy word with all boldness" (Acts 4:29). Paul, at Damascus, "preached boldly in the name of Jesus" (Acts 9:27). Paul and Barnabas, "spake out boldly" (Acts 13:46), and then later are said to have entered into the synagogue and to have spoken "boldly for the space of three months" (Acts 19:8). The apostle, in Rome, a prisoner of the government, nonetheless taught "the things concerning the Lord Jesus Christ with all boldness" (Acts 28:31). A concordance will list a surprisingly large number of such statements, these being but a few of those recorded. Those men were neither afraid nor ashamed to teach and preach the truth and with great emphasis, however much this may have jeopardized their welfare and personal safety.

We prove ourselves false to the Cause for which the Saviour died when we do not contend earnestly for the faith once delivered to the saints (Jude 3). Children of God are admonished to sanctify Christ as Lord in their hearts and "be ready always to give answer to every man that asketh you a reason concerning the hope that is in you, yet with meekness and fear" (1 Peter 3:15). This necessitates familiarity with, and dedication to, the sacred writings, and the will to defend them. We often sing,

> "I'm not ashamed to own my Lord,
> Nor to defend his cause;
> Maintain the honors of his word,
> The glory of his cross,"

yet, we are often remiss in doing so. The strength and permanence of the Cause of Christ depend on those who represent it; whether the slide to apostasy now so evident will turn into an avalanche will be determined, in large measure, by the degree of faithfulness we of the present day exhibit. Sadly, there are, in every conflict, the "summer soldiers," and the "sunshine patriots," who do not hesitate to abandon the fight when the guns of battle begin to roar; who insist that they do not believe in digression, but who often bitterly criticize the efforts of those who do oppose it. What shooting they do is usually limited to sniping at their own front line soldiers! If they think that only BB guns should be used in defense of the truth, instead of the heavy artillery, they ought at least to use their BB guns!

The leader in the rebellion in the kingdom of Israel which occurred about 975 B.C., and eventuated in division, the establishment of a false religion, a corrupted worship, and an apostate people, was the infamous Jeroboam. He is identified again and again in the Old Testament as "Jeroboam, the son of Nebat

who made Israel to sin" (2 Kings 10:29). Following that
tragic event, when Jeroboam is mentioned he is usually
referred to as the one "who made Israel to sin" (2 Kings
10:29). Following that tragic event, when Jeroboam is
mentioned he is usually referred to as the one "who
made Israel to sin." He did so by leading the people
to believe that Jehovah did not *specifically* forbid his
people to worship him at Bethel, and they were,
therefore, in the absence of such a prohibition, at
liberty to do so at will. The "hermeneutical principle"
is, by no means, a modern discovery! Those thus
deceived ended in apostasy and rejection, and finally
destruction. Jeroboam lives in history as the one "who
made Israel to sin." The church today is the "Israel of
God" (Galatians 6:16). If under a dispensation admittedly inferior to the sunlight age in which we live, God
looked with such great disfavor on a man who led
astray physical Israel, what must he think of those who
would cause spiritual Israel to sin in similar fashion in
our day?

A day of judgment awaits us all. The record of our
lives is being inscribed and from the record thus being
made our destiny will be determined. Whether we
shall appear among those who loved the Lord and who
defended his cause, as did Paul, or whether we shall
live in infamy throughout eternity as will "Jeroboam
the son of Nebat who made Israel to sin," is being
determined here and now by our response to the will
of God as set out in his word. We shall all appear in
that court of last resort (Romans 14:12). From the
heavenly verdict, to be announced at the Last Great
day, there can be no appeal.

DEBATING NOTES ON THE
DESIGN OF WATER BAPTISM*

The plan of salvation—that which the Lord requires of the alien sinner as conditions precedent to the forgiveness of sins—has been a fruitful field of controversy for centuries. With but few exceptions, all agree that there are conditions to be performed by the alien sinner in order to obtain salvation, but what these conditions are, their nature and relation to each other and to the plan of salvation, have long provided occasion for debate.

General, if not universal, agreement obtains regarding the utility of faith, repentance, and in some form, confession. I shall show in this speech that the scriptures as clearly demonstrate that baptism in water is equally essential to salvation. In so doing, the following propositions will be advanced: (1) God has a definite and prescribed law regarding the sinner's approach to him; (2) the sinner cannot be saved except through free and faithful compliance with this law; (3) baptism is a part of this law.

It is not claimed that (1) baptism, *by itself*, is for remission of sins; or that (2) baptism *alone*—that is, when not preceded by belief, repentance and confession of faith—is for the remission of sins; or that (3)

---

*It is believed that I have engaged in more public religious discussions than any man living, in or out of the church, today. In preparation for these debates, now embracing a period of a half century, I have had occasion to examine, in much detail, most books of the brotherhood touching these controversial matters and that of the denominational world, as well. In addition, I have accumulated many notes resulting from my experience in these efforts on a great variety of controversial themes. Here is a condensation of these notes dealing with those passages in the New Testament touching the essentiality of water baptism that I have found to be exceptionally effective. This material is included with the earnest hope that it will be helpful in assisting others to know and to teach the truth on this vital subject.

there is virtue or power or cleansing efficacy in water literally to remove sins. I simply assert, and shall engage to prove, that the Lord has made baptism, in water, along with belief, repentance and confession, a condition precedent to salvation.

(1) Israel, fleeing from the galling and intolerable bondage of Egypt (Exodus 14:13), saw "the salvation of the Lord" when Pharaoh and his hosts were overthrown and perished in the sea; and the people of God were brought safely and triumphantly through its waters, when they had reached the farther shore. They were delivered from the avenging hand of the Egyptian monarch by the waters of the sea; but, the efficacy was in the power of God—not in the water. Notwithstanding, had not Israel, by faith, entered and crossed this barrier, in compliance with the command of Jehovah, the people would have perished, as did Pharaoh and his armies, in the sea. *The waters of the Red Sea were, therefore, an instrument in the hands of God to save Israel.* We shall see that the scriptures clearly evidence the fact that baptism in water, when preceded by faith, repentance and confession is a similar instrument in his hand to save sinners today. (2) When fiery serpents plagued the camp of Israel, Moses caused to be erected in the midst of the camp a *brazen serpent,* and issued instructions to the afflicted people to look upon it and live! (Numbers 21:8). Obviously, the power to heal was not in the object of brass suspended in the camp of the Israelites, but in the command of God; yet, only through compliance with the command did Israel receive deliverance from the plague. (3) Namaan was required to dip *seven times* in the muddy waters of the Jordan river in order to be cleansed of his loathsome disease of leprosy (2 Kings 5:14). It is not of record that the waters of that historic river were before or after thus used; and we may be

sure that the power to heal was not inherent in its waters. Yet, Namaan was not healed until he dipped!

In similar fashion, though water possesses no inherent qualities enabling it literally to wash away sins, I shall demonstrate that the Bible as clearly teaches that only those who are subject to the gospel, and who humbly submit thereto, receive forgiveness of past, or alien, sins. Note that I said, "Those who are subject to the gospel"; I am not to be understood as affirming that (a) infants, (b) idiots, or (c) insane persons are required of God to comply with any conditions! These individuals, not accountable, are not subject to the gospel of Christ and stand in no need of salvation whatsoever. Those not answerable for their actions did not fall within the scope of these commands. They are *in a safe condition;* hence, not *lost,* and thus are in no sense subjects of God's plan to save.

Affirmed is this: an alien sinner (one who has not before made any response to God and is, therefore, not in the kingdom), who believes that Jesus is the Christ, the Son of God, has genuinely repented of all sins, and confessed faith in the Lord (Romans 10:10), is not promised forgiveness until having complied with the command to be baptized in water. This is made crystal clear by a simple induction of all passages mentioning baptism and salvation (or its equivalent) in the New Testament. Note that in *every instance* baptism is mentioned before salvation!

Mark 1:4: "John did baptize in the wilderness, and preach the baptism of repentance for the remission of sins."

Note the order: (1) Baptism. (2) Remission of sins.

Luke 3:3: "And he came into the country about Jordan, preaching the baptism of repentance for the remission of sins."

(1) Baptism. (2) Remission of sins.

Mark 16:16: "He that believeth and is baptized shall be saved."

(1) Baptism. (2) Salvation.

Acts 2:38: "Then Peter said unto them, Repent, and be baptized every one of you in the name of Jesus Christ for the remission of sins, and ye shall receive the gift of the Holy Spirit."

(1) Baptism. (2) Remission of sins.

Acts 22:16: "And now why tarriest thou? arise, and be baptized, and wash away thy sins, calling on the name of the Lord."

(1) Baptism. (2) Sins washed away.

1 Peter 3:21: "The like figure whereunto baptism doth also now save us, (not the putting away the filth of the flesh, but the answer of a good conscience toward God) by the resurrection of Jesus Christ."

(1) Baptism. (2) Salvation.

Is it not significant that in *every instance* when baptism and salvation (or what is equal to it) are mentioned together, salvation always came *only after baptism?*

The reason, to perceptive people, is obvious: baptism is the act in which one turns to God. It has already been shown that God has a law governing the alien sinner's approach to him, and that the sinner is not saved until he has complied with this law. We shall now see that it is in the act of baptism that one turns to God: Acts 3:19 (American Standard Version): "Repent ye therefore, *and turn again*, that your sins may be blotted out, that so there may come seasons of refreshing from the presence of the Lord." Hence, the sinner must "turn again," prior to having sins "blotted out." What is the turning act? (1) It is not belief: Acts 11:21: "A great number believed and turned unto the Lord." These believed and *turned*. Thus, they turned after they believed. The turning act followed belief. (2) It is not repentance. Paul preached

that men "should repent and turn to God" (Acts 11:21).
Their turning thus followed both faith and repentance.
What was the turning act? This parallel makes the
matter crystal clear:

Acts 2:38: Repent   and be baptized for remission of sins.
Acts 3:19: Repent   and *turn*   sins blotted out.

Each item in each verse perfectly corresponds to its
parallel. "Repent" in Acts 2:38 equals "repent" in Acts
3:19, "for remission of sins" in Acts 2:38 is equal to
sins "blotted out" in Acts 3:19; consequently, "be
baptized," in Acts 2:38, is exactly equal to "turn," in
Acts 3:19. It irrefutably follows that one turns to God
only in the act of baptism for the remission of sins
(Matthew 28:18-20).

A LOOK AT SPECIFIC PASSAGES
Mark 16:15, 16

"And he said unto them, Go ye into all the world
and preach the gospel to every creature. He that
believeth and is baptized shall be saved; but he that
believeth not shall be damned."

There is, on the face of this passage, the assumption
that man, in his unregenerate state, is (a) lost; (b) there
is a plan of salvation available to him; (c) with this plan
he must comply in order to be saved. It readily yields
itself to this analysis:

1. The obligation—"go."
2. The sphere—"into all the world."
3. The design—"preach the gospel."
4. The extent—"to every creature."
5. The conditions—belief and baptism.
6. The blessing—"shall be saved."
7. The alternative—"shall be damned."

That portion of the passage dealing with the conditions of salvation may properly be diagrammed and analyzed in this fashion:

"He that believeth and is baptized shall be saved."

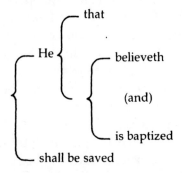

This is a complex, declarative sentence, of which "he that believeth and is baptized," is the complex subject. "He" is the simple subject, modified by a limiting or restrictive clause, "that believeth and is baptized," a simple element of the third class. ". . . that believeth and is baptized," is a partial, compound, subordinate, declarative sentence of which "that" is the simple subject, unmodified, of which subordinate sentence also "believeth and is baptized," is the compound predicate; of which principal sentence "shall be saved" is the simple predicate, unmodified." "And," is a copulative conjunction.

A "he" is under consideration. "He . . . shall be saved." Were the "he" unmodified, universal salvation would here, at least, be affirmed. But, the passage limits the "he" by means of a restrictive clause, "that believeth and is baptized."

What "he" is involved?

All who practice "infant baptism" say: "He that is baptized (when an infant) and later believes (as an adult) shall be saved."

All who teach salvation by faith only say: "He that believeth and is *not baptized* is saved."

The Lord said: "He that believeth *and is baptized* shall be saved."

Baptism and salvation in the passage we are examining, are joined by the coordinating conjunction, "and." It is the function of this conjunction to unite elements of equal rank. The rule of grammar is, "When two or more things are joined together by the coordinating conjunction, 'and,' and something is predicated of them, they stand related to that predicated of them in precisely the same sense." Since belief and baptism are united in this verse by this conjunction, salvation is predicated of both of them in "precisely the same sense."

The coordinating conjunction "and" has the force of the plus (+) sign—something added. The sentence, "He that believeth and is baptized shall be saved," is exactly equivalent to saying that "belief plus baptism equals salvation." Those who advocate salvation by faith only (as do all denominational churches and preachers), really teach that "belief minus baptism equals salvation!"

Consider, in this connection, the following simple equation:

	2	plus	2	=	4.
And,	belief	+	baptism	=	salvation.

	2	minus	2	=	0; therefore
But,	belief	−	baptism	=	nothing!

Moreover, advocates of the doctrine of salvation "by faith only," maintain that one may be saved and go to heaven if never baptized. Consider, for a moment, this remarkable contrast:

"He that believeth AND IS BAPTIZED shall be saved."
"He that believeth AND IS NOT BAPTIZED, shall be saved."

One of these statements must be false, being contradictory to the other. Should there be any difficulty on the part of those who respect the Lord and his word in determining which is true and which is false?

Jesus said: "He that believeth AND IS BAPTIZED shall be saved.
Men say: "He that believeth AND IS NOT BAPTIZED, shall be saved."

Let it be carefully noted that Jesus did not say, "is saved," and "shall be baptized." It is "IS BAPTIZED," and "SHALL BE" saved. Those who deny the essentiality of baptism, yet maintain that it is a condition of church membership, must change the tense of the verbs in order to conform to their perversion of this verse, thus making him say, "He that believeth IS SAVED, and SHALL THEN BE baptized."

Those who would strike baptism from the plan of salvation often point out that while the Lord said, "He that believeth and is baptized shall be saved," he simply added, "he that believeth not shall be damned," omitting, "and is not baptized," from the latter sentence, whence it is inferred that it must not be a condition of salvation if its omission is not a condition of damnation. Those offering this objection overlook the fact that the passage sets out two conditions of salvation, faith and baptism, each by our Lord being specified and equally necessary; whereas, one who does not believe need not add additional acts of disobedience, since "He that believeth not is condemned already" (John 3:18). Jesus further said, "He that believeth not God hath made him a liar" (1 John 5:10). Obviously, one who would thus insult the Creator need not advance to other acts of disobedience in order to be condemned! Furthermore, an unbeliever is not a subject of baptism. It is the believer who has the "power" (Greek, *exousia*, liberty of action), to become a son of God (John 1:11,12).

The Lord does not deal in nonsense, as would have been the case had he added the words, "and is not baptized," to the condemnatory section of Mark 16:16. These illustrations will make this clear:

1. He that diggeth a cistern and walleth it up with brick, shall receive $1,000.00; but he that diggeth it not shall receive nothing.

2. He that eateth and digesteth his food shall live; but he that eateth not shall die.

Should one add to the first illustration, "and does not wall it up," and to the second, "and does not digest his food?" To do so would be to resort to absurdity! As one cannot wall up a cistern never dug, nor digest food never eaten, so one cannot refuse to be baptized to whom baptism was never applicable. Only believers are subjects of baptism. Jesus said, "Except ye repent, ye shall all likewise perish" (Luke 13:3-5). He did not say, "Except ye repent and believe . . ." If, because he did not say, in Mark 16:16, "and is not baptized shall be damned," baptism is shown to be nonessential, it would follow that because Jesus did not say, "except ye repent and believe," in Luke 13:3, faith is therefore shown to be unnecessary. Let it be remembered and never forgotten: Jesus joined belief and baptism in Mark 16:16. That which the Lord joins let not men put asunder. He who would thus divorce what the Lord has joined is surely engaged in sorry business indeed!

There is a rule of interpretation which knows no exception:

"Where the Lord has promised salvation only on conditions he names, while it may depend on more conditions than those designated in any specific passage, it can never depend on fewer ones."

Mark 16:15,16 well illustrates this rule. It mentions two conditions, belief and baptism. It does not, however, mention all conditions essential to salvation, since neither the confession nor repentance is specifically included. They are implied, however, being elsewhere taught (Luke 13:3; Romans 10:10); and may, therefore be properly added, as conditions precedent to salvation; and, on the basis of this rule, baptism may not properly be subtracted. All passages dealing with salvation fall under it; and to urge that repentance, tholugh not mentioned, is implied, while rejecting baptism on the same grounds (as e.g. in John 3:16), is an unjustifiable and arbitrary action leading those who do so into grave error.

It is interesting and edifying to note that
Water baptism

1. Stands between the sinner and salvation (Mark 16:16)

2. Stands between the sinner and remission of sins (Acts 2:38)

3 Stands between the sinner and washing (Acts 22:16)

4. Stands between the sinner and calling (Acts 22:16)

5. Stands between the sinner and death of Christ (Romans 6:3)

6. Stands between the sinner and new creature (2 Corinthians 5:17)

7. Stands between the sinner and putting on Christ (Galatians 3:27)

8. Stands between the sinner and cleansing (Ephesians 5:26)

9. Stands between the sinner and sanctification (Ephesians 5:26)

10. Stands between the sinner and putting away sins (Colossians 2:11f)

11. Stands between the sinner and new life in Christ (Ephesians 2:6)

12. Stands between the sinner and quickened with Christ (Ephesians 2:5)

13. Stands between the sinner and forgiveness (Colossians 1:13)

14. Stands between the sinner and the kingdom (John 3:5)

15. Stands between the sinner and blood of Christ (John 19:34)

16. Stands between the sinner and a good conscience (1 Peter 3:21)

17. Stands between the sinner and promise thru Christ (Acts 2:39)

18. Stands between the sinner and the body of Christ (1 Corinthians 12:12)

19. Stands between the sinner and salvation (1 Peter 3:21)

20. Stands between the sinner and sonship (Galatians 3:26,27)

ACTS 2:37,38

"Now when they heard this, they were pricked in their heart, and said unto Peter and to the rest of the apostles, Men and brethren, what shall we do? Then Peter said unto them, Repent, and be baptized every one of you in the name of Jesus Christ for the remission of sins, and ye shall receive the gift of the Holy Ghost. For the promise is unto you, and to your children, and to all that are afar off, even as many as the Lord our God shall call."

It will at once be seen that Peter's response was in answer to the question, "Men and brethren, what shall we do?" Do for what? Obviously to obtain remission of sins for so Peter understood them, and proceeded to set out the answer, "Repent and be baptized . . . for the remission of sins." It follows, therefore, that whatever the response to such a query might have been under earlier dispensations, and prior to the establishment of the church which occurred on this day, the apostle Peter, by inspiration, gave the proper answer applicable to an alien sinner in this, the Christian age. If we regard his answer as an expression of one's obligation to God, aside from the specific reasons given, it becomes crystal clear what it is: "Men and brethren, what shall we do?" Answer: "Repent and be baptized for the remission of sins." If, however, we look at the verse from the standpoint of the reason given and the blessing attending the duty, we have it thus: "Men and brethren, what shall we do to obtain the remission of sins?" Again, the answer is unmistakable: "Repent and be baptized." In either instance, the meaning is obvious: It is the obligation of all accountable beings to "repent and be baptized for the remission of sins."

Grammatical analysis of the passage leads irresistibly to the same conclusion. The rule is,

"Coordinate connectives connect similar grammatical elements, and put them in equal ranks."

In the sentence, "Repent and be baptized for the remission of sins," the coordinate conjunction "and" is the connective. The verbs, "repent," and "be baptized," being similar grammatical elements, are put in equal ranks, and thus are related in precisely the same way to that affirmed of them—in this case, "the remission of sins." There is a second rule of grammar applicable here:

"When two or more elements are joined together by the "coordinating conjunction "and," and something is predicated of them, they stand related to that predicated of them in exactly the same sense." This may well be seen in the first verse of the Bible: "In the beginning God created the heaven and the earth" (Genesis 1:1). The nouns "heaven," and "earth," are joined by the coordinating conjunction "and." They thus stand related to that affirmed of them in precisely the same way, i.e., God created them. Though the words, "heaven," and "earth," differ greatly in significance, what is affirmed of them in this passage is exactly the same: God created them. Similarly, though "repentance," and "baptism," differ as to the nature of the actions each involves, they are identical in that which is affirmed of them by Peter: they are "for the remission of sins." What repentance is "for," baptism is "for," and Peter so asserts in this passage. Each, when taken together is "for the remission of sins." The following diagram and parallel establishing this fact cannot be successfully controverted:

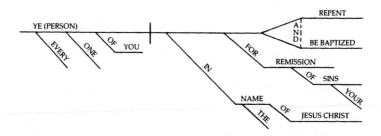

"Ye," is the subject; "repent and be baptized every one of you in the name of Jesus Christ for the remission of sins," is the compound predicate. "Ye" is modified by "person," (understood) which is in apposition with "ye," the subject, and is modified by "every," and "one," these being adjectival elements. "Repent and be baptized," are modified by the phrases, "in name" and "for remission," adverbial elements. "Name" is modified by the adjectival element "the," and the phrase, "of Jesus Christ," which is also an adjectival element, as is the phrase, "of sins." "Sins," is modified by "your," a possessive pronoun.

Without the modifiers, the passage reads: "Repent and be baptized for the remission of sins." A diagram of it, and a parallel evidences beyond reasonable doubt the meaning of this vital passage:

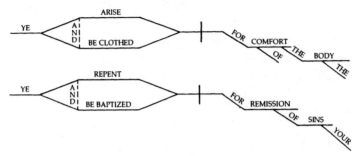

The word "for," in the sentence, "Repent and be baptized for the remission of sins," is translated from the Greek preposition, "eis." Henry Thayer, renowned lexicographer, defines it as "a preposition governing the Accusative, and denoting entrance into, or direction and limit: into, to, towards, for, among" (page 183). Moreover, on page 94 of his lexicon, Mr. Thayer cites Acts 2:38, and defines the phrase *eis aphesin hamartioon,* translated "for the remission of sins," in the King James Version, and "unto the remission of sins," in the American Standard Translation, to mean "to obtain the remission of sins." Arndt and Gingrich's Greek Lexicon, one of the most popular and widely used Greek dictionaries in use today, cites Acts 2:38, along with Matthew 26:28, Mark 1:4, Luke 3:3, to illustrate the usage, *eis aphesin hamartioon,* and defines the preposition and the phrase, "for forgiveness of sins, so that sins might be forgiven" (page 228).

An interesting and informative parallel, shedding further light on the significance of the preposition *eis,* the meaning of the word "for," in Acts 2:38, and the phrase, "remission of sins," of which it is a part follows:

The Lord said, "For this is my blood of the New Testament, which is shed for many for the remission of sins" (Matthew 26:28).

Peter responded to the query, "Men and brethren, what shall we do?" by saying, "Repent and be baptized . . . for the remission of sins" (Acts 2:38). We have earlier noted that the words, "for the remission of sins," translates the Greek phrase, *eis aphesin hamartioon.* and that *eis* is a preposition signifying direction and limit and means, according to all reliable lexicographers, "to obtain." *Aphesin,* accusative singular of *aphesis,* means "forgiveness," pardon of sins (prop. "the letting them go, as if they had not been committed.") (Thayer.) *Hamartioon,* plural of *hamartia,* is defined by the same authority as "a failing to hit the mark, sinning, that which is done wrong."

It will be observed that both passages—Matthew 26:28 and Acts 2:38—have the phrase, "for remission of sins," and the words are identical both in Greek and English.

Jesus shed his blood, "for remission of sins."

The Greek phrase is *eis aphesin hamartioon.*

Peter said, "Repent and be baptized for remission of sins."

The Greek phrase is, *eis aphesin hamartioon.*

Let it be carefully noted that in each instance, the phrase, translated "for remission of sins," is *eis aphesin hamartioon.*

Obviously, our Lord did not shed his blood "because" our sins are forgiven, but in order that they might be. The meaning of Acts 2:38 thus becomes clear: alien sinners are to "repent and be baptized," in order that their sins may be forgiven.

To this end, genuine Greek scholars, whatever may be their denominational preferences testify, among them some distinguished Baptist theologians. Dr. H. B. Hackett, in his commentary on Acts, wrote: "In order to the forgiveness of sins we connect, naturally, with both the preceding verbs. This clause ['for the remission of sins,' GNW] states the motive or object which should induce them to repent and be baptized. It enforces the entire obligation, not one part of it to the exclusion of the other" (page 53). This eminent Baptist scholar did not hesitate to state plainly the relationship of repentance and baptism, to remission of sins.

Dr. Alvah Hovey, who wrote the commentary on John in the most scholarly series of commentaries ever prepared in that denomination said with reference to Acts 2:38: "Repent and be baptized every one of you in (or upon) the name of Jesus Christ unto the remission (or forgiveness) of your sins (Acts 2:38 ASV). Here repentance and baptism are represented as leading to the forgiveness of sins." (Commentary on John, Appendix, page 420.) Dr. C. B. Williams, a long time professor of Greek in Union University, Jackson, Tennessee, a Baptist institution, who prepared and published a translation of the Greek Testament, rendered Acts 2:38, "Peter said unto them, You must repent, and as an expression of it, let every one of you be baptized in the name of Jesus Christ, *that you may have your sins forgiven.*" Did time and space permit, many other denominational scholars might similarly be cited.

When the Greek preposition *eis* stands between a command and a blessing, it always makes that command essential to that blessing. An induction of instances where the preposition *eis* and salvation, or its equivalent occur, demonstrates vividly this fact:

Believe . . . EIS . . . . Righteousness (Romans 10:10.)
Repent . . . EIS . . . . Life (Acts 11:18.)
Confess . . . EIS . . . . . . Salvation (Romans 10:10.)
Baptized . . . EIS . . . . Christ (Romans 6:3, 4)
Repent
and
Baptized . . . EIS . . . . . Remission of sins (Acts 2:38)

Advocates of the doctrine of salvation by faith only

(compare James 2:24-26), have sought to avoid the foregoing obvious conclusion by asserting that in Acts 2:38, "repent," is second person plural, and "be baptized," is third person singular, and that the two cannot properly be joined together to obtain the same result. This objection, however, is as invalid grammatically, as the "faith only" position is as false biblically.

The grammatical rule is, "A masculine noun in the singular, with the article, is often used collectively to denote the whole class. The singular in all such cases presents the distinctive characteristic more exclusively and more forcibly than the plural, designating, as the latter does, a multitude of individuals. Similar to this construction is the use of the singular to express, in reference to a plurality, an object which belongs to each of the individuals." Liddell & Scott, in their classic Greek lexicon, say: "The singular is often joined with a plural verb—they went home—every one of them. The singular is also put in apposition with a plural noun—fear seized them every one." (Eighth edition, New York, 1897. Page 428.) Thayer, in defining *ekastos* ("every one of you," Acts 2:38), says that this word, when "it denotes individuality, every one of many is often added appositively to nouns and pronouns and verbs in the plural."

This construction, and manner of speaking, is done by us all regularly, and it is absurd to say that it is impossible to associate a verb, second person plural, joined by "and" with a verb in the third person singular, to obtain a result dependent on both verbs. The following instances will demonstrate the falsity of the allegation.

"Ye children," (second person plural), "and every one of your ancestors" (third person singular), "descended from Adam and Eve."

"Come ye," (second person plural), "and be washed

every one of you" (third person singular), "for the cleansing of your bodies."

"Turn ye," (second person plural), "and be ye inoculated every one of you" (third person singular) "for the prevention of flu."

Note this biblical instance, "But ye," (second person plural), "that did cleave unto the Lord your God are alive every one of you" (third person singular), "this day" (Deuteronomy 4:4).

Compare the foregoing with the words of Peter, "Repent, and be baptized every one of you in the name of Jesus Christ for the remission of sins."

In the light of the foregoing facts, it is the sheerest folly to deny that baptism sustains the same relation to remission of sins that repentance does; and, since men are required to repent for (in order to) the remission of sins, and are here told also to be baptized for (in order to) the remission of sins, it follows that baptism is for (in order to) the remission of sins as much so and to the same extent as repentance is. Our Lord, in the great commission, enjoined baptism, as a condition of salvation, and sent the apostles abroad with instruction to make disciples of all nations by teaching them the gospel, and by baptizing them in order that they might be saved (Matthew 28:18-20; Mark 16:15,16). Peter, on the day of Pentecost, in the first public proclamation of this message specifically carried out the will of the Lord who said, "He that believeth AND IS BAPTIZED shall be saved," by telling his hearers, "Repent, and be baptized every one of you in the name of Jesus Christ for the remission of sins." To disregard, or to seek to avoid this clear and plain affirmation of the inspired apostle is not only to imperil one's soul, it is to put oneself into precisely the same position as that of the rebellious lawyers and Pharisees "who rejected the counsel of God against themselves, being not baptized of him" (Luke 7:29,30).

Strangely, in spite of, and despite this decisive teaching of the New Testament regarding the essentiality of baptism "for the remission of sins," there are those who oppose it on the ground that it places a third party between one and his God. This is not a valid objection for many reasons.

1. There is absolutely nothing in the scriptures which should lead one to suppose that there are not third parties connected with man's duty to God.

2. In every instance of conversion in the New Testament a third party was present. To confirm this, examine any of the cases of conversion in the book of Acts.

3. Under the plan of salvation today prevailing under this, the Christian dispensation it is impossible to comply with God's conditions leading to salvation without a third party being present. Nothing is taught more emphatically in the sacred writings than the fact that "third parties" are necessary in order to the proclamation of the great commission and the discharge of its details by preaching it and making disciples by baptizing them! (Matthew 28:18-20).

4. It "pleased God by the foolishness of preaching to save them that believe" (1 Corinthians 1:21). Were it possible to be saved without the presence and assistance either actually or substantially of a third party it would not please God!

It should never be forgotten that the *baptism* of the New Testament that is "for the remission of sins," is an *immersion* in water and "into the name of the Father and of the Son and of the Holy Spirit" (Matthew 28:18-20). The noun, "baptism," is the rendering of the Greek word *baptismos,* and it, in turn, derives from the root *bapto,* "to dip." Neither the root not any of its derivatives may properly be rendered other than to immerse or to dip, and no reliable scholar ever so rendered them. Biblical baptism can be administered only by being immersed in water. Paul, in Romans 6:3, 4 asserts, in so many words, that it is a *burial*. And, to it, only those capable of believing the gospel (Mark 16:16), are its subjects. Infants cannot comply with the obligations of salvation, and there is no instance of such in the Bible. Not being lost, they have no need of salvation. The doctrine of sprinkling, as a substitute for baptism, and "infant baptism" are equally false (Matthew 18:3).

GALATIANS 3:23-29

"But before faith came we were kept under the law, shut up unto the faith which should afterwards be revealed. Wherefore the law was our schoolmaster to bring us unto Christ, that we might be justified by faith. But after that faith is come, we are no longer under a schoolmaster. For ye are all the children of God by faith in Christ Jesus. For as many of you as have been baptized into Christ have put on Christ. There is neither Jew nor Greek, there is neither bond nor free, there is neither male nor female: for ye are all one in Christ Jesus. And if ye be Christ's, then are ye Abraham's seed, and heirs according to the promise." From this interesting and significant statement these conclusions follow:

1. There was a time "before faith came."
2. It (faith) was afterwards revealed.
3. It could not have been known before it was revealed.
4. Those who lived before it had been "revealed" could not have been saved by it.
5. Faith, as an assent of the mind—the act of believing— has from the earliest ages existed, and been a condition of salvation (Hebrews 11:1ff).
6. It follows, therefore, that the "faith" of the foregoing passage is not synonymous with "belief."

Faith, under the figure of the synecdoche (a part of the whole and the whole for a part), is often made to represent more, much more, than the act of believing. Occasionally, all the conditions of salvation are by it implied, (Romans 5:1, is an example of this). Sometimes it stands for God's entire scheme of redemption, in which case it signifies the gospel plan of salvation. Note this example: "Knowing that a man is not justified by the works of the law, but by THE FAITH of Jesus Christ, even we have believed in Jesus Christ, that we might be justified by THE FAITH of Christ" (Galatians 2:16). Clearly, the "faith of Jesus Christ," is not belief that Christ exercises, but the system of faith of which he is the Author—the gospel. In the Greek text, the article appears before the word *faith* several times in the foregoing passage which, if translated, would read "Before THE FAITH came we were kept under the law . . . Ye are all children of God by THE FAITH in Christ Jesus."

The "faith" of the passage is thus conclusively shown to be a system of faith, i.e., the gospel, the belief of which enables one to have the privilege ("right of action," John 1:11,12), to become a child of God.

Affirmed is that the Galatians (these being the antecedent of the personal pronoun "ye") were children of God by a system of faith, otherwise identified in the scriptures as the gospel (Romans 1:13-17).

They were children of God, "in Christ Jesus," the sphere in which this right became a reality. Thus, in Christ they were required to be before the blessings of sonship were theirs. Into Christ it was, then, necessary for them to pass. We shall, in a moment, see how they entered into this sphere.

It is sometimes urged that the passage teaches that the Galatians became children of God as the result of their having believed (or trusted) in Christ. There are two conclusive reasons why this cannot possibly be. (1) We have observed already that "the faith" of the passage is not synonymous with belief, but designates the gospel system of salvation. Literally, the verse runs, "Ye are all children of God by a faith system—the gospel." (2) Were the objection factual, the phrase "in Christ," would, of necessity, be in the accusative case—the case of the object in the Greek text. But, it is not in the accusative case, but in the locative—the case of sphere or location, and signifies that the *Galatians were children of God by a system of faith in the sphere of Christ.* In this sphere then must one be to be a child of God by His system of faith.

Thus, the passage locates salvation—in Christ.

1. Is it reached by merely believing? No.
2. Is it by faith only or faith alone? No.
3. Is it by faith OUT OF CHRIST? Certainly not!

The Galatians were children of God IN CHRIST.
How did they get into Christ?

The verse following (Galatians 3:27), tells us plainly, clearly, unmistakably.

"For as many of you as have been baptized into Christ have put on Christ."

The preposition *into* is a term denoting relationship. The Galatians, at the time when Paul penned the passage under study, were "in Christ." They are said to sustain this position because they had been baptized *into* him. Prior to their baptism, in water, they were *out of Christ.* Not until they were baptized were they in him, in whom alone are all spiritual blessings (Ephesians 1:3).

The American Standard translation of Galatians 3:26, 27, with closer attention to the tenses of the verbs reads,

"For ye are all sons of God, through faith in Christ

Jesus. For as many of you as were baptized into Christ did put on Christ."

Let it be noted that the verb of verse 26 is in the present tense, "ye *are* all sons of God in Christ Jesus." At the time Paul penned these words the Galatians were sons of God. The verb is in the present tense. However, in the verse following (Galatians 3:27), the verb changes to the past: "For as many of you as *were baptized* (past tense) into Christ did put on Christ." Why the change in the tenses? Why did he write, "Ye ARE sons . . . " but . . . you WERE BAPTIZED into Christ?

In the nature of the case it had to be. The only way in which it was possible for Paul, the apostle, to write that the Galatians *are* (presently) sons of God, was because he was also able to point out that they *had been* (previously) baptized!

Therefore, You ARE if you WERE!

You are what? Sons of God if you were what? If you were baptized into him! It must follow, for all thoughtful people respectful of the authority of God's word and desirous of doing his will, that only those who have believed the gospel, have repented of their sins, have confessed their faith and have been baptized INTO CHRIST, may properly be styled sons of God.

It is edifying to observe how verse 27 is joined to verse 26:

"For ye are all the children of God by faith in Christ Jesus. FOR as many of you as have been baptized into Christ have put on Christ." The word "for" as here used is not a preposition, but a conjunction; and its lexical significance is "to introduce the reason." Stated in verse 26 is a conclusion. This conclusion is that the Galatians were children of God in Christ Jesus. "For," (to introduce the reason): they had been baptized INTO CHRIST.

These incontrovertible facts should be deeply etched into our minds and inscribed in our hearts. Verse 26 *locates* salvation. (In Christ.) Verse 27 tells *how* it is reached—by being baptized into HIM. The text affirms that one is a child of God by faith when "in Christ." But, one is baptized into Christ; therefore, one is a child of God by faith only following baptism (immersion) in water. Those who have so done are,

1. In Christ. (Galatians 3:27).
2. Are heirs according to the promise God made to Abraham (verse 29).
3. In a relationship where there is neither Jew nor Greek, neither bond nor free, neither male nor female, where all have equal blessings.
4. Are children of God by faith.

Consequently, those who have not been baptized,
1. Are not in Christ.
2. Are not heirs according to the promise.
3. Are in a relationship where distinctions exist.
4. Are not children of God by faith.

But, it may be said, did not the Lord, in John 3:16, say that "whosoever believeth in him should not perish but have everlasting life," thus making salvation dependent on believing, but mentioning nothing about water baptism, hence, in effect, excluding it from his plan to save? If so, *he excluded repentance from the plan of salvation as well, because he did not mention it in this passage either!* But, we will be told, "Repentance is taught as essential elsewhere in the New Testament," as indeed it is, and so also is water baptism, as I have already abundantly shown. We must not overlook the rule earlier given that
"Where salvation is promised to a person, or affirmed of him on certain named conditions, though it may depend on MORE conditions than those named, it can never depend on LESS."
Neither in John 3:16, nor elsewhere in the scriptures, is salvation conditioned on faith only; indeed, it is

expressly said not to be: "Ye see then how that by works a man is justified, and not by faith only. . . . For as the body without the spirit is dead, so faith without works is dead also" (James 2:24,26).

It would be well, at this juncture, to see exactly what is said in John 3:16. "For God so loved the world, that he gave his only begotten Son, that whosoever believeth in him should not perish, but have everlasting life."

Some questions are in order: Did the Lord say,

1. Whosoever believeth Christ should not perish? No.
2. Did he say, "Whosoever believeth *out of Christ* should not perish?" No.

Let it be observed that under consideration here is a believer—not just any believer, but a positioned one. The position of the believer contemplated here is *in Christ*. Of him the promise of life is affirmed. Why? Because he is a believer? No, see especially John 12:42, 43. Why, then? because he is *in Christ*. Note, in this connection, the context of the passage in the American Standard translation:

"And as Moses lifted up the serpent in the wilderness, even so must the Son of man be lifted up; that whosoever believeth may in him have eternal life. For God so loved the world, that he gave his only begotten Son, that whosoever believeth on him should not perish, but have eternal life" (John 3:14-16). Verse 15 reads, "That whosoever believeth may *in him* have eternal life." Note the prepositional phrase, "in him." Only a certain believer is promised eternal life. What believer? The one "in him." In whom? Christ Jesus our Lord. But how does one get into him? Having believed the gospel, having repented of one's sins, having confessed one's faith in Christ, one is then baptized INTO him (Galatians 3:27; Romans 6:3, 4).

ACTS 22:16

Saul of Tarsus, persecutor of Christians, and carrying letters of authority from the chief priests in Jerusalem to seize and to bind and to bring to Jerusalem for punishment those who called on the name of the Lord, was on a mission to Damascus, a city of Syria, in order to pursue his infamous designs. As he drew near that distant city, there "shown from heaven a great light round about" him, and he heard a voice saying, "Saul, Saul, why persecutest thou me?" He answered, "Who art thou, Lord?" The answer came, "I am Jesus of Nazareth, whom thou persecutest." Saul, in response, said, "What shall I do, Lord?" Jesus answered, "Arise, and go into Damascus: and there it shall be told thee of all things which are appointed for thee to do."

The determined persecutor, blinded by a light above the brightness of the Syrian sun, was "led by the hand of them that were with" him, and eventually was brought into Damascus. Meantime, Ananias, a gospel preacher, had been sent to him, and on approaching him, said: "The God of our fathers hath chosen thee, that thou shouldest know his will, and see that Just One, and shouldest hear the voice of his mouth. For thou shalt be his witness unto all men of what thou hast seen and heard. And now why tarriest thou? arise, and be baptized, and wash away thy sins, calling on the name of the Lord" (Acts 9:1-20; 22:1:21).

Saul, having *believed* on Jesus, having *repented of his sins*, and having *confessed* Christ, as evidenced by his appeal to Jesus for some intimation of his duty and his response thereto, was told,

"And now why tarriest thou? arise, and be baptized, and wash away thy sins, calling on the name of the Lord."

An analysis of the passage reveals that there are three commands:

1. Arise.
2. Be baptized.
3. Wash away sins.

"Calling on the name of the Lord."

The preceding commands are joined by the copulative conjunction, *and*. Each was obligatory on Saul, and all were necessary in order to his forgiveness. The contention sometimes offered that Saul's sins were forgiven prior to his baptism, or, that he was baptized because his sins were already forgiven, is in direct conflict with what the passage says: "Arise, (the first condition), "be baptized" (second condition), *and* (by so doing, this being an additional action required) "wash away" sins. Note a parallel:

Arise, take aspirin, and sweat away thy fever.
Arise, be baptized, and wash away thy sins.

Aspirin taken because fever is already gone???
Here, as always, in this, the Christian age, baptism, in water, stood between the sinner and remission of sins. There is an exact parallel here with Acts 2:38.
1. Repent and be baptized . . . for remission of sins.
2. Arise, be baptized and wash away thy sins.

Note that washing in this passage is not baptism, but follows it, just as remission of sins was not baptism but followed it as it does in Acts 2:38.
It is often alleged that Saul was saved at the moment he fell to the earth on the Damascus road and, therefore, long before he was baptized.

When was Saul saved?

1. When the light appeared? If so, before he knew who Jesus is.
2. When he asked what to do? If so, before he knew he was lost.
3. When sent into the city? If so, before Jesus knew it.
4. While praying? If so, before Ananias knew it.
5. Why praying and fasting? If so, a very miserable "Christian."
6. When Ananias laid hands upon him? Did not know then what to do.
7. Before he was baptized? If so, before his sins were washed away.

Thus, if Saul of Tarsus was saved on the Damascus road, the Lord did not know it, those traveling with Saul did not know it, Saul did not know it, and Ananias did not know it! If Saul was saved before he was baptized, he was saved and yet in his sins! Is it not strange, in the light of these facts, that anyone would deny that it was necessary for Saul, in order to be saved to "arise, and be baptized and wash away thy sins, calling on the name of the Lord?" Or, that if such was his duty, as indeed it was, it is any less ours? See, especially in this connection, Philippians 4:9.

What is the significance of the words, "calling on the name of the Lord?" The rule of grammar is that a participle, following an injunction, describes the manner in which the action is carried out. Note this example:

"Cleanse the floor, sweeping it," i.e., cleanse it, by sweeping it. "Sweeping" indicates the manner in which the action (cleanse) is carried out. Here is a statement to this end in the scriptures: "It shall come to pass that whosoever shall call upon the name of the Lord shall be saved" (Acts 2:21).

Hence, "be baptized, and wash away thy sins, calling on the name of the Lord," i.e., calling on the Lord by being baptized. To "call" on the Lord is much, much more than saying, "Lord, Lord." "Not every one that saith unto me, Lord, Lord, shall enter into the kingdom of heaven; but he that doeth the will of my Father which is in heaven" (Matthew 7:21).

"Water cannot *literally* wash away sins," we are told. No. Neither does blood literally wash away sins. But, our Lord had to die in order that our sins might be forgiven (Matthew 26:28); and Saul, in being told what he *must* do to have remission of sins (Acts 9:6), was required to "arise, and be baptized, and wash away thy sins, calling on the name of the Lord." Thus, baptism is in order to, or "for" remission of sins (Acts 2:38).

1 PETER 3:18-22

"For Christ hath once suffered for sins, the just for the unjust, that he might bring us to God, being put to death in the flesh, but quickened by the Spirit: by which also he went and preached unto the spirits in prison; which sometime were disobedient, when once the longsuffering of God waited in the days of Noah, while the ark was a preparing, wherein few, that is, eight souls were saved by water. The like figure whereunto even baptism doth also now save us (not the putting away of the filth of the flesh, but the answer of a good conscience toward God), by the resurrection of Jesus Christ: who is gone into heaven, and is on the right hand of God; angels and authorities and powers being made subject unto him."

The salvation of Noah and his family is said to have been a "figure" (American Standard version: *antitype*) of our salvation in this, the Christian age, from the world of sin. As the waters of the flood was the line of demarcation separating the old world and that washed by the flood, so baptism is said here to be the dividing line between the world of sinful people and the people of the Lord. There are those who say that baptism is itself merely a figure, and thus an empty and meaningless thing. The passage does not say that baptism is a figure. The figure (antitype) was in the deliverance of Noah and his family by the flood prefiguring the deliverance from the world of sin available to those who submit to baptism—the dividing line between the sinful and the saved today.

Only a substance can cast a shadow. Noah's salvation was the shadow (accomplished by means of the waters of the flood), as our salvation (achieved through the waters of baptism) is the substance. If it be argued that Noah's salvation, because it is described as a "figure" (type), means that it is an empty and insignificant thing, note what such an argument does for heaven:

"Christ is not entered into the holy places made with hands, which are the FIGURES of the true; but into heaven itself, there to appear in the presence of God for us" (Hebrews 9:24).

Holy places on earth . . . . "THE FIGURE?"
Heaven . . . . "THE SUBSTANCE?"

Noah's salvation . . . . "THE FIGURE?"
Baptism . . . . "THE SUBSTANCE?"

1. God used WATER to deliver Noah and his family.
2. God uses WATER to deliver us from a sinful state.

The entire Mosaic economy was a FIGURE or TYPE of Christianity; are we then to conclude that there is no real salvation in Christianity today?

The objection is occasionally offered that baptism must not be a condition of salvation because 1 Peter 3:21 asserts that it is "the answer of a good conscience." But, a good conscience is not salvation. Paul, then Saul of Tarsus, had a good conscience while persecuting Christians! (Acts 23:1).

The passage says, we are told, that it is not the function of baptism to save because it is specifically said not to remove "the filth of the flesh." But, the filth of the *flesh* is not synonymous with the scarlet stain of sin on the soul! "Filth," from the Greek word "rupos," simply signifies that which is dirty. This command of God—to be baptized—was not designed to serve as a bath to remove dirt, but a condition precedent on the basis of which God removes the guilt of sin from our souls. It is sometimes said that Noah and his family were saved before the waters came. But, such an objection is against the text itself! It says eight souls, consisting of Noah and his family, were "saved by water." Were they?

Any "explanation" of 1 Peter 3:21, which asserts that we ARE NOT saved by baptism is not an explanation; it is a *contradiction*.

Let this question be seriously considered:
From WHAT DOES BAPTISM save?

Not from sickness or physical infirmity,
Not from sorrow, grief, and death.
Not from persecution and evil treatment.

It is the final act of obedience in God's plan to save the sinner from the guilt of sin (Mark 16:15,16).

When does BAPTISM save?

Not at some future date, since the passage declares that it NOW saves.

Which of the following statements is true:

BAPTISM DOTH ALSO N O W SAVE US
BAPTISM DOTH ALSO N O T SAVE US

HOW WAS NOAH SAVED:

1. By grace: He "found favor in the eyes of the Lord" (Genesis 6:8).
2. By faith: "By faith Noah prepared an ark." (Hebrews 11:7).
3. By obedience: "By faith Noah prepared an ark to the saving of his house" (Hebrews 11:7).
4. By water: "Eight souls were saved by water" (1 Peter 3:20).

In spite of the overwhelming evidence in the scriptures that the Lord has made baptism in water, when preceded by belief, repentance, and confession, a condition precedent to salvation there are those who cite Paul's statement in Romans 4:3,4, in an effort to prove that salvation is by faith (by which those who thus do mean by merely believing); and that baptism cannot be a condition of salvation (which they assume is a "work" in the sense used by Paul) because "works" are by the apostle excluded. But, inasmuch as James (equally inspired) declares that we are justified by works, it must follow that these writers use the term in different senses.

Paul (Romans 4:3,4), cites Genesis 15:6 to show justification by faith. James (2:21,22) cites Genesis 15:6, to show justification by works! There is no contradiction, because each shows what he means by "works."

Paul: WE ARE NOT justified by works.
James: We ARE justified by works.

Paul: *Boasting* ("whereof to glory") Romans 4:2.
James: *Obedience* ("faith made perfect") James 2:21, 22.

Hence, Paul *excludes* meritorious works.
James *includes* acts of obedience, one of which is baptism.

It is often urged that Paul wrote of the justification of Abraham as an unpardoned sinner; whereas, James, in his reference to that illustrious father, writes of his justification as a child of God. This objection is obviously without merit since it would make Abraham an unpardoned sinner for *twenty-five years while walking in harmony with the expressed will of God!* Note the events in his life which occurred while he was yet in his sins according to this absurd contention:

1. His call in Ur of Chaldees
2. Sojourn in Haran
3. Entrance into Canaan
4. Sojourn in Bethel
5. Descent into Egypt
6. Return to Bethel
7. Separation from Lot
8. Removal to Hebron
9. Deliverance of Lot
10. Paying tithes to Melchizedek
11. Faith counted for righteousness

THEN, and only then JUSTIFIED?

Such a conclusion is neither proper nor reasonable in the light of the foregoing facts.

Faith blesses, only when it is strong enough to lead its possessor to obedience. This is evident in the lexical significance of the word *pistis* translated "faith" in the New Testament. Thayer, in his Greek Lexicon of the New Testament, defines it as "used especially of the faith by which a man embraces Jesus; i.e. a conviction, full of joy, trust, that Jesus is the Messiah—the one divinely appointed author of salvation in the kingdom of God, conjoined with obedience to Christ" (1886 edition, page 511). Note particularly the explanatory phrase, "conjoined with obedience to Christ."

Faith then, in its comprehensive sense, is conviction joined with obedience. In demonstration of the fact that only when it manifests itself in obedience is it a blessing, it is said that Jesus SAW THE FAITH OF

THOSE WHO ASSISTED THE PALSIED MAN of Mark 2; obviously, it is not meant by this that Jesus was able to see with his eyes their act of believing; what is meant is that he saw the physical actions which proved that they did indeed believe in the power of Jesus in the fact that they brought the sick man, under difficulty, to him. Faith, in the true biblical sense, is something one can see! One cannot see the mental action of believing, however; and it is thus evident that the faith that saves is the faith that manifests itself in action.

There are numerous instances in the scriptures where people were blessed because of their faith, and there are other cases where, notwithstanding they believed, no blessing came. Let the following instance of the former be noted:

Titus 3:8: These "believed in God," and were "careful to maintain good works." These were baptized believers—members of the church.

1 Timothy 4:12: "Be thou an example to the believers," i.e. believers who were faithful members of the body of Christ.

Acts 18:8: "And Crispus . . . believed." This observation was made regarding the disciple in connection with Paul's preaching in Corinth. Nothing is said in this passage, however, about his baptism; yet, in 1 Corinthians 1:14, Paul mentioned that he baptized Crispus at Corinth! His believing included baptism. Indeed, it is said that at this same time, "many of the Corinthians hearing, believed and were baptized" (1 Corinthians 18:8). They were simply obeying their Lord who said, "He that believeth and is baptized shall be saved" (Mark 16:16).

There were some in that day who, though they believed, were not saved, because they would not complete their obedience by submitting to the commands of Christ:

John 12:41, 42: "Nevertheless among the chief rulers also many believed on him; but because of the Pharisees they did not confess him, lest they should be put out of the synagogue: for they loved the praise of men more than the praise of God."

James 2:19: "Thou believest that there is one God; thou doest well; the devils also believe, and tremble."

It is clear from these instances that an unsaved believer is a disobedient believer!

Chapter 11, of the book of Hebrews is Inspiration's Hall of Fame. In the marvelous recital of faithfulness and fidelity there appearing, grand old men out of an ancient past, worthy patriarchs, prophets, priests and kings, are made to move before us in majestic array, in demonstration of the faith that blesses. In every instance there appearing, the mention of faith is followed by a *verb of action* thus demonstrating that faith, in order to bless, must be followed by an overt act, or otherwise it is a dead faith (James 2:20-26). Note these remarkable and impressive examples:

BY FAITH . ABEL . *OFFERED* . OBTAINED WITNESS
BY FAITH . NOAH . *PREPARED* . SAVED HIS HOUSE
BY FAITH . ABRAHAM . *OBEYED* . RECEIVED INHERITANCE
BY FAITH . MOSES . *CHOSE* . RECOMPENSE OF REWARD
BY FAITH . ISRAEL . *CROSSED* . DELIVERED FROM EGYPT
BY FAITH . RAHAB . *RECEIVED SPIES* . PERISHED NOT.

THE FAITH THAT BLESSES IS
THE FAITH THAT OBEYS!

NOTES OF TRAVEL*

From my earliest acquaintance with Christianity, Palestine—the land of its birth—has held for me an unwavering and ever-increasing fascination. This interest was greatly intensified and heightened when, many years ago as a student in Freed-Hardeman College, Henderson, Tennessee, it was my honored privilege to sit at the feet of that incomparable teacher and preacher, my beloved brother and valued friend, N. B. Hardeman, and study the history and geography of the Bible Lands form Hurlbut's "Bible Atlas."

Under brother Hardeman's sublime guidance, mountain and plain, rivers and seas, oceans and deserts were unforgettably etched in memory and are as vivid today, many years later, as they were when first learned. And, there was born at the time a tremendous urge to visit the sacred places of Europe, Egypt and Asia, and to see especially the country honored above all others as the birthplace of our Lord.

This life-long ambition was wonderfully realized when, in company with, and through the kindly generosity of brother and sister W. Vernon Morris, Visalia, California, I have been privileged to visit the cities of Rome, Athens, Corinth, Cairo, and the countries of Jordan and Israel.

I closed a splendid meeting with the Lake Shore Drive congregation in Shreveport, Louisiana, immedi-

---

*Some years ago, following my first tour of middle Eastern countries, and Bible lands, a trip made possible through the kindness and generosity of brother and sister Vernon Morris, of Visalia, California (brother Morris has long since gone on to be with the Lord), I assembled and wrote these notes of travel resulting from that thrilling and exciting and unforgettable event. I include these observations here with the hope that those who have not traveled in lands made sacred by the great and good of the ages, and where Christianity began, will find these chronicles interesting and edifying, and those who have journeyed there in reading them will derive some profit and pleasure from comparing my observations and experiences with theirs.

ately returned to Memphis, Tennessee, and early the next day, boarded an American Airlines plane for New York. That night was spent in the historic old Waldorf Astoria Hotel, where I met brother and sister Morris who had earlier flown here from California.

During the afternoon of May 1, we checked in with Trans-World Airlines at Idlewild International Airport, and shortly before 5 P.M., we boarded the giant TWA Skyliner which was to bear us safely through cloud and sky over the thousands of miles of ocean, mountains and plain and the next day to set us gently down in the "Eternal City"—Rome—the first extended stop of our tour.

The magical moment had arrived, and the sombre realization possessed us that we were on the verge of one of life's most momentous experiences. We committed ourselves into the care of him but for whom we would never have undertaken such a journey; and, from this time forward there was not a moment when we were conscious of fear, difficulty or danger.

The great ship moved easily along the runways, paused briefly at the end for the usual check-list and then, with a tremendous roar from its four powerful engines leaped forward, the earth fell away, New York's breathtaking skyline receded into the background, Long Island was beneath us for a few fleeting moments, and we were flying northeastward along the historic coast of New England. Soon, New Haven appeared on our left, and to our right was Providence. Boston was west of us, Cape Cod passed beneath us, and we were soon out to sea, high above the shimmering waters of the blue Atlantic.

Before we could scarcely realize it, we were over Nova Scotia, and its cities of Yarmouth, Halifax and Sydney were visible. Again we headed for the open sea, and the sheen of its waters turned from burnished gold to molten silver as the sun, a brilliant flame of fire, sank in the distant haze, and the sable garments of the night enveloped us high in the skies. Minutes later, the cheery twinkle of lights below told us that we were over Newfoundland and we knew that Gander, where then planes which follow the northern route to Europe stopped for operational reasons, was just ahead.

We descended from the plane at Gander and were met with a cold, biting wind out of the star-studded night as we rushed to the waiting room of the Terminal while the plane was serviced for its long ocean flight to Paris.

After a brief period of waiting, our flight was called, and we were again aboard, eager to be on our way. The captain and co-pilots, the engineers and radio men, the stewardess and purser—nine crew members— exhibited none of the excitement characteristic of those of us who were making our first crossing. With confidence born of long experience the crew lifted the giant plane into the darkness of the night and headed eastward over the Atlantic Ocean for a flight to terminate in Paris, France.

We flew eastward and toward the sun, and we were surprised to note that at twelve o'clock midnight, the first grey streamers of dawn were appearing on the horizon. Soon, the sun arose, a livid ball of flaming fire straight up out of the sea, enveloping the cloud-banks in unspeakable radiance, their iridescence providing us with endless delight. Through giant chasms in the clouds below us, the ocean was occasionally visible, its blue background relieved here and there by daubs of white which evidenced the crest of its waves rolling ceaselessly on.

At length, the strikingly beautiful coastline of Ireland appeared, minutes later we were passing over the southern coast of England, the English Channel was soon in view and crossed, and we were over the hills of Normandy, historic old France where, for centuries, great armies have marched across its battlefields, and in whose soil sleep multitudes of men who have made the supreme sacrifice. Versailles was visible from the plane, and as the ship gradually descended for its landing at Orly Field in Paris, we marvelled at the quaint homes which dotted the countryside, and found much pleasure in watching the well-kept fields pass beneath us, their geometric arrangement affording an ever-changing panorama as far as the eye could see.

The stop in Paris was brief, and we were again airborne, our plane the same as that in which we had flown from New York, but now with a French crew. Our flight was over fruitful gardens, rich, fertile fields, and vineyards which stretched mile after mile below us. Our attention was directed to Belfort, famous for its millenniums of strife because of its situation on a pass between mountains leading to France. Over the Jura Mountains we passed, by Basle in Switzerland, and then the descent to Zurich, believed by many to be the most beautifully located of all Swiss cities.

From Zurich we flew south to Rome, passing over the Alps, their snow-covered peaks presenting a scene of indescribable beauty. Lovely mountain lakes, such as Lucerne, slipped beneath us, and we strained our eyes toward the distant horizon to catch a glimpse of the famous Jungfrau, rising 13,668 feet above sea level. We passed over Milan, Genoa, flew out over the Gulf of Genoa, across the Ligurian Sea, over Elba, and then to Rome.

Rome—"The Eternal City"

Our approach to Rome was fraught with much reflection. As the plane circled for its landing at Ciampino Airport, our eyes followed the horizon to the seven hills of this great city and we realized that here we were for the first time to stand upon ground made sacred by the footsteps of Paul, the apostle. We—brother and sister Morris and I—commented, as the plane landed, on the vast difference between our approach and his. We were arriving by speedy plane, with credentials of admission, and reservations at one of her best hotels; the apostle came into the city on foot, a prisoner bound with chains!

We learned here—at the Ciampino Airport—a lesson which we would often need, that patience in passing customs is essential, and that things must be done *their* way, not *ours*! Representatives from our travel agency were waiting and we were soon on our way into the city, approximately nine miles away. En route there, we saw the first evidence of antiquity, ruins of the old Roman Aqueduct which more than nineteen hundred years ago brought water to the imperial city. Sections of it are still in a splendid state of preservation.

Our reservations were at Hotel Excelsior. Our arrival there was in the late afternoon and after we had checked into the hotel, we took a stroll through the streets and among the shops and cafes. We marvelled at the bedlam and confusion which characterized the late evening traffic, we were intrigued by the hundreds who sat sipping coffee at tables along the streets and we found many things to interest us in shops which were along the way. We ate pizza in a small Italian cafe and had our first experience (with many amusing ones to follow) of attempting to make ourselves understood and to pay our bill in their currency!

We began our sightseeing tour of Rome in a private car with a chauffeur and an English-speaking guide. After a brief stop at the tomb of Keats, we drove through the historic streets of the old city to the Pantheon, a building antedating the Christian era and originally erected as a pagan temple for purposes of idolatrous worship. Rightly regarded as the most perfect of the classical monuments of Roman antiquity, it is a tremendous circular structure with walls twenty feet thick and entered through doors thirty-two feet high and fourteen feet wide. In it is the tomb of Raphael, and around its interior are niches which once contained the statues of Jupiter, Mars, Romulus, Aeneas and Julius Caesar.

Our next stop was at the Vatican, seat and capitol of Roman Catholicism. We moved through what appeared to be endless corridors in the world-famous Sistine Chapel, marvelling at the fabulous and priceless collections of gems, paintings, and sculptures assembled there. No words of ours are adequate to describe the treasures which are exhibited in it. We stood in St. Peter's square at high noon, and watched the pope appear briefly at a window high up in Vatican City. We entered St. Peter's Cathedral, largest and costliest church on earth, believed by Catholics to be built over the tomb of Peter. Seven hundred and thirty feet long and three hundred and eighty-four feet wide, it is commodious enough to contain eighty thousand people. In it is the huge bronze statue of Peter, the right foot of which is slightly extended and the toes of which are no longer there, having been literally kissed away by the millions of devout Catholics who have thus humbled themselves before it. Around its walls are statues of every pope the Church has had, and under it are the tombs. We wearied of the magnificence and wealth which characterized the headquarters of this Ecclesiastical Empire, and noted that in its very shadow its duped subjects live in poverty.

In the afternoon we visited one of the catacombs of the city, an underground burial place, along whose corridors niches had been dug out and into which bodies had been inserted. Inscriptions, paintings, markers, and objects found in these places have contributed much to our knowledge of the years immediately following the beginning of the Christian era.

Our most thrilling experience of this day was to drive out St. Sebastian's Gate, alongside the Circus Maximus and by Caracalla's baths to the Appian Way, famous for the fact that along it Paul wearily traveled into the city to perfect his appeal to Caesar. Traces of the old pavement remain, and we dismounted from the car and walked meditatively along its way, mindful of the fact that we were traversing the route and perhaps walking on the same stones over which Paul came en route to the city.

As the evening shadows lengthened, we re-entered the ancient walls and drove to the Colosseum, begun by Vespasian and built by Jewish prisoners in the first century after Christ. Here the elite of Rome entertained themselves by witnessing the deaths of condemned men by lions; here too, multitudes of Christians died, preferring so to do rather than to renounce their faith in the Lord. The Colosseum is a huge amphitheater which was capable of seating tens of thousands of people, and at whose base tunnels ran outside, some to carry the blood of the victims and others their bodies. It may well have been such a fate that Paul avoided and to which he alluded when he said: "Notwithstanding the Lord stood with me, and strengthened me . . . and I was delivered out of the mouth of the lion" (2 Timothy 4:17.) These words were penned, on the occasion of his last imprisonment in Rome almost in the shadow of this monument to Roman cruelty.

En route to our hotel we paused briefly at the Tomb of the Unknown Soldier, and saw nearby the balcony from which the pompous and boastful egoist, Benito Mussolini would appear, stripped to his waist, and make his rabble-rousing speeches, before his ignoble demise.

On the next day we visited the "Church of St. Peter in Chains," and saw the famous statue of Moses by Michelangelo; we saw, and made pictures of the sacred stairway brought from Jerusalem up whose twenty-eight steps our Lord is alleged to have walked when he entered the presence of Pilate. It may be mounted only on one's knees, and many people were doing this when we were there. It is needless to mention that we did not follow the usual pattern, but remained at their foot.

Our next point of interest was the Roman Forum, situated between the Capitoline and Palatine hills. In this area was the ancient senate house, the temple of Vesta where the sacred flame was kept ever-more burning, and the various pagan edifices of worship dedicated to the gods of Rome. Near the eastern approach to the Forum is the famous Arch of Titus, built to commemorate his triumph over the Jews on the occasion of the destruction of Jerusalem, A.D. 70. Along the walls were the palaces of the Emperors, and here the greatest of them all was slain, and at this place Mark Antony delivered the funeral oration.

Nearby, and meeting all the demands of the case, is the traditional prison where Paul was incarcerated. We descended into it along a flight of steps; but, when Paul was there the only entrance was through an opening two feet in diameter straight down from the top twelve feet above. This aperture alone supplied such light and ventilation as the cell had. Through this opening in the ceiling prisoners were let down. The room is circular in form, and approximately twelve feet across; and, near one side is a spring the waters of which flowed out through a sewer into the Tiber. Saddened from the contemplation of the suffering the faithful apostle experienced here, we came away with an awareness of the zeal and fidelity of Paul that we had not hitherto known. We could not help wondering what our reactions would have been had our experience been his. At this point our tour in Rome terminated, and we returned to the hotel, preparatory to our trip to Ciampino Airport and our flight to Athens, Greece.

The Glory That Was Greece

Our flight from Rome to Athens, Greece, was aboard a British European Airways plane, powered by four turbo-prop Rolls Royce engines, using kerosene for fuel, the seats of which, in harmony with British practice, then faced toward the rear of the plane. Virtually vibrationless, this marvelous aircraft bore us through blue Mediterranean skies at an altitude of twenty-three thousand five hundred feet. Brother and sister Morris and I agreed that this was the finest plane on which we had to that time flown.

Once airborne, our course was, for a brief period, overland, and toward the south; but, in a few minutes our direction of flight was altered slightly to the southeast; and, for nearly an hour we were above the Tyrrhenian Sea. We came at length to the south of Italy, crossed the "toe" of the Italian "boot" and, veering a bit more eastward than south, we flew over the Mediterranean to the Peloponnesus of Greece, past the Gulf of Corinth, over the ancient city of that name, across the Corinthian Isthmus, and then to Athens.

Only on the flight across the Mediterranean did we experience any stormy weather; and this was of little consequence. The turbulence was at the level of flight—23,500 feet—and the captain and crew simply brought the great ship *down under the storm* and we were conscious of no danger or difficulty whatsoever.

Below us, as the plane swooped into the Athens airport was the harbor of Piraeus, famed in song and story, and out of which Paul sailed en route to Jerusalem on his second missionary journey; and about us were the storied monuments of the glory that was Greece—a glory long since departed. The customs officials were exceedingly courteous here, our travel representatives were waiting with private car to escort us to hotel Acropolis where we found comfortable quarters and some of the most tasty meals of the entire trip.

Early the next day, we began our tour of the city. Our first stop was at the Archaeological Museum where we were privileged to see Greece's most precious treasures of antiquity—tokens of a civilization so remote that the periods thereof are designated by millenniums. Artifacts of great variety are there sheltered, many of which antedate the Christian era. We marvelled at the skill which characterized the ancient peoples of Greece who lived centuries before Grecian culture came to be regarded as the highest possible attainment, and before Themistocles brought immortal glory to the nation by his decisive victory over the Persians at Salamis.

The Acropolis claimed our attention next, and for hours we moved amid its ruins, charmed by this centuries-old evidence of Greece's greatness. We passed through the magnificent Propylaea, erected during the time of Pericles, the Golden Age of Athens—the entrance to the Acropolis, and looked upon the Parthenon, pride of the Grecian world and the most perfect example of ancient art. It was constructed of a lovely Pentelic marble, and originally consisted of forty-six Doric columns, on a platform two hundred twenty-eight feet long and a hundred feet wide. There were seventeen columns on each side and eight on each end. These supported a roof consisting of thin tiles of Parian marble. It was built during the years 447 and 438 B.C., as a temple for idolatrous worship. Though now in ruins, enough of the building remains to indicate its original beauty. Nearby is the temple of Athena and in the vicinity is the Erechtheum with its Porch of the Maidens.

From the Acropolis one looks out over an area more historic, perhaps, than any other place on earth. To the right is the Tower of the Winds, erected in the first century. Slightly to the left of this is the Agora, the center of the social, political and commercial life of Athens, from the sixth century A.D. The "agora" was the "market" to which reference is made in Acts 17:17. It was a vast area, comprising many buildings. Beyond it and to the left is the temple of Theseus, designed for idolatrous purposes and the best preserved of all the Greek temples. Directly across from the present entrance to the Acropolis is the Areopagus, Mars Hill on which Paul delivered the sermon recorded in Acts 17. This was, to the writer, by far the most interesting thing observed in Athens. We are powerless to describe the emotions which tugged at our hearts as we climbed to its summit, and read the sermon which Paul preached there. Still farther to the left is the theatre of Dionysus, an open-air amphitheatre where the masterpieces of Aeschylus, Sophocles, Euripides, and Aristophanes were played to the elite of Athens centuries before Christ came to the earth. And next is seen the remains of the temple of Zeus, largest of all the temples of Greece and one of the largest of the ancient world. It was built out of the indescribably beautiful Pentelic marble, with one hundred four Corinthian columns arranged in double rows on either side, and in triple rows at each end. The temple was three hundred fifty-four feet long, one hundred thirty-five feet wide, and approximately ninety feet high. About fifteen columns remain, sufficient to evidence the hugeness and loveliness of the original structure. Beyond was the ancient Greek stadium, built

248 Shall We Know One Another in Heaven?

under the direction of Lycurgus, the orator about 330
B.C., and capable of caring for fifty thousand specta-
tors.

As we gazed upon these vestiges of ancient
Athenian idolatry, we were able better than ever before
to appreciate Luke's words in Acts 17:16: "Now while
Paul waited for them at Athens, his spirit was stirred
in him, when he saw the city *wholly given to idolatry*."
And, we could understand why, under these circumstances, Paul's labors were not as fruitful as in other
places.

On Lord's day morning, brother and sister Morris
and I worshipped after the New Testament pattern in
their hotel room, and later in the day traveled, by
automobile, to Corinth, approximately forty miles
distant from Athens, accompanied by an English-
speaking guide. Our route was, for the most part,
along the coast of the Aegean Sea, over the isthmus
separating the mainland of Greece from the Peloponnesus, and through New Corinth situated on the
Ionian Sea. After lunch in New Corinth, a city of
approximately thirty thousand people, we drove to the
ruins of the ancient Corinth, some eight or ten miles
distant, the most important commercial and political
center of Greece in Paul's time. It was, in that day, an
exceeding wicked and corrupt metropolis, a symbol of
lewdness and licentiousness. To "Corinthianize" was
to engage in ungodly living, dissolute and depraved
conduct. Here Paul preached for eighteen months,
meanwhile supporting himself by making tents; and
to the congregation here he wrote epistles, two of
which have come down to us. Much excavation has
been done in the area of the old city, and the spade
has uncovered many evidences of the size and
characteristics of old Corinth. We walked amid the
ruins of the market-place, the forum, the *"bema"*
(Judgment seat, Acts 18:12-17), and the temple of

Apollo. Nothing remains of its former greatness. Then, a proud, populous city, the commercial and political crossroads of the world, today weeds and thistles grow in the midst of its ruins, and a miserable village of poverty-stricken individuals, numbering perhaps four or five hundred people, live on its borders.

Its glory is gone, and the grandeur which character-ized it in its day of greatness is no more. The ships of the world no longer enter its harbor, and the babble of business is no longer heard in its streets. Silent are the voices of her orators, her statesmen, and men of renown, they sleep in unmarked graves in the midst of desolation, decay and ruin. Such is the destiny of all who sow to the flesh as did Corinth in the hour of her glory.

Egypt—Land of the Pharaohs

Our flight from Athens, Greece, to Cairo, Egypt was on Sunday night and by Trans-World Airlines. Our route took us over numerous small islands of the Aegean Sea, between Rhodes and Crete, and over the Mediterranean for nearly seven hundred miles. We passed over Alexandria, Egypt, the lights of which constituted one of the most spectacular displays we saw on the trip; and we reflected at length on its ancient history and glory. There, the greatest of the ancient libraries was assembled; there, too, was begun the translation of the Old Testament from Hebrew into Greek, the *Septuagint* Version, 287 B.C. The city takes its name from, and was built by, Alexander the Great in the fourth century before Christ.

Soon after passing over Alexandria, our plane began its descent for Cairo, and its airport, Air Leban, where we arrived shortly after midnight. Our accommoda-tions were at Hotel Semiramis.

Our first stop was in front of the mansion where Farouk, former ruler of Egypt, lived in lavish luxury before his downfall and consequent removal from the country. From here, we visited various Mosques, shrines of Mohammedan worship, where before entering, we were required to place sandals over our shoes. Into these, the faithful assemble five times a day for prayers, ever facing toward Mecca, the birthplace of Mohammed, and the most sacred city of earth to all Mohammedans. Rising above each mosque is the familiar minaret, a slender tower with a platform around the top, from which the call to prayer is made five times daily. Some of these places of worship date to the sixth century, A.D., and are of varying degrees of splendor and ornate design. There are no seats, and the worshipers sit on the floor and prostrate themselves in their devotions. Ninety-five per cent of the people of Egypt subscribe to this religion; and the percentage is even higher in some other Arab lands.

We spent a never-to-be-forgotten hour in the Egyptian Museum, where is assembled the greatest and most valuable collection of ancient Egyptian lore in the world. There, we were carried back through the ages into the most remote periods of the world's history, and privileged to gaze upon objects which were already old when the children of Israel were slaves in the land. We saw, and marvelled at, the fabulous collection of articles taken from king Tutankhamen's tomb, and reflected on the vanity which evidently characterized the kings of ancient Egypt, in their efforts to perpetuate their memory and to attain to the type of immortality which they coveted.

A brief visit to the bazaars of the city intrigued us, and the narrow, winding streets of much of the city revealed levels of poverty below that which we had thus far seen on the trip. Dirty, unkempt adults, and filthy, ragged children, roamed the streets in great numbers; and the dwellings in these areas were unsanitary hovels. In other sections of the city were mansions in which lived the very rich; and we were impressed here, as often elsewhere in the Middle East, that there is virtually no middle class; one is either wealthy or exceedingly poor. While western clothing is in evidence, the natives, for the most part, follow the Mohammedan custom of wearing Bedouin garments, consisting of a flowing skirt reaching almost to the ground and a head-covering made of a shawl laid over the head and tied with a cord around the head, the shawl extending for some inches between the shoulders.

That which interested us most in Egypt was our visit to the pyramids and the Sphinx, ancient tokens of Egypt's greatness. We traveled by automobile from Cairo to the vicinity of the pyramids, a distance of ten or twelve miles, where brother Morris and I mounted camels for the short desert ride to their base. Sister Morris chose the more sedate sand cart for transportation. Here, the Arabs who led the camels claimed more of our attention than the pyramids! There was a violent disagreement between two of them touching who was to lead the camel brother Morris rode; and it was finally terminated by the intervention of a policeman. These Arabs first amused, then irritated and finally greatly annoyed us by their constant bantering for tips. It was their custom to walk close beside the camel, and in the most honeyed fashion possible to ask for money. We were reminded every moment that we must give it to them before we returned, otherwise the owner of the camel would not allow them to receive it. Brother McGarvey relates that on the occasion of his visit there in 1879 he was subjected to the same annoyances. (Lands of the Bible, page 431.) These camel drivers had acquired a collection of American descriptives and with these we were constantly regaled, on the assumption evidently that we would be more generous in our tips. Among these were "super colossal," "hotsy-totsy," "fine and dandy."

Numerous pyramids lie in irregular lines along a cliff facing the valley of the Nile and the city of Cairo. The mightiest of these is Cheops, a gigantic structure which required one hundred thousand men twenty years to construct. Its base is a square, each side of which is seven hundred sixty-one feet and six inches, the height is approximately four hundred fifty feet, with thirty feet of the pinnacle missing. This massive pile of masonry covers *thirteen acres of ground!* The stones out of which it is constructed vary in size from two to six feet in thickness, and were quarried about twelve miles distant. How they were transported to the spot and raised to their elevations, no one knows. Near the center of the north wall is an entrance, closed when we were there, to the interior. Vast chambers, which may have been intended for the tomb of an ancient monarch, are inside, but no mummy has been found there. Other pyramids in the vicinity, though not quite so large, are equally interesting.

A few hundred yards from the pyramid Cheops is the celebrated Sphinx, a synonym for the mysterious, the inscrutable, the unknown. Why it was built, by whom and in what age are matters about which the past is as silent as the Sphinx itself. It is a gigantic structure with the body of a lion crouched, and the head of a man. It is sixty-six feet high, one hundred twenty-three feet long, and the width of the face is thirteen feet, eight inches. It was built out of the cliff on which it stands, by chiselling away the rock into the form and features it possesses. Facing the east, it continues to gaze, as it has done through the centuries, toward the rising sun.

In the immediate vicinity of the Sphinx is the Granite temple, constructed of red granite, highly polished, with columns four feet square and twelve feet in height, in rows and supporting enormous beams of rock of the same type. The walls are of the same material and fit so perfectly that mortar or cement was never used. The corners were hewn out of the solid rock, and the joints were made to fit where they meet. For thousands of years the shifting sands of the Egyptian desert hid this marvelous building from human eyes; the spade and shovel have again brought it to light, but without revealing to us its history or design. Questions which clamor for solution remain unanswered: How were these huge stones moved from their quarries to this location? Why was the engineering skill evidenced in the building lost for so many centuries? To what purpose was it erected? We do not, and perhaps shall never know.

This entrancing day ended with a restful ride in a sailboat on the historic Nile which flowed past our hotel. As we glided upon its bosom, we reflected on the contributions which it had made through the centuries to the culture of the land and people of ancient Egypt, and remembered that to it they had ever been indebted for their very lives. It enriched their land by its annual deposit of silt, it brought life-giving moisture to their rainless climate, and supplied them with fish for their tables. It is a lovely stream, placid, quiet, gentle, flowing peaceably through valleys green and fertile, an invaluable part of a historic heritage.

Flight to Jerusalem

Our departure from Cairo, Egypt to Jerusalem followed and we journeyed to that historic place via Beirut, Lebanon. We traveled from Beirut to Jerusalem on Middle East Airlines, the captain of the plane was an American!

The runways of the great new Beirut International airport end just short of the Mediterranean Sea, and our plane was scarcely airborne before we were out over its blue waters. Circling, to gain altitude, the plane passed over the city of Beirut; and, for a few fleeting moments, a grand panorama of the ancient Phoenician plain from old Byblos on the north to the windswept coasts of Tyre and Sidon on the south, unfolded before our eyes. Below us was truly historic ground; here, armies both ancient and modern had swirled through its borders and made history in its narrow corridor.

Directly ahead of us was the Lebanon range, mountains famed for the fact that out of them came the hewn timbers for the magnificent temple of Solomon in Jerusalem. We were informed that varieties of these same fabulous "cedars of Lebanon" still subsist on the slopes of this storied range. In the distance, Mount Hermon, shrouded in clouds and wrapped in a mantle of snow, was occasionally visible. Below us was the "Valley of Mizpah," to the left, ancient Baalbek.

Soon, we were in the vicinity of Damascus, oldest city in the world, but glimpses of which we were privileged to have through the cloudbanks below us.

Our course had thus far been southeastward, to avoid violating the territory of Israel with whom the Arabs were technically in a state of war. We now turned to the south, and our first landmark was the Pharpar, along whose course Paul is believed to have traveled en route to Damascus, just prior to his conversion. Very shortly we were over the Hieromax, a stream which Hurlbut (Bible Atlas, page 13) identifies as the Yarmuk, whose channel carries water from the highlands of Bashan to the Jordan.

We were now about to experience the inexpressible thrill of seeing, for the first time, the Sea of Galilee! At first but a blob of blue in the distance, and only partially visible through the haze, we were, nevertheless, thrillingly aware of the fact that we were gazing on an area in which Jesus did much of his teaching and his mighty works, and whose history is inextricably interwoven with the cause we love; and the realization filled us with indescribable emotion. We were later to walk along its sacred shore, fall asleep to the soft swish of its gentle waves and see the early morning beams of the rising sun turn its lovely bosom into a million radiant gems. In a lifetime of travel and observation, this writer has seen nothing in nature which surpasses in simple beauty ". . . blue Galilee, where Jesus loved so much to be."

Our flight followed the Jordan valley; and the historic river was now and then visible, a tortuous thread weaving in and out of deep canyons as it made its way southward to the Dead Sea. Below were the mountains of Gilead, and in the distance was old Gerasa, one of the cities of the Decapolis.

Turning westward to fly the narrow corridor into Jerusalem, again to avoid passing over territory belonging to the State of Israel, our plane crossed the Jordan and in a few minutes was over the mountains of Judea. Again, as we gazed upon the rolling hills below us, our emotions defied analysis. Here angels had announced the birth of the Lord of Glory; deity had taken upon itself human flesh and had condescended to be born into the world; over its hills Jesus had walked and talked with his disciples; and to this area he had come from distant Galilee to be baptized by John. An awareness of these facts made us impatient to be down where these events occurred—to see at firsthand the historic places made sacred by Christ and his apostles.

Shortly before we arrived at the Jerusalem airport, the captain of the ship (with whom we had earlier visited momentarily, and who had ascertained the occasion of our visit to Jerusalem) sent the stewardess back to inquire if I would like to come up into the cockpit and watch them land the plane in Jerusalem. I accepted this invitation with alacrity and was thus privileged to witness our approach to the holy city and to see, in the most advantageous fashion, its general features.

The captain directed attention to ancient Jericho on our left, and beyond it the Dead Sea. Rising sharply from its banks was Mount Nebo, from whose "lofty heights" Moses looked upon the Promised Land. Above Jericho we could see Quarantania, the traditional Mount of Temptation, a gaunt, barren elevation, unrelieved by any sign of life or vegetation. As the plane circled to land at the Jerusalem airport, the captain pointed out the Mount of Olives, the site of the ancient temple of Solomon, the Dome of the Rock (where Abraham offered Isaac), roads to Bethany and Bethlehem and other historic points we were soon to see firsthand.

Once on the ground, we passed through customs with a minimum of difficulty. Our flight from Beirut had required approximately one hour and thirty minutes, during which time we had flown over three countries, and an area whose history has more powerfully influenced the world than any other on earth. So long as the world stands, its history will continue to exercise a tremendous force in the lives of men, and the events which there occurred in the long, long ago, will project themselves into all eternity. Small in area, of little significance economically, commercially or politically, its importance transcends historically that of all the rest of the earth.

A representative of our hotel was waiting at the airport for us; the drive into the city was brief, and we were soon registered at the American Colony Hotel.

Jerusalem and Its Environs

We began our tour of the Holy City early in the day. Our guide was a clean-cut young Arab of splendid attainments; the driver a Greek; the automobile a late model American built machine.

From the American Colony Hotel—our quarters while in Arab Jerusalem—we went directly to the Mount of Olives. Our route took us by the Tomb of the Kings, eastward from the city through the valley of Jehoshaphat, across the brook Kedron at a point just north of Absalom's Tomb, and then upward, along its western slope, to the summit. En route, one passes "the church of the Virgin Mary" on the left, the Garden of Gethsemane on the right. A paved road has been built to the top. The elevation is slightly over 2,500 feet above sea level, approximately 400 feet above the Kedron. Olive trees grow on its sides, patches of wheat and clumps of fig trees supply sufficient color to make the effect very pleasing.

We were taken directly to the traditional spot where Jesus ascended. On it a chapel had been erected and the usual evidences of Catholicism were abundant. Here, as often elsewhere, the traditional view is in conflict with New Testament teaching. Jesus ascended from the Mount of Olives, but from near Bethany (Luke 24:50), and hence from some point on the opposite side of the Mount. We were privileged to ascend to the roof of a building nearby, and to enjoy the finest view of Jerusalem to be had anywhere in the vicinity.

Looking eastward, Bethany was at our feet; a bit farther, Jericho; and beyond Jericho, Jordan and the Dead Sea. In the greater distance was the eastern tableland with Nebo rising gracefully in the soft haze. Turning back to the west there was Mount Scopus, Mount Moriah, Mount Zion, and the Hill of Evil Counsel. Jerusalem was directly in front, the Garden of Gethsemane immediately below and between. We were sobered with the realization that somewhere near the place we were standing—possibly on the very spot—Jesus had uttered his bitter cry over the wayward and rebellious city. (Luke 19:41-46.)

Leaving Olivet, we crossed the valley of Jehoshaphat, and entered the city of Jerusalem through "St. Stephen's Gate," an imposing entrance providing access to the city through the great wall which surrounds it. We followed a narrow street for a few hundred feet, and then turned to our right into a walled area, where tradition says Jesus was tried and condemned. The spot meets the historical demands of the case, and may indeed be the place where Pilate's judgment hall stood. Nearby is the site of his house and a wall which separates the temple area from the street is allegedly built on the same foundation at the Roman Procurator's house. In the vicinity is the pool of Bethesda.

From the judgment hall to Calvary is the *Via Dolorosa* (the way of the cross), with its fourteen stations. Along this route is alleged to have occurred the events which the scriptures mention in connection with his painful and agonizing march from Pilate's Hall to Golgotha. In addition, Catholic superstition has fabricated many others. We were shown where the cross was placed upon the shoulders of Jesus, where he stumbled and twice fell under its weight; where Simon of Cyrene was compelled to bear it. We were little impressed by these and other obviously unfounded traditions of exact places where these events occurred. We knew, however, that somewhere in the vicinity, our Lord *was* condemned, *did* bear the cross, and *was* forced to make the agonizing march to Calvary; and our hearts burned within us.

The "Church of the Holy Sepulchre" contains the traditional tomb of Jesus. About it a tremendous mass of misinformation has accumulated through the years,

and there is little reason to believe the stories which
the guides relate concerning it. We were, for example,
shown not only the tomb where Jesus was laid, but the
exact spot where the cross was found, a break in the
rocks which occurred during the earthquake which
followed his tragic death. (Matthew 27:50-53.)

We strolled meditatively about the temple area,
gazed with wondering eyes on the grounds where
Solomon's magnificent temple once stood, and were
deeply stirred by the realization that here, in this very
spot, our dear Lord had walked and talked, and his
disciples had preached and prayed! The "Dome of the
Rock," a gigantic Moslem house of worship—
sometimes called the Mosque of Omer—now covers a
portion of the ancient sanctuary area, and nearby is a
similar structure, the Mosque El Aska. In front of this
building is a fountain, and at the time we were there,
numerous Mohammedans were performing their ablu-
tions preparatory to worship. Inside both buildings
were many engaged in their devotions, sitting in
characteristic style on the floor, and bowing toward
Mecca.

The most important of these Mosques, the Dome of
the Rock, is so designated because of a huge rock in its
center, and its most prominent feature. The rock is
approximately six feet high, fifty feet long, and of
varying widths from twenty-eight to thirty-eight feet.
Around it is a substantial barrier, prohibiting direct
contact with it.

Many traditions, both Jewish and Moslem, cluster
about it. The Jews believe that it is the exact spot where
Abraham prepared an altar to offer Isaac; the rock
where Jacob pillowed his head when he saw the angels
ascending and descending on the ladder which
reached up to heaven, and which he called Bethel, the
"House of God"; and the place where Jeremiah

concealed the ark of the covenant when Jerusalem was
overwhelmed by the Babylonians.

Mohammedans believe that from it their founder—
Mohammed—ascended to heaven; that it originally
came from Paradise; that it bears the footprints of
Mohammad; and that a prayer uttered here is more
effective than a thousand elsewhere.

Stripped of such superstitious speculations, the facts
are that it is on the very eminence of Mount Moriah;
it is just such a spot as Abraham would have selected
for his trying task; and it is, most certainly, within the
general area where the temple of Solomon stood. We
regarded it, therefore, with the greatest interest.

On the western border of the temple area is the
famous "wailing wall," of the Jews. Before the war
with the Arabs resulted in their expulsion from this
portion of the city of Jerusalem, each Friday afternoon
large numbers of them came there to weep over the
desolation of the nation, the temple and the people.
This was as near as they were privileged to approach
the temple area.

We were in Arab Jerusalem on the eve of the great
Mohammedan feast of Ramadan; and its narrow,
winding streets were choked with pilgrims who had
come there for this important Moslem festival. Clothed
in their colorful dress, Bedouin from the desert,
grim-faced sheiks of the shifting sands, had left their
flocks and tents to come to the holy city to mingle in
the festivities with the Fellahin of the cities and villages
of Transjordan during the gala days which celebrated
the termination of a lengthy fast. Their flowing
headdress, the long robes which extended nearly to
the ground, and the dignified bearing which ever
characterized them, combined to create an impression
we shall not soon forget.

In the afternoon we went to the Garden of
Gethsemane, and stood in reverie somewhere near the

place where Jesus prayed his bitter prayer, and the disciples, from weariness, slept. We drove to Bethlehem, saw the "Church of the Nativity," where Jesus is believed to have been born; and, on the return trip, stopped briefly at the Tomb of Rachel. We were taken to the "Garden Tomb," a second traditional spot where Jesus was buried and, in our opinion, more nearly in harmony with scripture requirements than the tomb in the "Church of the Holy Sepulchre." The Garden Tomb is so designated because it is in a garden (John 19:41); and, nearby, there is the "place of the skull," a natural formation in the side of a hill, resembling a human skull. The "Garden Tomb" is outside the wall of the city, thus conforming to the New Testament record. (Cf. Matthew 28:11; Hebrews 13:12.)

Travels in Judea and Samaria

Very early in the morning brother and sister Morris and I left our lodgings at the American Colony Hotel in Jerusalem, Jordan, in an automobile driven by a Greek and with an Arab as our guide, Bethany was our first stop. Our route was along the valley of Jehoshaphat, over the brook Kedron, and then, by a gradual incline, over the slope of Olivet, and down the eastern side. Bethany the home of Mary, Martha and Lazarus (John 11), is, today, a small Arab village, with all the usual evidences of poverty characteristic of such. It is situated on the eastern side of the Mount of Olives approximately two miles from Jerusalem. Here Jesus spent many happy hours in the home of his friends, Mary, Martha and Lazarus; and to this place was he called when sickness laid Lazarus low. The spot where he met his sorrowing friends is designated, and we descended into the tomb where the clarion call, "Lazarus, come forth!" was heard, and the dead man sprang immediately into life. (John 11:1-44.) The tomb, carved out of solid rock, is reached down a flight of twenty-six steps.

From Bethany, we took the road from Jerusalem to Jericho. Now a paved thoroughfare, it follows the original route down which Jesus and his disciples journeyed, and made famous by the story of the good Samaritan. The distance from Jerusalem to Jericho is approximately twenty miles, the road a crooked, winding one as it threads its way through desolate canyons, and over sharp elevations. The entire area is one of bleak abandonment; there are no signs of life, no flocks, no fowls of the air, no human habitations; and the hills are unrelieved save for a scrubby, brownish type of grass which merely heightens the monotony of the landscape. For centuries, robbers infested the area, preying on the unfortunate travelers forced to pass that way. The descent from Jerusalem to the Jordan Valley is an exceedingly sharp one—from 2,700 feet *above* sea level to 1,300 feet *below* sea level.

En route, we passed a fountain which we believe to be that designated in Joshua 15:7 as "the waters of Enshemesh"; and, a bit farther, we gazed with high emotion on the ruins of the Old Samaritan Inn where the man was carried who fell among thieves. This historic place is approximately half way between Jerusalem and Jericho. Shortly before entering the Jordan Valley we passed over the "brook Cherith" where Elijah hid and was fed by ravens. (1 Kings 17:1-7.)

We motored through modern Jericho, a pleasant appearing place where, because of irrigation, vegetables, citrus fruits, bananas, and almonds flourish in profusion, and came to the site of ancient Jericho, near where the Israelites crossed the Jordan, when they entered the promised land, and camped at Gilgal two miles distant. Here, we saw the excavations which allegedly have reached the levels of the walls which fell when the Israelites, in compliance with the command of Jehovah, marched around them. Nearby is the famous watering place—Elisha's fountain—which, for centuries has quenched the thirst of tired and dusty travelers in the area. We saw what appeared to be an endless procession of Arab women carrying water in huge jars gracefully balanced on their heads to a refugee camp in the vicinity.

Overlooking ancient Jericho is Quarantania, the traditional Mount of Temptation. (Matthew 4:1-11.) Its aspect is grim and foreboding, an unlovely mass of rock, one hundred fifty feet high, about half of a mile wide, browned by the passing of the years and barren of vegetation, and with little evidence that it is indeed the place where Jesus emerged triumphantly from his conflict with the prince of the power of the air.

One of our greatest thrills was to stand at the spot where it is believed our Lord was baptized at the hands of John in the river Jordan. Here, the river is at least forty feet wide, and in the dry season, fifteen feet deep. The stream is always muddy, we are told; and, it flows swiftly at all times. Whether this is the exact spot where the event occurred, we could not, of course, know; but, we are certain that it took place somewhere in that vicinity, and our hearts stirred within us.

The Dead Sea, into which the Jordan empties, next claimed our attention, and we looked upon it with intense interest. The terminus of the Jordan, it is forty-five miles long, and from three to nine miles wide. It is the lowest body of water on earth—approximately thirteen hundred feet below sea level—and in places its depth reaches another thirteen hundred feet. Its mineral content is twenty-six per cent, as compared to ocean water which is approximately four per cent! It weighs in excess of twelve pounds per gallon, compared to slightly more than ten pounds per gallon for ocean water. The high mineral

content is due to the centuries' long deposit of such
from the Jordan river, the water of which evaporates,
leaving behind its deposits. All the minerals, including
chloride of magnesium, sodium, calcium, potassium,
are in solution, and the water is beautiful and clear. It
is, however, extremely nauseating to the taste, and
no life, either vegetable or animal, can survive in its
waters. Best known to the world today as the "Dead
Sea," such a designation is not found in the Bible. The
scriptures refer to it as the "Salt Sea," the "Sea of
Arabah," and "The Sea of the Plain." There is an
ancient tradition that the wicked cities of Sodom and
Gomorrah are at its bottom. We believe that there is a
reasonable ground for this tradition. The location is
suitable; the Arabs designate it as Bahr Lut (the Sea of
Lot), because of their belief that such occurred; and the
Talmud also recites the story. In the mighty conflagra-
tion which engulfed them under the righteous indignation of an offended God, the topography of the area
might well have been altered, as tradition asserts, until
the waters of Jordan formed the forbidding sea.

In the afternoon, we drove northward for forty miles
through historic territory to Shechem, believed by
many scholars to be identical with Sychar, the modern
name of which is Nablus. En route the sites of ancient
Ai, Ramah the ancestral home of Samuel, and other
sacred places were pointed out. We entered the pass
between Mount Gerizim, "the mount of blessing," and
Mount Ebal, "the mount of cursing," and stopped at
"Jacob's Well," where we quenched our thirst as did
Jesus in the long, long ago. It was here that he met "the
woman of Samaria," probed deeply into her past,
taught her the requisites of acceptable worship and
revealed to her his Messiahship. (John 4:1-42). We
lifted our eyes to the summit of Old Gerizim and saw,
in fancy, the woman point to a temple there, and say:
"Our fathers worshipped in this mountain; and ye

say, that in Jerusalem is the place where men ought to worship" (John 4:20). We thought of that momentous occasion when Joshua assembled the children of Israel in the area, "half of them over against mount Gerizim, and half of them over against mount Ebal; as Moses the servant of the Lord had commanded before," read the blessings and cursings and all the people shouted "Amen!" (Joshua 8:33-35).

We entered Nablus, drove along the slope of Gerizim, and visited the Samaritan synagogue, where a remnant of the ancient race continues to adhere to the traditions of their fathers. We were informed that only three hundred Samaritans were in existence, and that Gerizim is the most sacred spot on earth to them. They subsist, in large measure, by tips which they receive from travelers desirous of seeing their synagogue, and the ancient roll containing the Samaritan Pentateuch which they fondly believe and aver to date back to Moses. The patriarch with whom we talked declared that he was a direct descendent (more than a hundred generations removed) of Aaron himself!

As the shadows lengthened, we turned our faces toward Jerusalem, and drove through the villages of Samaria and Judea mindful of the fact that all about us were sacred scenes hallowed by the presence of our Lord and his disciples. The land has indeed become to us "a fifth gospel," corroborative evidence of the truth of the divine record. It was good to be there!

Final Notes on a Tour of the Holy Land

We checked out of the American Colony Hotel in Jerusalem, Jordan; and, with some uneasiness, traversed, on foot, the "no man's land"—then a strip one hundred yards wide—between Arab Jerusalem and Jewish Jerusalem. Neither Jews nor Arabs could accompany us through this area; and, on either side, soldiers watched the strip behind machine gun emplacements. Our entry was through the Mandelbaum Gate; our quarters at King David Hotel. We were now in the State of Israel.

A half day of sightseeing took us through the valley of Hinnom (Tophet) where, in the days of Israel's idolatry, children were sacrificed to the fire-god Molech (2 Kings 23:10; 2 Chronicles 28:3; 33:5); to the summit of Mount Zion, once in the days of the Jebusites, the sole area of Jerusalem, and now the site of the upper room where the Lord's supper was instituted; and to Ein Karem, a small village which is believed to be "the city in the hill country of Judea," where Mary, mother of Jesus, visited Elizabeth, and where John the Baptist was born (Luke 1).

On the day following, we departed from Jerusalem, taking the road northward, our destination Galilee. Our route was through Lydda where Aeneas, sick of the palsy eight years, was made whole (Acts 9:33,34), when Peter came there; by Beth-horon and the valley of Ajalon where the sun stood still at the command of Joshua (Joshua 10:12-14), through the plain of Esdraelon, a flat area famous for centuries as the "bread-basket" of Palestine, and the battlefield of countless contests; between Mount Tabor on our left, Mount Gilboa on our right; and alongside the "Hill of Migiddo," the scene of millenniums of strife and where the Premillennialists allege the final triumph of truth over error will occur when Jesus, on a white horse, leads an army into actual combat with the foe! A more absurd and impossible theory was never advanced.

Shortly before our descent to the Jordan Valley, we passed the "Horns of Hattin," twin peaks from which there is a gentle decline, and from early centuries, the traditional spot where Jesus delivered the Sermon on the Mount.

About four miles distant, we crossed the brow of a hill, and below us, in breathtaking beauty, was Tiberias, and the brilliantly blue waters of the Sea of Galilee. We confess our utter inability to express the profound effect the view of this magnificent sea exercised upon us. The road sharply descends to a point about 580 feet below sea level, and to the city of Tiberias located on the shore of the lake. The Sea of Galilee is approximately seven miles wide and twelve miles long. Its waters gradually deepen to a depth of one hundred sixty-five feet. We spent a never-to-be-forgotten night in a hotel, the foundations of which were laid by the lovely waters of this historic sea.

A drive around its borders took us through the village of Magdala, where Mary Magdalene was born; to Capernaum, home of Jesus during his public ministry; and to the traditional site of the feeding of the five thousand nearby. We were profoundly impressed with the fact that in this immediate area Jesus was most active during his earthly sojourn.

Early the next morning—on Lord's day—the three of us (brother and sister W. Vernon Morris and I) assembled in their hotel room, read selections from the New Testament touching our Lord's activities about the Sea of Galilee, sang and prayed, and partook of the Lord's supper. We were saddened with the realization that here, amid the scenes which gave Christianity its birth, the cause of the Lord is unknown.

Leaving Tiberias, we ascended to the Esdraelon plain, and turning westward, drove to Nazareth. En route, we passed through Cana of Galilee where Jesus, on the occasion of the wedding which he attended there, turned water into wine. We visited the "Well of Mary," saw the traditional cave where Mary, Joseph and Jesus lived, and the hill of precipitation where the aroused citizens of Nazareth sought to destroy Jesus. (Luke 4:29). We saw little in present-day Nazareth to

admire. Its streets are narrow and filthy, and wretched-
ness and poverty abound. We hastened our departure
from a city the glory of which has long since departed
and the cause which gave it world-wide prominence
is unknown.

We visited Acre, crossed the Kishon, and entered
Haifa, a comparatively modern Israelite city. We
ascended to the top of Carmel which overlooks the city,
and marvelled at the magnificent view of the city and
harbor from that point. We visited the grotto where
Elijah is alleged to have had his conflict with the
prophets of Baal, and remembered the triumph which
Jehovah gained through his faithful prophet over the
minions of heathen gods. As evening approached, we
registered at Hotel Zion in Haifa.

On the morrow, we drove through the lush Sharon
plain, its fruitful fields for centuries the "salad-bowl"
of the maritime plain; our route took us by huge
factories engaged, we suspect, in turning out war
material for war with Arab nations; and we saw much
other evidence of a nation geared for war.

We stopped by Old Caesarea, where Paul was
imprisoned for two years prior to his appeal to Caesar,
and now a wholly abandoned place. Not a soul inhabits
the once famous harbor town of Palestine. We stood
on the shore amid the ruins of its former glory, and
thought of the days when it was one of the most
important of the Mediterranean coastal cities. Cities
flourish, decline and die and their glory departs; but
God's handiwork goes on forever. Though but little
remains at Caesarea of its once proud status, the
waters of the Mediterranean still wash its shores
exactly as they did in the long, long ago.

We entered Tel Aviv, Israel's largest and most
modern city, and claimed our reservations at Hotel
Dan. In the afternoon, we drove to Joppa and stood
on the shore near where Peter received his call to come

to Caesarea. Other points of interest in the area were shown us, and as the day ended, we completed our itinerary. We saw many things and went to many places, limitations of space and time do not allow to detail in this narrative. We covered approximately 20,000 miles in about twenty days, and visited in more than a dozen different countries. It was the richest, most fruitful and educational similar period I have ever experienced. I shall evermore be profoundly grateful to God whose watchful care brought us safely back, and to brother and sister W. Vernon Morris who made the trip financially possible, and whose genial companionship throughout the trip added immeasurably to its pleasure.

We rested in Tel Aviv for a day, and on Wednesday, May 16, at 9 A.M., we left that city by Sabena Air Lines. We crossed the Mediterranean, stopped briefly in Athens, Greece, flew over the Alps to Frankfurt, Germany, and on to Brussels, Belgium, where brother and sister Morris took a plane to Paris for brief visits there and in London. After some hours layover, I boarded a plane which made stops in Manchester, England, and Shannon, Ireland; and, then at midnight, began the long flight across the Atlantic. An operational stop was made in Gander, Newfoundland, and we landed shortly after noon, May 17, in New York. I hurried over to the Newark airport, and claimed reservations on an Eastern Airlines plane, arriving in Memphis that evening. Two days later, I was in Texas to begin a gospel meeting!

Author's Note: Since these notes were written, Israel, in other conflicts with the Arabs, has extended its control over the land from the Great Sea through the Jordan plain, and from the borders of Lebanon to Palestine's original southern limits.